Cognitive Psychology and Emotional Disorders

THE WILEY SERIES IN CLINICAL PSYCHOLOGY

Series Editor:

Fraser N. Watts

MRC Applied Psychology Unit
Cambridge

Severe Learning Disability
and Psychological Handicap
John Clements

Cognitive Psychology
and Emotional Disorders
J. Mark G. Williams, Fraser N. Watts,
Colin MacLeod and Andrew Mathews

Attribution Theory
in Clinical Psychology
Friedrich Försterling

Community Care in Practice
Services for the Continuing Care Client
Edited by Anthony Lavender
and Frank Holloway

Further titles in preparation

Cognitive Psychology and Emotional Disorders

J. Mark G. Williams
Fraser N. Watts
Medical Research Council
Applied Psychology Unit
Cambridge, UK

Colin MacLeod
Andrew Mathews
Psychology Department
St George's Hospital Medical School
Tooting, London, UK

JOHN WILEY & SONS
Chichester · New York · Brisbane · Toronto · Singapore

Copyright © 1988 by John Wiley & Sons Ltd.

Library of Congress Cataloging-in-Publication Data:

Cognitive psychology and emotional disorders/J. Mark G. Williams ...
   [et al.].
   p. cm. — (The Wiley series in clinical psychology)
   Bibliography: p.
   Includes index.
   ISBN 0 471 91845 8
   1. Affective disorders.   2. Anxiety.   3. Cognition.   I. Williams,
   J. Mark G.   II. Series.
   [DNLM: 1. Affective Symptoms—psychology.   2. Anxiety Disorders—
   psychology.   3. Cognition.   WM 171 C6757]
   RC537.C624 1988
   616.85′2—dc19
   DNLM/DLC
   for Library of Congress   87–31739
                                                                 CIP

British Library Cataloguing in Publication Data available
ISBN 0 471 91845 8

Typeset by Witwell Ltd, Southport
Printed and bound in Great Britain by Biddles Ltd, Guildford

Contents

Series Editor's Preface

This is the second of a new series of texts in clinical psychology. Some, such as this volume, will present distillations of work in a specialist area where exciting advances are currently being made. Others, such as John Clements' earlier book on Severe Learning Disability, will present an authoritative, up-to-date introduction to one of the core fields of clinical psychology. Where possible the books will be written by a single author or — as in this case — by a small group of authors working as a team. They will therefore have the coherence which is often lacking in edited books.

Clinical psychology is a field with permeable frontiers. It has close links with many other professions and scientific disciplines. We hope, therefore, that the series will have a broad appeal to all those who are concerned with the application of psychological knowledge to clinical problems. The present book, which concerns the application of experimental cognitive psychology to particular clinical disorders, will interest cognitive psychologists as much as clinical psychologists. Equally, we hope that psychiatrists and other professionals who are interested in cognitive approaches to emotional problems will also find this book a valuable resource.

Cognitive therapies for disorders of anxiety and depression have become very widely used in clinical practice and have been shown to be among the most effective psychological treatments currently available. This book focuses, not on the techniques themselves, but on the theoretical assumptions on which they are predicated. It aims to present a coherent and critical review of relevant research, together with a theoretical framework based on them. Such a framework can enable clinicians to make increasingly precise observations about the exact nature of their patients' cognitive dysfunctions.

Fraser Watts

Preface

This book has grown out of regular meetings which have taken place over the last few years between the authors to discuss matters of mutual research interest. The study of emotional disorders from the standpoint of cognitive psychology is very new, and it is difficult to know the appropriate time to put down in writing the current state of the evidence and current speculations about causation and mechanism. The disadvantages are obvious: the field has not yet reached a steady state. The danger is that today's speculation will seem naive tomorrow in the light of further evidence. Yet already the field has some coherence and clarity. First, it is now more obvious what are the tractable questions (for example, to what extent do different types of patient differ in the types of bias in information-processing they show?) Second, it is clearer which experimental paradigms are useful, and which are less so for examining such biases (for example, depth of processing paradigms have yielded a great deal of evidence, but lexical decision paradigms have not). The experiments which allow us to come to these preliminary conclusions are scattered throughout the literature. This book attempts to draw them together in order to be able to observe the regularities that may be emerging. Having drawn them together the book aims to make explicit what the connections may be between them.

We shall concentrate on disorders of anxiety and depression, not only because they are the commonest forms of psychopathology, but also because it is these emotional disorders which have been most studied by experimental cognitive psychologists. Other disorders, such as mania and hypomania, aggression and psychopathy, have not been subject to so detailed and systematic an enquiry.

Following a general introduction to the integration of cognition and emotion (Chapter 1) and to the information-processing paradigm (Chapter 2) the book reviews the core areas where experimental cognitive paradigms have been applied to emotional disorders. Consideration is given in Chapter 3 to research on cognitive impairments — how emotional disturbance affects performance on neutral tasks. This represented the earliest attempt to apply information-processing concepts, and laid the groundwork for much of the later research.

The more recent work has been largely concerned with investigating the processing of emotionally valent information. Chapter 4 examines the research on attentional biases, and Chapter 5, that on memory biases. Such biased processing has often been explained within schema theory, and this contention is critically examined in Chapter 6.

Chapters 7 and 8 move away from considering underlying biases and focus on how the phenomenology of emotionally disordered individuals can best be understood. In Chapter 7 this involves a discussion of current theories of mental imagery, and their implications for emotional pathology. In Chapter 8, the way in which normal heuristics and biases contribute to judgements made by patients with emotional disorders is considered.

The final two chapters give a theoretical overview in order to integrate the research. Many of the findings discussed in the book raise the issue of the relation between conscious and nonconscious processing. Chapter 9 therefore discusses this in detail. Its conclusion is that, though there can be a dissociation between conscious and nonconscious processing, experimental investigation of the latter is not precluded. The final chapter builds upon this conclusion, suggesting the need to distinguish between two different types of processing operating at encoding (an automatic priming process and a strategic elaboration process) with a parallel distinction at retrieval (a 'remembering without awareness' aspect and a 'strategic recollection' aspect). Evidence that different emotional disorders affect different aspects within this processing model is reviewed.

In writing this book, there has been much discussion of all the chapters by all the authors. However, specific members of the group took main responsibility for particular chapters as follows: Chapter 1, 3 and 7, Fraser Watts; Chapter 2, 6 (with AM) and 9, Colin MacLeod;* Chapter 6 (with CM) and 8, Andrew Mathews; Chapters 4, 5 and 10, Mark Williams.

We gratefully acknowledge helpful discussions at various stages in the production of the book with several colleagues: Alan Baddeley, John Duncan, Phil Johnson-Laird, Andrew MacLeod, Anthony Marcel and John Teasdale. Thanks are also due to Tim Dalgleish for help with proof-reading and indexing the manuscript. Much of our own research which is reported in the book has been supported by the Medical Research Council of Great Britain.

Mark Williams
Fraser Watts
Colin MacLeod
Andrew Mathews

August 1987

*Colin MacLeod is now at the Department of Psychology, School of Social Enquiry, Murdoch University, Perth, W. Australia 6150.

Chapter 1

The Cognitive Approach to Emotional Disorders

Recent years have seen the development of a body of psychological work, both empirical and theoretical, on the application of cognitive psychology to the investigation of emotional disorders. Our intention in this book is to review that body of work, and to consider its clinical and scientific implications. We hope that clinical psychologists whose primary concern is with the assessment and treatment of patients with emotional disorders will value the opportunity to appraise a body of fundamental research on these conditions that is still relatively novel and is attracting considerable interest. However, we believe that the body of work with which we are concerned is potentially of broader interest. The cognitive psychology of emotional disorders is only one aspect of an increasing general interest in the connection between emotion and cognition. Also, psychologists with a primary interest in the information-processing paradigm have become more interested in applying concepts and paradigms to everyday phenomena; emotional disorders represent one such application.

The purpose of this introductory chapter is to set the cognitive investigation of emotional disorders in the broader context of cognitive approaches to emotional phenomena. This will proceed through five stages.

1. First, we shall place our own interest in the cognitive investigation of emotional disorders in the context of recent general interest in the connection between cognition and emotion.
2. Next, we shall present a brief conceptualization of emotion and emotional disorders, raising issues which are pertinent to cognitive investigations.
3. Third, we shall describe some of the cognitive processing phenomena suggested by clinical observations, and indicate the experimental paradigms available for their investigation.
4. Fourth, we shall review the variety of cognitive approaches to emotional disorders that have been attempted recently, and explain the distinctive features of the approach grounded in cognitive psychology with which this book will be concerned.

5. Finally, developing this point, we shall discuss the value of distinguishing
    between different levels of the cognitive system in the way that recent
    hierarchical theories of emotion have done.

1.1 COGNITION AND EMOTION

Discussions of the relationship between cognition and emotion tend to focus
either on the effects of emotion on cognitive processes or on the role of
cognitive processes in the genesis of emotional states, and these will be
considered in turn.

Work on the effects of emotion on cognitive functioning can introduce
'emotion' at at least three different points. One concerns the materials used.
Attention and memory for emotional materials diverge at many points from
those that apply with neutral materials even in 'normal' subjects who are not
emotionally aroused. The effects are often quite subtle, such as the well-
known phenomenon reported by Kleinsmith and Kaplan (1963) that
emotional materials are less well remembered at short retention intervals but
better remembered at longer intervals.

Emotion can also be introduced through the subject, and there are two
possible ways in which this can happen. 'Normal' subjects can experience a
temporary state of emotional arousal, or subjects can have chronic emotional
arousal and preoccupations. Either 'state' or 'trait' emotion in subjects can
affect cognitive processing, the clearest results being seen in subjects who have
both, i.e. people with chronic emotional vulnerability experiencing acute
emotional arousal. Cognitive processing in subjects with emotional disorders
or in states of emotional arousal is generally less efficient, and the evidence
relating to this will be reviewed in Chapter 3.

Finally, there can be interaction between the emotional content of materials
and the emotional state or preoccupations of subjects. Most of the cognitive
phenomena considered in this book fall into this category, and involve the use
of experimental materials of relevance to patients with particular emotional
disorders. It appears that the effects of emotion on cognition are particularly
powerful in such paradigms.

Effects of cognitive processes on emotional states have also been studied.
For example, the theories of Lazarus (1966) and Scherer (1984) emphasize that
whether events lead to emotional reactions depends on how they are
appraised. Scherer's theory postulates a series of five stimulus evaluation
checks for (a) novelty, (b) intrinsic pleasantness, (c) goal/need significance, (d)
coping potential, and (e) norm/self compatibility. Cognitive representations,
such as thoughts and images, can also affect emotion (see Chapter 7) and
clinical theorists (e.g. Teasdale, 1983a) have often emphasized that there is a
reciprocal relationship between cognition and mood, in which mood is affected
by cognition as well as vice versa.

However, the assumption that cognition influences or determines emotion has recently become controversial, and Zajonc has argued that emotion is potentially independent of cognition (Zajonc, 1980, 1984; Zajonc et al., 1982). The import of the 'potentially' in this statement is that affect and cognition *can* function independently; it is not being suggested that affect is necessarily or always independent of cognition. The argument that emotion can be independent of cognition has not gone unchallenged (e.g. Lazarus, 1982, 1984; Mandler, 1982). The debate over Zajonc's position has been fuelled by different views about scientific theories and their verification. Zajonc feels that Lazarus's view that emotional reactions are mediated by cognitive appraisal is effectively unverifiable because Lazarus's definition of cognitive appraisal is so broad as to include phenomena that are unobservable. Lazarus regards this as an unnecessarily positivist stance that does not sufficiently allow for scientific constructs which are tied, not to a single measure, but to a network of observations which jointly support the construct concerned.

It is now widely agreed that this debate has depended, to a large extent, on how the key terms of 'cognition' and 'emotion' are defined, especially by what is meant by cognition (e.g. Watts, 1983; Leventhal and Scherer, 1987). One empirical fact that Zajonc regards as a 'crucial' piece of evidence for his position (Zajonc et al., 1982, p. 216) concerns the phenomenon of previously exposed stimuli being preferred to those that have not been exposed. Zajonc is impressed by the fact that this does not depend on 'awareness of recognition of the object as familiar' and takes this as support for his position; but clearly at best it only shows that affective changes are not necessarily based on *conscious* awareness. There would thus be fairly wide support for a reformulated version of Zajonc's thesis that emotion can be independent of *conscious* cognitive processes (Mandler, 1982). Some of the evidence to show that emotional reactions can be produced by stimuli of which people are not consciously aware will be reviewed in Chapter 4. However, to conclude from this that 'cognition' is not involved in the production of emotional reactions is to use 'cognition' in a limited and idiosyncratic way.

The general debate about the relationship between emotion and cognition has led to a parallel debate in the clinical literature. Rachman (1981), accepting Zajonc's conclusion about the relative independence of affect and cognition, drew out its clinical implications. Though noting that Zajonc had not suggested that affect is *wholly* independent of cognition, the clinical conclusions that Rachman drew seem to go beyond what follows legitimately from the actual evidence Zajonc marshalls. Among these is the proposition that the current emphasis on behaviourally-based treatments should be maintained rather than relying instead on cognitive treatments. This might be correct, but it does not follow from Zajonc's thesis. The fact that affect can be independent of conscious cognition justifies caution about whether or not cognitive treatments for emotional disorders will be effective. However, it certainly does not by itself justify the conclusion that they will be *in*effective; this is an empirical matter. It should also be noted that many forms of cognitive therapy, such as Beck's treatment of anxiety, use corrective experience as well as verbally-mediated work on conscious cognition. Rachman's paper stimulated a subsequent debate in the clinical literature which is beyond the scope of this chapter, but which can be followed in Watts (1983), Greenberg and Safran (1984a), Rachman (1984), Mahoney (1984), and Greenberg and Safran (1984b).

1.2 EMOTION AND EMOTIONAL DISORDERS

A clear understanding of the role of cognition in emotion depends on a clear conceptualization of emotion. Important issues are: what range of phenomena are to be included in 'emotion', differences between emotions in the role of cognition, and differences between short and long-term aspects of emotion.

The debate between Zajonc and Lazarus has been based on a very general concept of emotion or 'affect'. Where Zajonc was specific, he indicated that he was mainly concerned with affective judgement or preferences (Russell and Woudzia, 1986), but it is not clear that what may be true of preferences is true of more general emotional reactions.

Emotion is a multifaceted phenomenon and it has been widely accepted that comprehensive theories of emotion must include its different facets. Lang (1985) specifies behavioural, physiological and cognitive components. Scherer (1984) has proposed a similar model with five components: cognitive processing of stimuli, motivation, physiological activation, motor behaviour and subjective feeling state. The information-processing approach to emotion does not exclude non-cognitive components of emotion, nor regard them as in any way secondary. Some cognitive approaches to emotional disorders suggestive cognitive factors are 'primary'. It seems to us that the interrelationship between the different facets of emotion are such that no one of them is likely to be primary to all the others (Watts, in press). We are also not proposing a reductionist approach to emotional disorders in which all other aspects of emotion are held to be derived from and explained by cognitive factors. Rather, we see the cognitive approach as making a valuable contribution to the study of emotional disorders as one among a number of different perspectives.

It is important to distinguish between different emotions, partly because they vary in the extent to which they are associated with cognitive interpretations of the situations that produce them. A distinction can be made between basic and complex emotions, though it is not clear that it is better to consider them as dichotomized in this way rather than being arranged along a continuum. Oatley and Johnson-Laird (1987) propose that complex emotions are founded on basic emotions, but also include a 'propositional evaluation which is social and includes reference to the self'. Basic emotions (happiness, sadness, anxiety, anger, disgust) are seen as universal. but complex emotions take different forms in different cultures. Remorse would be an example of a complex emotion, based on sadness, but incorporating mutual plans and specific beliefs about the self. Cognitive elaboration in remorse is thus more extensive than in sadness. Emotions with extensive cognitive elaboration are perhaps more likely to be long-term; the propositional content of complex emotions such as remorse can take the form of repetitive ruminations that serve to maintain them. It is important to begin to make such distinctions, because the effects on information-processing of simple and complex emotions are likely to be different.

The emotional states of anxiety and depression which are the primary subject of this book are multifaceted. In patients with anxiety states there are likely to be acute and intense emotional reactions with a strong autonomic component, but also long-term cognitive elaboration around themes of danger and risk. Depression is perhaps less likely to include acute reactions to specific stimuli, but is more pervasive in its effects. This pervasiveness seems to be partly what is meant by calling depression a disorder of 'mood'. We shall return in the final chapter to differences between the cognitive processes involved in anxiety and depression.

Emotional disorders by definition involve long-term emotional disturbance and preoccupations. They are probably not unique in this, depending in part on how widely the category of 'disorder' is drawn. Certainly, there are many people who are not 'patients' who have long-term emotional reactions. Overlaid on these long-term features there can be varying degrees of acute emotional arousal. Recent research is tending to show that it is subjects who have acute emotional reactions against a background of chronic increased emotionality who show cognitive effects most clearly (e.g. Covington et al., 1986). The general picture that is emerging is that long-term disorders create cognitive 'structures' which are 'activated' at times of acute emotional arousal.

1.3 THE INVESTIGATION OF COGNITIVE PHENOMENA

To elucidate the nature of the approach to emotional disorders from cognitive psychology, it will be helpful to consider the range of information-processing phenomena which is suggested by clinical observation and the kinds of experimental paradigm available for their investigation.

Many patients with emotional disorders are preoccupied with upsetting experiences. Anxious people may be preoccupied with occasions when they have panicked and with the risk of similar events in the future. Depressed patients may be preoccupied with their failures or with times when they felt let down by people. Though patients have often had more such experiences than people in the ordinary population, their preoccupation with them often seems to exceed what is explicable on this basis. Why this excessive preoccupation? Several explanations suggest themselves. One is that emotional disorders may (a) increase the extent to which people *notice* stressful events, (b) increase the *effect* of these events on cognitive functioning, or (c) increase the frequency with which these events are *recalled*. Each of these is clinically plausible, though it cannot be assumed without investigation that they are necessarily all correct.

Clinical observations of depressed patients might suggest that they are particularly likely to notice things that are consistent with their depressed mood. Perhaps 'negative' things are particularly likely to be noticed. Some depressed people may be particularly inclined to notice criticism of their competence; others to notice a lack of affection and intimacy. Alternatively, emotional preoccupations may be due to stressful events having more *effect* on people with emotional disorders than on others. For example, an insulting comment by a supervisor at work may be more likely to produce distressing ruminations that interfere with concentration and task performance. Yet again, depressed people seem more likely to *remember* things that are relevant to their mood state. Upsetting events, such as criticism or a lack of support, may be well remembered by patients, not only because of how they were 'encoded' at the time, but because depressed patients are predisposed selectively to remember and rehearse such events. From a clinical point of view both explanations are plausible.

A variety of experimental paradigms are available to investigate such phenomena. For example, systematic biases in attention can be studied in the laboratory, though in order to do so it is often necessary to work with stimuli that simulate the relevant real-life phenomena. Individual words or phrases are often useful, even when taken out of the interpersonal context in which they have greatest significance. In designing such an experiment, it is necessary to use methods to ensure that the stimuli are not too easily noticed, such as presenting them at low visual or auditory intensities, presenting other distracting stimuli at the same time, or presenting stimuli which are ambiguous. It is only when a situation is created in which people vary in the sensitivity with which they detect the target stimuli that the effects of emotional disorders can be examined. In a similar way, the disruptive effects of upsetting events can be investigated by using stimuli that are a simulation of the relevant real-life events, such as words that represent central emotional concerns. If people are given carefully selected tasks to perform with such words it is possible to demonstrate the disruptive impact of emotional stimuli in patients. Finally, the accessibility of upsetting events can be investigated by testing people's ability to recall them.

A central aim of research is, of course, to design an experiment that can be interpreted relatively unambiguously. Two examples relating to selective recall will illustrate this point. If people are depressed both when negative events occur and when they remember them, it is not clear whether it is mood at the time the events occur (i.e. at encoding) or mood when they are remembered (i.e. at retrieval), or the similarity of mood at the two points which is responsible for the effect. By using artificial mood-induction procedures to create depressed mood at encoding but not at retrieval in some subjects, and depressed mood at retrieval but not at encoding in others, it is possible to disentangle the processes involved. Another issue relates to the pool of memories from which people draw when remembering particular events. It is possible that depressed people selectively recall negative events because such things have happened to them more often. To examine whether particular negative events are especially likely to be remembered if they happen to depressed people, it is necessary to work with a determinate number of memories. For this purpose, it is helpful to present a specially constructed list of words which are relevant to a depressed mood state. Using slightly artificial materials of this kind results in an experiment that is less ambiguous to interpret. There is a constant tension in research on information processing in emotional disorders between research which is somewhat artificial but relatively unambiguous, and research which is more naturalistic but less easy to interpret. Both have their place and they can enrich each other. Detailed accounts of the kinds of paradigm that are available and the results that can be obtained from them will be presented in subsequent chapters.

1.4 COGNITIVE APPROACHES TO EMOTIONAL DISORDERS

The approach to emotional disorders from the standpoint of experimental cognitive psychology can be contrasted with other contemporary 'cognitive' approaches to emotional disorders. Cognitive approaches of emotional phenomena are now widely accepted, but they are very varied in their foci. For example, the reformulated learned helplessness model of depression (Abramson et al., 1978; Peterson and Seligman, 1984) focuses on the attribution of negative events to internal, stable and global factors. In contrast, Meichenbaum (1977) and Beck (Beck et al., 1979; Beck and Emery, 1985) have given particular emphasis to the role of recurrent anxious and depressive thoughts in emotional disorders. Most clinicians who refer to 'cognitive' approaches to emotional disorders probably have in mind approaches such as these. Though they are clearly able to elucidate important features of emotional disorders and have led to treatment methods of worthwhile power, there has been a lack of precision in clinical theorizing about cognitive aspects of emotional disorders.

In interpreting the cognitive phenomena found in emotional disorders, researchers have made use of concepts such as 'schema' derived from cognitive theory (see Chapter 6). A contrast can be made between descriptive and explanatory uses of such terms. At a descriptive level, it is possible to try simply to *translate* clinical accounts of the cognitive phenomena found in emotional disorders into such apparently theoretical terms. Many uses of the concept of 'schema' by clinical theorists have been of this descriptive kind. We shall, in contrast, try to keep a distinction between theoretical concepts and the phenomena they purport to explain. This makes it possible to question whether a particular theoretical account of a cognitive phenomenon is the correct one. Another example would be the concept of an associative network which has been so widely employed in describing depressive memory bias that the question has sometimes ceased to be raised of whether this is the correct theoretical account. In fact, we shall argue in Chapter 5 that, though it has served a useful function in stimulating research on memory bias, there are some phenomena, such as the retrieval strategies used by depressed patients for remembering positive events, that it cannot easily accommodate.

The information-processing approach to emotional disorders also promises to provide a wider range of methodologies for investigating the bases of dysfunctional thoughts. In particular, it provides an experimental paradigm which can avoid the problems of self-report methods. In pursuing a cognitive processing approach, we shall omit from consideration much of the questionnaire data on which research on cognitive dysfunction in emotional disorders has hitherto been based. However, we shall consider research on cognitive *events*, such as images, thoughts and judgements (Chapters 7 and 8), and attempt to relate these to basic cognitive processes.

The common element in cognitive approaches to emotion based on phenomena such as appraisals, attributions and beliefs, is the conceptual primacy that they give to *conscious* cognition. Though they do not claim that the cognitive processes associated with emotional reactions or disorders are necessarily conscious, they describe them in terminology appropriate to their conscious forms. For example, though attributions may occur at an implicit level that is outside conscious awareness, the concept of attribution is based on the responses given when questions of causality are consciously considered.

Cognitive psychology is potentially able to take a broader view in two important respects. First, it is specifically concerned not only with conscious phenomena such as judgements, but also with cognitive processes such as encoding that that can proceed without awareness, and frequently do so. Secondly, it is at least as concerned with cognitive *processes* as with the *content* of cognitions. It would be a mistake to suggest that theorists such as Beck have neglected processes. For example, the concept of over-generalization which has an important place in his theory would be one example of a process concept. However, we would argue that an approach grounded in general cognitive psychology which has long been concerned with such processes as selective attention, encoding and retrieval, is better equipped to provide an account of the cognitive processes that characterize emotional disorders.

1.5 COGNITIVE LEVELS

One particular advantage of cognitive psychology's concern with both conscious and non-conscious aspects of cognition is its ability to give an account of the relationship between the two. The connection (or lack of it) between different cognitive levels may be particularly important when considering emotion. It is a common clinical observation about patients with emotional disorders that there is a partial dissociation between rational and automatic cognitive processes. People with simple phobias are good examples. They often believe that there is no reason to be frightened of their phobic object (spiders, for example), and consequently feel that their phobia is stupid and irrational. Nevertheless, in the presence of the phobic object they automatically become frightened, and cannot help doing so. Sometimes depressed patients show a somewhat similar dissociation, though less clearly. For example, a depressed person may feel whenever he is slighted by someone else that he is thoroughly unlovable and unattractive, though he may also be able to recognize at a rational level that he actually has at least as many attractive qualities as the average person.

Such consideration suggested the relevance of a hierarchical model of emotion, such as that proposed by Howard Leventhal, which distinguishes between the effects of emotion at different levels of the cognitive system (Leventhal, 1984). (Peter Lang has proposed a somewhat similar model that will be discussed in Chapter 7.) The lowest level in Leventhal's scheme is a 'sensorimotor' one which operates without volitional effort. Next, there is a 'schematic' level which contains concrete representations of specific emotional events and experiences. Schemata stored from previous emotional episodes influence the processing of current events, and are activated automatically. The highest level is a conceptual one and is based on the capacity to draw propositional conclusions about two or more emotional episodes; this level operates by conscious volition.

Leventhal and Scherer (1987) have recently argued that it would be more fruitful than discussing whether or not cognition and emotion are potentially independent of each other, as Zajonc and Lazarus have done, to examine exactly how cognition is involved in different kinds of emotional reaction. They apply the hierarchical model of emotion to help to elucidate how cognition is involved in different aspects of emotion. Clearly, only limited stimulus processing is involved at the sensorimotor level, but they suggest that, at the higher levels, increasingly complex stimulus appraisals occur. For example, checks for 'pleasantness' are based on innate preferences at the sensorimotor level, on learned preferences at the schematic level, and on recalled, anticipated or derived evaluations at the conceptual level.

Leventhal's model is a highly detailed one, and this is only the briefest indication of its scope. However, it will be clear that some such distinctions are helpful in conceptualizing the kinds of dissociation between different facets of emotional disorders. For example, when spider phobics say that they know that spiders are not really frightening, they are operating at the conceptual level. Nevertheless, when faced with a spider, they show strong 'sensorimotor' reactions of anxiety. Also, at what Leventhal calls the 'schematic' level, they have vivid and sometimes intrusive memories of particular occasions when spiders have made them panic.

It may be somewhat misleading to talk here about discrete 'levels'. Though there is a strong case for some kind of hierarchical model of the cognitive aspects of emotion, to talk of levels may imply too sharp a separation between the components of the hierarchical cognitive system. Outside the context of emotion, many cognitive theorists have included hierarchical features in models of the cognitive system, though these have often been more subtle than hierarchical theories of emotion. Some indication of the ways in which hierarchical structures have been incorporated in cognitive systems will be given in the next chapter. However, several clinically important questions arise from this kind of hierarchical model of the cognitive aspects of depression. One is the relative effect of mood state on the various levels. For example, clinical observations suggest that automatic thoughts are particularly important in maintaining depressive mood state, though there has been little attempt to compare their depressogenic effect with that resulting from the activation of sensorimotor or conceptual levels of depression. Another question relates to the relative time-course of emotional dysfunction at the various levels. For example, is the conceptual level one of the more stable aspects of depression?

An approach to emotional disorders based on cognitive psychology offers a way of exploring the relationships between different levels. Clearly, there are influences in both directions (a theme that will be developed in the next chapter). Low-level cognitive processes can feed upwards and affect higher-level judgements. High-level assumptions can also feed downwards and affect how individual events are processed. The extent of these two kinds of influence is a matter for empirical investigation; cognitive psychology provides a relevant set of experimental techniques for doing so.

A hierarchical approach also has implications for the investigation of treatment processes (see also Greenberg and Safran, 1984a). Successful treatment of an emotional disorder must include modification of all levels at which reactions are disordered. This must include, for a phobic patient, reaching the point at which he no longer reacts with involuntary anxiety to the phobic stimulus. Similarly, for a depressed patient, it must include being able to experience being criticized without showing an exaggerated 'catastrophic' reaction. How is this best achieved? Because of the dissociation that can take place between different levels, there is a danger that therapeutic work at one level will not affect other levels. For example, therapies that operate at the conceptual level cannot necessarily be assumed to have effects at the sensorimotor level. Current 'cognitive' methods of treating depression involve such a complex of component techniques that it is difficult to disentangle scientifically which components are working at which level. We currently need a more varied range of measures relating to the different cognitive levels at which emotional disorder can be manifest.

1.6 AN INTEGRATIVE FRAMEWORK

The cognitive processing framework with which we are concerned promises to provide a broad integrative framework within which the effects of various different kinds of treatment can be considered. We have already argued its relevance to cognitive therapies for emotional disorders. It is also relevant to behaviour therapy. For example, it is widely recognized that an important feature of the behavioural treatment of phobic anxiety is systematic exposure to the phobic stimulus. One of the issues that arises is how the patient processes the phobic stimulus: there is a danger of a patient showing 'cognitive avoidance' which is likely to interfere with the therapeutic value of exposure treatment (Foa and Kozak, 1986). The information-processing perspective is relevant to investigating the kind of processing that takes place during stimulus exposure (see Chapter 4).

Similarly, the information-processing perspective is relevant to psycho-dynamic approaches to emotional disorders. Because the informational perspective focuses primarily on processes that can proceed without phenomenal experience, it can provide a meeting-point with the psycho-dynamic interest in non-conscious processes. The concepts of the unconscious in information-processing and psychodynamic psychology are, of course, not identical. The important issue is whether people remain unconscious of material, not just because of the informational limits of consciousness, but because they are motivated by anxiety to do so. There are currently signs of a growing integration of information-processing and psychodynamic psy-chology (Erdelyi, 1985; Wegman, 1985). It is beyond our purpose here to consider this issue in detail, but such trends at least suggest that an information-processing approach to emotional disorders should not be regarded as incompatible with a psychodynamic one (see Chapter 9).

There is also potential scope for relating the information-processing approach to biological and social factors. For example, connections can be made between some of the cognitive dysfunction found in depression and the disruption of circadian rhythms (Healy and Williams, in press). There are also indications that social context can have important effects on cognitive processing, and that it may also be possible to apply the kind of methodologies described in this book to studying the processing of social events in emotional disorders (Loewenstein and Hokanson, 1986). This will enhance the clinical importance of the cognitive approach to emotional disorders (Coyne and Gotlib, 1983, 1986).

For the present, we see the main contribution of the cognitive processing approach to emotional disorders in enhancing our understanding of them. The research described in this book has already led to advances in our understanding of how cognitive processes, such as attention and memory, are affected in emotional disorders. One of the next stages will be to formulate a theory of the dysfunctions found in disorders of anxiety and depression; we have attempted in the final chapter to sketch the kind of theoretical framework that we believe will be needed to provide a theoretical synthesis of the developing body of data. We also return in the final chapter to the question of implications for clinical practice. For example, we may be approaching the point where some of the investigatory techniques we describe have a clinical application, such as in exploring the effects of treatment. However, for the time being, cognitive psychology promises to contribute more to the general understanding of emotional disorders than to advances in clinical techniques.

Chapter 2

The Information-processing Paradigm

Consider the following transcript from a hypothetical patient, MF., attending a psychology out-patient clinic as a GP referral:

'I feel so low and depressed that everything is just too much effort. I can't even manage very simple jobs without getting distracted or confused. I just can't concentrate any more. And I feel afraid all the time too. Society is so dangerous nowadays. Everything I read in the papers is about some terrible accident, or about violence. It's not even safe on the streets — everywhere I look there are dangers. But I can get anxious even when I'm just sitting quietly, thinking about nothing. Anxiety just seems to come out of the blue and sweeps over me. I am doing less and less nowadays, and seldom see friends any more. Whenever I'm out socially I get uncomfortable. People find it difficult to accept me now. It's clear that they either find me boring or embarrassing, so I prefer to avoid these situations...'

What is wrong with MF? A simplistic answer may involve formulating a diagnosis for this patient, such as mixed anxiety and depressive neurosis. However, such a label does nothing to increase our understanding of his problems. Each abnormal symptom indicates that something about MF is functioning maladaptively, and we can only understand the nature of this patient's condition if we can accurately describe those fundamental processes which are giving rise to his specific problems. But what kind of model should we construct? A careful look at the transcript above will reveal a number of important cognitive operations which may potentially contribute to the emotional distress suffered by MF. For example, his description suggests the possibility not only of some general impairment in cognitive functioning, but also of processing biases, such as enhanced perceptual salience for threat-related stimuli, distorted probability judgements concerning the likelihood of dangerous events, inferential biases in the way ambiguous situations are interpreted, and so on. Each of these issues, and more, will be considered in greater detail within the main chapters of this book. In this current chapter we offer a very general introduction to one particular approach to psychological modelling, based on the information-processing paradigm, and indicate its potential for generating plausible hypotheses to explain various symptoms associated with the affective disorders.

Before beginning, however, we should stress the necessary limitations of this overview. Cognitive psychology is a young and diverse discipline which is continually evolving. With each shift in emphasis new levels of explanation and corresponding new theoretical concepts emerge, sometimes only briefly before their utility is effectively challenged. For the purposes of this general introduction it would be inappropriate to focus upon the developing frontiers of cognitive science. Rather, we shall attempt to introduce some of the central themes which have traditionally characterized the information-processing paradigm and which have survived in some or other guise, throughout its various stages of development. This will inevitably result in a rather historic orientation, but should familiarize the reader with the kinds of enduring issue which are most pervasive in applied cognitive research.

2.1 THE NATURE OF SCIENTIFIC PARADIGMS

Theorists typically draw on a particular set of conceptual structures and processes, and rely upon a conventional series of assumptions, when formulating hypothetical models. In effect, they utilize the components of a pre-existing 'construction kit', which both facilitates model design and constrains the range of possibilities. The 'construction kit' employed to develop any model represents the scientific paradigm adopted by the model builder. A scientific paradigm is neither right nor wrong: we do not normally attempt to prove or disprove it. However, it can be judged more or less fruitful on the basis of its ability to produce models which can accommodate and predict relevant data. Indeed, Kuhn (1962) argues that major scientific advances are marked not simply by the emergence of innovative models, but by the adoption of new, more fruitful paradigms to generate such models.

In its short history, psychology has witnessed the development of several alternative paradigms. Psychoanalytical models construe man's activities as attempts to reduce tension between conflicting internal drives and values, and the external constraints imposed by reality. Behavioural models consider man primarily as a basic learning device, and try to account for current activity in terms of an individual's classical and instrumental conditioning history. Cognitive models, however, characterize man as a complex information-processing system, and attempt to describe human experience and activity in terms of the integrated operation of fundamental processing mechanisms which act upon, and are themselves acted upon, by the flow of information through the system. Importing the concept of information from communication science in the 1950s freed theoretical psychology from the constraints of S-R behaviourism. By demonstrating that even simple behaviours, such as choice reaction-time responses, were dependent upon such variables as the number of stimuli in the set (Hicks, 1953) stimulus frequency (Hyman, 1952) and the provision of context (Crossman, 1953), the concept of discrete linkages between each stimulus and its response was overthrown. This recognition that the brain deals with information, rather than simply responds to specific stimuli, allowed psychologists to discuss internal representations without commitment to any particular neurological or biochemical framework. Regardless of their physical nature, such internal representations could now be considered in terms of the type and amount of information which they contained.

The past decade or so has witnessed a growing recognition that cognitive processes may play an important role in the development and maintenance of neurotic disorders. Thus, clinical theorists have begun to suggest that idiosyncracies in the way information is processed may lead to styles of thinking which characterise (and perhaps constitute) the affective neuroses (e.g. Beck, 1976). As discussed in Chapter 1, however, such accounts have often failed to exploit fully the rich potential offered by the information-processing paradigm to model the nature of these hypothetical individual differences. The remainder of the current chapter introduces some of the important concepts which have historically characterized this paradigm.

2.2 CAPACITY LIMITATIONS

One common characteristic of all information-processing devices is that they are to some degree constrained by available capacity. Accordingly, information-processing models of the brain typically characterize it as a limited capacity system, and certain features of human experience and activity are considered to reflect constraints on available processing capacity. While it may be self-evident that we cannot do all things simultaneously with full efficiency, there are a number of ways in which capacity limitations can be conceptualized. One option has been to postulate that cognitive processes require 'resources' to operate (or 'effort' or 'attention', e.g. Kahneman, 1973; Shiffrin, 1976; Roediger et al., 1977; Hasher and Zacks, 1979; Kahneman and Treisman, 1984), and that these resources are allocated in continuous modulated quantities from some common undifferentiated reservoir. Subject and task parameters will determine the amount of resources required for a particular process to operate. Processes which make relatively small demands upon the resource pool may therefore proceed simultaneously, but whenever the overall requirements exceed the capacity of the resource pool, this will not be possible.

While this simple formulation of capacity limitation is appealing, and has been incorporated in a number of useful models, it is inconsistent with the observation that interference between tasks often appears to reflect task structure rather than task difficulty (e.g. Baddeley, 1974; McLeod, 1977, 1978;

Kinsbourne and Hicks; 1978). That is, one task may cause severe interference when performed simultaneously with one other kind of task, yet little interference when performed simultaneously with a different task of equal difficulty. This has led a number of researchers to put forward structural accounts of capacity limitations (e.g. Welford, 1967; Keele, 1973; Kerr, 1973; Fodor, 1983; Broadbent, 1984). According to such formulations, capacity limitations reflect competition between tasks for specific information-processing mechanisms or structures necessary for performance. Tasks which need to use a common processing structure cannot easily be performed at the same time without some interference, whereas those which do not share common structures can efficiently proceed simultaneously.

Certain alternative accounts of capacity limitations have integrated resource-based and structural-based formulations into a common conceptual framework (e.g. Kantowitz and Knight, 1976; Kinsbourne and Hicks, 1978; Navon and Gopher, 1979a, 1979b; Sanders, 1979; Wickens, 1979, 1984). The suggestion is that tasks draw for their performance upon a number of structure-specific reservoirs of processing resources. That is, the processing system incorporates a number of mechanisms, each having its own capacity, and these structures can share or divide their limited processing resources between concurrent activities (e.g. Long, 1976). Wickens (1984), for example, suggests that such reservoirs can be characterized along at least the three following dimensions: (a) stimulus characteristics, such as sensory modality; (b) internal codes, which may be structural, phonetic, semantic, etc.; (c) response mode, which may, for instance, be manual or verbal. There is indeed considerable evidence that resources can be differentiated on the basis of such factors as input modality (e.g. Baddeley and Liberman, 1980; Rollins and Hendricks, 1980), requirements for short-term storage (Baddeley and Hitch, 1974; Baddeley, 1986), means of response (e.g. Wickens, 1984), and even the hemisphere of the brain primarily involved in processing an input (e.g. Friedman et al., 1982; Friedman and Polson, 1981).

More recently, a number of researchers have attempted to characterize capacity limitations in terms of neither resource limitations nor structural competition, but as a consequence of skill limitations in the parallel coordination of multiple cognitive processes (e.g. Spelke, Hirst and Neisser, 1976; Hirst et al., 1980; Hirst, 1986; Hirst and Kalmar, 1987). According to such accounts, limited skill in segregating two or more messages may result in inappropriate transformations to either or both inputs. Such 'cross-talk' between tasks leads to the breakdown in processing which characterizes overloaded cognitive systems.

How might such concepts be employed to illuminate a possible basis for some of the symptoms reported by our hypothetical patient MF? One feature of his condition was that simple tasks seemed excessively arduous, and concentration difficult to maintain. The information-processing paradigm, by highlighting the limited capacity nature of the cognitive system, suggests the possibility that such symptoms may be a consequence of severe restrictions in available processing capacity. More specific hypotheses can be derived from resource-based, structural or skill-based accounts of such capacity limitations. Indeed, a considerable literature now exists which attempts to characterise certain mood-related cognitive deficits, particularly those associated with anxiety, in precisely this way (e.g. Wine, 1971; Morris *et al.*, 1977). This will be discussed more fully in Chapter 3.

2.3 SELECTIVE PROCESSING

Regardless of their precise nature, capacity limitations within the cognitive system will inevitably lead to competition, and frequently to selectivity in processing. This differential processing of simultaneous sources of information is commonly termed selective attention, and the reader is directed to recent reviews by Broadbent (1982), Kahneman and Treisman (1984), Shiffrin (1985) and Johnston and Dark (1986).

While certain aspects of selectivity may reflect simple stimulus characteristics such as intensity, it is also clear that selectivity can be under internal control. The cognitive system can, through various priming techniques, be set to process information selectively in a particular sensory modality (e.g. Anthony and Graham, 1983; Hillyard and Kutas, 1983; Oatman, 1984), from a particular semantic area (e.g. Carr *et al.*, 1982; Johnston and Dark, 1982, 1985), or from a particular spatial and/or temporal domain (e.g. Palmer, 1975; Snyder and Uranowitz, 1978).

A number of important controversies have emerged within the field of selective attention. For example, some theorists have emphasized mechanisms of selectivity based on physical differences between relevant and irrelevant inputs, which operate early in the processing continuum (e.g. Broadbent, 1958). There is, however, considerable evidence that an irrelevant unattended message may nevertheless undergo some semantic processing (e.g. Treisman, 1960; Deutsch and Deutsch, 1963; Broadbent, 1971, 1982). On the basis of such observations some theorists have emphasized mechanisms of selectivity operating late in the processing continuum on the basis of semantic information. Such early controversy over the locus of selectivity has, however, largely been replaced by the view that it is pervasive throughout the processing continuum (Erdelyi, 1974).

Another underlying controversy, emphasized by Johnston and Dark (1986) but recognised by William James in 1890, distinguishes those approaches which construe selective attention as the *cause* of differential processing (e.g. Lundh, 1979; Duncan, 1980; Broadbent, 1982; Marcel, 1983b; Kahneman *et al.*, 1983; Shiffrin, 1985), and those which construe it as a *consequence* of differential processing (e.g. Neisser, 1976; Hochberg, 1978; Johnston and Dark, 1986). The former approach requires that a selective attentional system operates upon the records of some separate, large-capacity, nonconscious system to determine which lines of processing are pursued to completion and/or result in a conscious representation. One problem with such an attempt is that it 'explains' mechanisms of selective attention by postulating a selective attentional system which itself possesses the capability to select — inviting the infinite regress characteristic of homunculus-based theories. The alternative view is that differential processing occurs through the mechanistic priming of processing structures. Such priming may be relative chronic, leading to semi-permanent processing advantages for certain domains of information, or may be a transient result of current cognitive activity. According to this account, selectivity in a current input is the *passive* result, through priming, of prior processing activity, and attention is simply the resultant phenomenal correlate of such priming.

Whatever model of selective attention is adopted, one major requirement for an information-processing model of any particular activity is to accommodate the observed patterns of selectivity which commonly occur. Why is one thing noticed more easily than another? Why is one particular interpretation more obvious than an alternative? Why is one item of information stored more efficiently than another item? Why is one fact recalled more easily than another, equally well-learned fact? And so on. Acceptable cognitive models must be capable of answering such questions.

The emphasis which the information-processing paradigm places on selective factors in cognitive processing once again suggests a possible hypothesis to accommodate some of MF's symptoms. His comments appear to indicate a gross over-awareness of certain aspects of his environment; particularly those aspects which convey threat-related information concerned with real or imagined dangers. One could postulate that fundamental biases in the selective functions that determine which inputs are most completely processed may underlie this subjective experience. There is a long-standing, though not unchallenged, view expressed in the cognitive literature that selective functions may operate to inhibit the subsequent processing of emotionally threatening inputs (e.g. Broadbent and Gregory, 1967; Bruner and Postman, 1947a, 1947b; Erdelyi, 1974). If such 'defensive' patterns of selectivity are inoperative for MF, or if his selective functions operate using different criteria which favour the processing of emotionally threatening information, then such information will ultimately become over-represented in his conscious experience. There is now considerable evidence that people do indeed show basic individual differences in the way their selective functions operate when dealing with emotionally threatening inputs (e.g. Byrne, 1961; Miller and Mangan, 1983), and a number of studies now suggest that particular patterns of selective processing may underlie various features of anxiety (cf. Eysenck, MacLeod and Mathews, in press) and depression (e.g.

Teasdale and Taylor, 1981; Clark and Teasdale, 1982; Mathews and Bradley, 1983).

2.4 STAGES OF PROCESSING

So far we have suggested that cognitive models characterize the brain as an overcrowded, limited-capacity system, designed to process the most important aspects of the available information. We have not yet discussed how this processing might take place. Clearly, there have been numerous models proposed for many different kinds of cognitive activity. Let us consider, however, some of the common features which often appear in models developed from the information-processing paradigm. The cognitive approach is typically reductionistic. Attempts to formulate a model for any complex process usually involve identifying and organizing the simpler component subprocesses which are involved. The simplest models which emerge can be characterized as linear sequences of independent processing stages. Each stage accepts information from the preceding stage, conducts some operation on it, and produces an output to be acted upon by the following stage. One attraction of this stages-of-processing approach lies in its potential to reveal basic, invariant, component subprocesses which may constitute the building-blocks of cognition. If these could be exhaustively identified, it has been argued, then models of higher-order processes may simply involve assembling those invariant subprocesses in an appropriate sequence, much like constructing a complex circuit from simple electrical components.

Given this incentive it is perhaps not surprising that a great deal of research effort, particularly in the early 1970s, has been directed at identifying the component stages of processing which underlie more complex cognitive operations. Frequently, this has involved the application of additive factors and subtraction methodology to reaction-time data (e.g. Sternberg, 1969; Pachella, 1974). The additive factors method involves introducing various experimental manipulations to a particular task, either singly or in pairs, which will plausibly increase the time taken to perform the whole task. If two different manipulations produce additive effects on performance time then, it is argued, they must affect different processing stages, whereas if their effect is interactive they are considered to influence the same stage. By imposing a large number of such manipulations on any task it must therefore be possible to identify the number of processing stages involved and, by considering the kinds of manipulation which affect each, what these stages most plausibly reflect. The subtraction method can be used to refine further an already formulated stages of processing model by employing task variants which will eliminate the need for one particular theoretical stage, and calculating the duration of this 'subtracted' stage from the magnitude of the time-saving. The precise influence of subsequent novel task manipulations can then be predicted on the basis of the model and these parameters.

Both methods are based on important assumptions which are vulnerable to criticism, and therefore the techniques have a controversial history (cf. Pieters, 1983; Broadbent, 1984). The most important assumptions are that information should be processed through stages in a strict *serial* order, and that the functioning of each stage (in particular its temporal duration) must be entirely independent from the processing outcomes of any other stage. As will be argued later in this chapter, there are plausible alternatives to both these possibilities.

While models based on linear independent processing stages may be limited, the principle of reducing complex mental operations to discrete component processes has obvious advantages, and has remained a pervasive characteristic of cognitive research. Contemporary theorists commonly conceptualize the cognitive system as a collection of processing modules, each module concerned with a particular type of computation or transformation (e.g. Johnson-Laird, 1983a, 1983b; Fodor, 1983). Some modules receive information directly from the environment, whereas some take inputs from other modules. Some are relatively self-contained, or 'cognitively impenetrable', while others may be under intentional control. The way in which such modules are organized in order to perform a specific task may, however, be considerably more complex than a simple linear sequence.

Identification of fundamental component operations increases the potential specificity of hypotheses concerning the cognitive basis of MF's symptoms. We have considered that his concentration difficulties may reflect restrictions in available processing resources, and his preoccupation with threat-related information may arise from biased selection procedures. Perhaps we can also identify the fundamental processing operations which may be involved. Such an approach has indeed been adopted with some success. For example, one recent account of the cognitive deficits associated with high levels of anxiety not only implicates reduced processing capacity, but also identifies the stage where this capacity restriction occurs. Thus, Eysenck (1979a, 1979b) interprets the available data to show that reductions in the capacity of working memory (Baddeley and Hitch, 1974; Baddeley, 1986), which serves as a temporary store for intermediate processing results, appear to underlie some cognitive impairments. Similarly, it may be possible to identify the particular component operations most involved in the biased selective processing which, it has been hypothesized, could explain MF's subjective preoccupation with certain categories of unpleasant information. Available evidence suggests that early perceptual stages may involve biased selectivity in anxiety (e.g. Mathews and MacLeod, 1985, 1986) and stages involving the retrieval of information from memory may be biased in depression (e.g. Clark and Teasdale, 1982; Mathews and Bradley, 1983).

However, one should be aware of the potential problems which accompany too rigid an adherence to the simplistic application of the above approach. For example, there is the problem of determining which processes represent the invariant building-blocks of cognitive. Just because two separate types of complex process each involve, let us say, a binary decision stage, this does not mean that the component process is identical in both tasks. The subtraction method can sometimes be usefully applied in such situations to determine whether the duration of this operation is comparable in both tasks — a necessary but insufficient condition for the argument that the component process is one and the same in each task. A more sophisticated technique has been suggested by R. Sternberg (1977) which uses the subtraction method, but involves the measurement of individual differences in the time taken to perform the component stage. If this same pattern of individual differences is also found when examining the relevant processing operation in the other task, then this adds considerable strength to the argument that the same component process is occurring.

2.5 SERIAL vs. PARALLEL PROCESSING

It has already been mentioned that serious limitations on the value of simplistic stages of processing research become apparent when one considers the plausibility of the necessary assumptions which underlie some of its methodology.

Consider the assumption of seriality. It is well recognized that the brain is quite capable of conducting both serial and parallel processing. In the former case a string of operations is conducted in sequence, whereas in the latter a number of operations all take place simultaneously. For example, Jonides and Gleitman (1972) report results from a task in which subjects must search for a particular target letter among a visually presented display of distractor letters. If this involves the sequential examination of every letter to determine if each is a target then the comparison operations are said to occur serially. If all letters are simultaneously evaluated to determine whether any is a target then comparison operations are said to occur in parallel. It is possible to determine whether this task involves serial or parallel processing by varying the number of letters which appear on any trial. This manipulation will influence decision time only if the relevant comparisons are conducted in serial. The results of this study showed that both serial and parallel operations are possible. The typical finding when searching for a target letter among distractor letters, or a target number among distractor numbers, was that decision latency depends upon set size, indicating serial processing. If, however, the target is a number embedded in distractor letters, or a letter embedded in distractor numbers, then the decision latency is quite independent of set size, indicating parallel processing. Intriguingly, Jonides and Gleitman have shown that the occurrence of serial or parallel processing does not simply depend upon the physical similarity or dissimilarity of the target and the distractors. This is clearly shown when a target is the symbol 0. Subjects instructed to search for this target can be told to look for either the number zero, or the letter 'O'. When the target is labelled zero, and shown with number distractors then serial comparisons are found to occur, leading to longer decision latencies with larger set sizes. When identical displays are presented, but the target symbol is simply labelled as the letter 'O', then decision latency is independent of set size, indicating that comparisons occurred in parallel. Thus both serial and parallel processing appear to be possible depending upon the precise details of the task. Indeed, the most powerful contemporary computational models of human cognition place particular emphasis on the parallel nature of component processes (e.g. McClelland and Rumelhart, 1985, 1986; Hinton, McClelland and Rumelhart, 1986).

2.6 PARALLEL CONTINGENT PROCESSING

The kinds of cognitive operation which can be modelled using a stages-of-processing approach must not only be serial in nature but require that the accuracy of later stages are dependent upon the prior successful completion of earlier stages. That is, the stages are logically contingent upon one another. However, a number of theorists have questioned the view that one component process must be completed before a contingent second process can start. An alternative possibility is that the output of a process may be continually available to other processes (cf. Posner and McLeod, 1982). For example, Norman and Bobrow (1975) suggest that the continuous output of each process may be a set of quantities, each indicating the current probability that one of a number of possible conclusions about the input is correct. If so, then a subsequent processing stage could begin to make use of this output even before the earlier stage was completed. Indeed, all stages may be simultaneously operative, although the accuracy, and possibly the processing rate, of later stages remains contingent on the continuously available results of earlier processes as they proceed. Turvey (1973) has termed such accounts parallel-contingent models, and this hypothetical relationship between processing stages is implicit in various theories of language comprehension (e.g. McClelland and Rumelhart, 1981), pattern identification (e.g. Selfridge, 1959; Turvey, 1973), word recognition (e.g. LaBerge and Samuels, 1974; McClelland, 1976; Henderson, 1977), and memory retrieval (e.g. Wickelgren, 1976). In an analysis of such 'cascade models', McClelland (1979) has demonstrated that additive factors and subtraction methodology may no longer be applicable, except under very specific circumstances. He shows, for example, that experimental manipulations which increase processing difficulty by influencing the asymptotic output of particular processing stages will all produce interactive effects, even when they affect different stages.

2.7 BOTTOM-UP vs. TOP-DOWN PROCESSING

One problem, therefore, with simplistic stages of processing research reflects its reliance on the assumption of strictly serial-independent stages. The possibility that stages may be related in a parallel-contingent manner means that operation at later stages may overlap with, and be qualitatively influenced by, the output from earlier stages. When one moves on to consider more complex cognitive operations, rather than simple input–output chains, it becomes clear that low-level operations may also be influenced by the results of higher-level operations. Most cognitive activity is not simply a passive response to an input. Rather, it tends to be goal-directed. We try to understand, to reach decisions, to solve problems, to remember particular details, and so on. Thus, typically, each operation of a processing sequence should take the system closer to the desired goal. However, it is only when the later operations are performed that it becomes apparent whether or not this goal has been achieved. If not, then the earlier stages of the processing chain must be modified adaptively. Thus, feedback from the later processing operations modify, or may even cause the reorganization of, earlier processing stages. Most aspects of cognitive functioning are therefore less accurately characterized as simple linear chains of processing stages, linking input to output, than as non-linear processing loops in which information is transferred in both directions. Those models which concentrate upon the way in which low-level basic processes lead to higher-order representations are often termed 'bottom-up' models. Those which emphasize how higher-order representations influence basic low-level operations are termed 'top down' models (cf. Sanford, 1985).

The distinction between top-down and bottom-up approaches can be illustrated with reference to many kinds of cognitive operation, including lexical processing (cf. McClelland and Rumelhart, 1981); solving mathematical equations (e.g. Ranney, 1987); other problems (e.g. Carroll, Thomas and Malhotra, 1980; Silver, 1981; Sanford, 1983) and comprehension of complex situations (e.g. Clark and Marshall, 1981; Sanford and Garrod, 1981; Shadbolt, 1983).

As an illustrative example let us consider perceptual processing. The question most basic to research on visual perception is this: how do we process information to yield an accurate internal representation of the external world impinging on the retina? Bottom-up models are typified by workers in *scene analysis*, a branch of artificial intelligence concerned with establishing a visual grammar to explain how basic elements are combined to yield complex percepts (cf. Frisby, 1980; Marr, 1980, 1982; Stent, 1981). Such programmes attempt to arrive at identified objects through successive stages of analysis and integration of the light input (cf. Kolers, 1983).

A completely bottom-up account of perception requires a massive amount of processing for every perceptual input and, furthermore, is not entirely consistent with certain available data. For example, it is possible to construct quite different objects which, when viewed monocularly from one particular angle, will project an identical retinal image. If one of these objects is a familiar structure, such as a chair, whereas the other is a meaningless structure, then both objects will be perceived as a chair when viewed in this way (cf. Haber and Hershenson, 1973).

Thus the pre-existing higher-order representation for chair controls the manner in which the current input is structured. There are a great many similar examples where familiar or expected higher-order pre-existing concepts will determine the way in which lower-level aspects of a current input, such as size (e.g. Bolles and Bailey, 1956; Gogel and Newton, 1969) colour (e.g. Duncker, 1939; Bruner, Postman and Rodrigues, 1951; Harper, 1953) or form (e.g. Leeper, 1935) are perceived. Those models of perception which consider low-level, more basic processes to be influenced by higher-order representations typify the top-down approach.

It is more realistic to accept the existence of both bottom-up and top-down operations, and to produce models which account for the relationship between these two different aspects of processing. Neisser (1976), for example, characterizes the interaction between bottom-up and top-down processes in perception as involving a cycle. An initial, brief, bottom-up phase will generate a hypothesis about what is being perceived. Expectations derived from this hypothesis will guide the next intake cycle, in a top-down manner, towards particular aspects of the stimulus. The selected aspects of the stimulus will then be briefly processed in a bottom-up manner, possibly modifying the hypothesis and leading to altered expectations which guide the next intake cycle; and so on. Through this cycling of bottom-up and top-down operations, each may influence the other in a way which maximizes efficiency.

As has already been indicated, top-down processing is certainly not limited to perception, and various areas of data seem to require a similar cyclical view. Consider, for example, the processes involved in comprehending the following simple event description.

> Jane was invited to Jack's birthday party. She wondered if he would like a kite. She went to her room and shook her piggy bank. It made no sound. (Charniak, 1972)

While this is very easy to understand, it cannot reasonably be argued that our comprehension of the overall situation simply reflects our cumulative understanding of its elements in a bottom-up manner. Nowhere is it stated that Jane wants to buy Jack a kite for his birthday present, or that she has no money to do so — yet that is most people's understanding of the story. Indeed, our understanding of each of the explicitly presented elements is only possible in the light of our overall understanding of the situation. We can only interpret the reasons for shaking the piggy bank, and the consequences of its silence, if we already appreciate the point of the story. Thus pre-existing information about birthday parties, present purchasing and piggy banks must be brought to bear in a top-down manner in order to extract the true meaning of this input. The common understanding that Jane is a child, for instance, is not supplied by the text, but reflects previously stored sets of assumptions.

Clearly, the kinds of higher order representations capable of influencing comprehension processes in a top-down manner must be quite complex. One common suggestion is that much knowledge of the world is organized into convenient 'packets', 'modules' or 'schemata', which represent conventional stereotypical situations and activities (e.g. Bartlett, 1932; Minsky, 1975; Schank and Abelson, 1977; Sanford and Garrod, 1982). These prototypical representations contain a considerable amount of default information; that is, information which is generally true in a particular situation, but which may be modified by the input. They also contain empty 'slots' which require a certain kind of information to be supplied. The comprehension process initially involves identifying the most appropriate module to accommodate the available information, perhaps on the basis of an initial bottom-up analysis. Thereafter this module will exert a top-down influence, determining the way in which the information must be organized and interpreted in order to be most efficiently incorporated. Therefore, the way in which the input is ultimately understood will be largely determined by pre-existing knowledge structures, and these structures will supply the additional information which allows inferencing and general elaborative processing. Similar schematic-based accounts have been suggested for the comprehension of stories (Rumelhart, 1975), and for the retrieval of information from long-term memory (Bara, 1983).

A fuller discussion of schemata can be found in Chapter 6. For the present, however, the most important point to note is that the way a complex situation is interpreted or recalled may depend upon the range of prototypical schemata stored in long-term memory, which are capable of accommodating the available details. Such representations are presumably acquired through direct or vicarious learning experiences, and it is thus highly probable that there will be a great deal of individual differences in the nature of the schemata which are stored, and in their relative accessibility. If so, then the same event may be processed in very dissimilar ways by two individuals, differing in the particular schemata available to organize the input. Disproportionately numerous or accessible schemata which function to organize information in ways which yield threatening or unpleasant interpretations may underlie the tendency, seen in anxious and depressed patients, to form appraisals or mental models (Johnson-Laird, 1983; Power and Champion, 1986) of their current environment which intensify their negative mood state. Perhaps, therefore,

MF's observation that in social situations people tend to reject him and find him boring or embarrassing may reflect the schemata which this patient has stored to accommodate prototypical social situations. Those schemata may contain default information that is consistent with such a view, and which therefore become incorporated into his subjective appraisal of any particular social interaction. Additionally, his prototypical schemata may contain slots which operate to collect evidence that he is being rejected and judged negatively. Innocuous or ambiguous aspects of social interactions, such as pauses in conversation or half-smiles, may therefore be actively misinterpreted due to the top-down influence which the schemata exert on the organization of the input.

2.8 CONTROL HIERARCHIES

We have moved from simple models involving linear sequences of processing stages to more complex accounts involving the transfer of information in both directions, and more closely resembling processing loops. Thus complex perceptual representations both result from and also affect more basic perceptual processes. We have considered similar accounts of comprehension, and analogous models exist for a wide range of processes, such as motor skills learning (e.g. Poulton, 1957) and problem-solving (e.g. Wason and Shapiro, 1971; Wason, 1971). However, such accounts typically deal with the relationship between the component stages involved in one particular kind of cognitive activity. It is unrealistic to conceptualize the brain as an assortment of totally unrelated processing systems. Rather, quite different kinds of cognitive activity often interact very closely with one another. Motor skills learning is closely associated with perceptual processing; problem-solving often relies upon the retrieval of appropriate information from memory, just as certain kinds of memory retrieval sometimes appear to require a degree of problem-solving, and so on. How should we conceptualize the relationship between all the different kinds of cognitive activity of which the brain is capable? The most compelling view, initiated by Bartlett (1941) and Craik (1966), restated by Broadbent (1977b), and implicit in many contemporary models (e.g. Johnson-Laird, 1983a, 1983b; Norman and Shallice, 1986; Oatley and Johnson-Laird, 1987), is that multiple cognitive activities may occur in parallel within an individual, organized through a hierarchical structure of control. The processes at higher levels in this hierarchy are concerned with behaviour which extends over a wider range of space and time than those operating at lower levels. Those processes operating at higher levels also control those processes operating at lower levels; i.e. the lower levels are organized by higher levels. It is important not to confuse this notion of levels with the concept of stages discussed earlier in this chapter. Within any level, a self-contained cognitive activity can proceed quite independently, with component processes interacting in a bottom-up and top-down manner within this level, as required. However, this cognitive activity will usually be initiated by processes operating on a higher level, and these initiating processes may also ultimately utilize the results of the lower level cognitive operations.

The idea that complex human behaviour may involve a hierarchy of self-contained processing programmes, with each level in the hierarchy controlling the operation of lower levels, is perhaps best illustrated by considering a particular complex human activity such as, let us say, driving a car. Higher-level processes will determine the destination, thus setting goals for subordinate processes involved in maintaining the appropriate route. At this next level of control, short-term goals will be set for even lower-level processes which decide upon the appropriate manoeuvre in any particular location, and these processes in turn set the goals for the motor programmes, operating at still lower levels, which ultimately deal with pedal-pushing, gear-changing and steering. The goals of the lowest-level processes may change several times a second, whereas the goals at the highest level of control is maintained throughout the journey.

This complex skill will be poorly performed if any of the fundamental low level processes are not efficiently conducted — for example, if the steering is loose, gear-changing stiff or the brakes spongey. Alternatively, difficulties may be encountered even when all those components processes function properly, if they are not efficiently coordinated by the control structure. If superordinate level processes set inappropriate goals for lower-level processes then the car driver may set out for the wrong destination, fail to negotiate junctions correctly, or mix up elementary manoeuvres by changing gear before depressing the clutch, and so on. Both faulty low-level component processes or poor control structure will result in a deficit in travelling ability.

Exactly the same reasoning can be applied when we consider cognitive defects, such as the confusion, distractability and poor concentration reported by our hypothetical patient, MF. Such impairments may possibly reflect dysfunctional abnormalities in basic cognitive processes such as memory access, or perceptual analysis. Alternatively, it may be the case that all the basic processing mechanisms are quite intact, but the higher levels of control, which formulate long-term goals and delegate appropriate short-term sub-goals to the lower levels, are not operating efficiently. Some researchers emphasize the former possibility when attempting to explain cognitive deficits associated with mood disorders such as depression. Thus, for example, it has been argued that these deficits reflect impaired long-term memory retrieval (Sternberg and Jarvik, 1976; Henry et al., 1973). However, other researchers associate such cognitive deficits with inefficiencies in control procedures. In a recent review of the literature, for example, Weingartner and Silberman (1982) note that failures tend only to occur when depressed patients must actively analyse information in an elaborative manner; that is, the deficit is manifest in those tasks requiring a high degree of strategic control over lower-level cognitive operations. More passive processing tasks tend not to differentiate depressed subjects from controls. These findings will be discussed in more detail in Chapter 10.

2.9 AUTOMATIC vs. STRATEGIC PROCESSES

Those researchers concerned with developing linear stages of processing models for certain cognitive activities often assumed that they could ultimately identify the unchanging stereotyped sequences of operations – the fundamental processing mechanisms – which give rise to this activity. Recognition that the cognitive system may more accurately be characterized as a complex hierarchical organization of control procedures gives rise to an alternative possibility. Perhaps the same cognitive task may be performed in a qualitatively different manner by different individuals, or even by the same individual on different occasions. Indeed, the evidence consistent with such a view is now overwhelming.

For example, individuals may differ in the strategies they employ to perform spatial tasks (e.g. Kyllonen, Woltz and Lohman, 1981; Cooper and Marshall, 1985), to store and retrieve information from memory (e.g. O'Sullivan and Pressley, 1984) and in the learning of complex skills such as mathematics (e.g. Briars, 1983). Clearly, then, certain aspects of information-processing can be strategically flexible, capable of adapting to changing conditions and achieving the same end by more than one means (cf. Dillon and Schmeck, 1983; Broadbent, 1984; Dillon, 1985).

A useful distinction can be drawn between those processes which are 'automatic', or incapable of flexibility, and those which are 'controlled', or strategically modifiable (Schneider and Shiffrin, 1977; Shiffrin and Schneider, 1977; Hasher and Zacks, 1979; Schneider and Fisk, 1984; Schneider, Dumais and Shiffrin, 1984). An automatic process involves a sequence of operations which are activated, without the need for attention or conscious effort, in response to a particular internal or external input configuration. Such a process operates through a relatively permanent set of associative connections which link its component operations, and these connections may either be innately determined or result from extensive and consistent training. Since automatic processes do not require attentional resources in order to function they are little constrained by capacity limitations, and numerous automatic processes may operate in parallel. A controlled process is a temporary sequence of operations activated under the control of, and maintained through attention by, the subject. Controlled processes are therefore tightly constrained by capacity limitations, and only one such sequence at a time may occur without interference, except when two sequences are so slow that they can be serially interlaced. Despite this apparent disadvantage, however, the inherent flexibility of controlled processes allows them to be set up, altered and adaptively applied in novel situations for which automatic sequences have never been learned.

Shiffrin and Schneider (1977) investigated controlled and automatic processing in search tasks, where subjects were required to establish whether an item from a particular memory set was present in a visually presented display. Initially, performance was relatively slow and enormously affected by memory load, indicating a limited capacity serial-comparison process. Provided that the same set of items was maintained as the search targets however, this process appeared to change qualitatively over several thousands of practice trials. Detection speed and accuracy not only improved greatly, but also became independent of memory load, indicating the development of capacity independent, parallel-comparison processes. When a new set of target items was then introduced, and the old set of items employed as distractors in the visual display, then performance not only deteriorated sharply but dropped below the level obtained at the start of training, when controlled search was first utilized. Eventually, these inappropriate automatic-attention responses could be unlearned, and new sets of appropriate automatic responses learned, but only after a very considerable amount of retraining. On the basis of this and similar observations, Schneider *et al.* (1984) argue that automatic and controlled operations serve different information-processing functions. Automatic processing is assumed to perform consistent and invariant component operations, interrupting ongoing controlled processing in order to reallocate attention, and to bias and prime controlled processing. Controlled processing is instrumental in the development of new automatic processing, and is essential to deal with novel tasks. Therefore:

(a) Automatic processes, once established, proceed independently from con-
    trolled processes. Thus, after reversal, although the subject is actively
    trying to respond to a particular stimulus set, he cannot easily prevent the
    occurrence of responses to inappropriate set items which have become
    automatized.
(b) Related to this, while controlled processes cannot easily modify automatic
    processes, the reverse is not also true. Once an automatic-attention
    response has been established this can direct attention (i.e. can direct
    controlled processing) automatically to the target, regardless of
    concurrent input or memory load, to enable conscious detection to occur.

It has been argued that evaluation of the emotional quality of a stimulus input is an automatic process which can proceed entirely in the absence of awareness, and may be little affected by controlled operations (Zajonc, 1980). Furthermore, there is evidence (reviewed in Chapter 4) which indicates that patients suffering from anxiety disorders appear to show an automatic-attention response to stimulus items which are inherently threatening (e.g. Mathews and MacLeod, 1986). Consider the implications of this kind of information-processing for our patient MF. He reports experiencing episodes of anxiety 'out of the blue' even when he is thinking about nothing at all. However, he can only comment on those thought processes which are attentionally mediated or controlled. According to the information-processing paradigm, he will be processing much information automatically, and this appears to include emotional appraisal processes. The emotions he experiences may not, therefore, be independent of his environment, but rather may represent an appropriate response to evaluations which have been made quite automatically. Clearly, this argument depends upon the limitations of conscious awareness, and Chapter 9 will consider this topic in more detail. Another comment, made by MF, may also be illuminated by the above considerations. He notes that 'everything I read in the papers is about some terrible accident, or about violence', and that 'everywhere I look there are dangers'. Shiffrin and Schneider's hypothetical automatic-attentional responses may be highly relevant here. If, at some time in the past, MF has actively attended to certain cues which indicate potential dangers, then such attentional biases may have become automatized, as demonstrated by Mathews and MacLeod (1986). Perhaps a more accurate description of MF's condition would involve rephrasing his comments as follows: 'Every newspaper report of terrible accidents and violence, I will read,' or 'Everywhere there are dangers, I will look.' The unlearning of such automatic responses may only be possible after a very extensive period of practice.

2.10 CONCLUDING REMARKS

This chapter has avoided examining detailed models for particular cognitive activities, and has instead considered some of the more general conceptual issues central to the information-processing paradigm. We have seen how the brain can be characterized as a system dealing with internal representations which convey information. Capacity limitations, however they are conceptualized, will often cause bottlenecks which necessitate selective processing of certain representations in preference to others. Complex cognitive operations can more easily be modelled by reducing them to their simpler components or stages although certain methods for achieving this reduction are dependent on controversial assumptions. Certainly, it is unlikely that all cognitive operations involve linear sequences of stages which transmit information in a single direction. For example, some processes will involve the simultaneous activity of several operations in parallel rather than in series. Also, the transfer of information from later stages to earlier stages may be a common characteristic of much cognitive activity, which will thus involve a cyclic interaction of bottom-up operations driven by the stimulus and top-down operations driven by higher-order, long-term representations in memory. Just as any particular kind of cognitive process will involve component operations, much complex human activity must involve the coordination of many different cognitive processes. We have seen how the brain may be conceptually organized as a hierarchical system of processing levels, with the higher levels setting superordinate goals over extended time-periods, and delegating appropriate shorter-term subgoals to those processes operating at lower levels. Certain aspects of this system may thus be strategicaly and adaptively modifiable, though various low-level operations and certain well-learned processing sequences may be performed auto-matically in response to external or internal input configurations. Each possibility brings its own advantages and limitations.

The information-processing paradigm has rich potential for modelling individual differences. Human experience and activity will be mediated by available processing capacity, and by the priorities of selective functions which allocate this capacity. It will be affected by the nature and efficiency of the processing stages which analyse information, and constrained by the range of available long-term representations or schemata which exert top-down control over perception, comprehension, memory retrieval and other cognitive processes. The organization of the control structure, and the goals set at each level, will almost certainly be idiosyncratic, as will the degree to which certain processing sequences may have become automatized, and so forth. In the main chapters of this book we will discuss how those particular individual differences associated with the affective disorders can be illuminated by the adoption of the information-processing paradigm.

Chapter 3

Cognitive Impairments

Having set out the general approach to cognitive functioning that has been taken in current experimental psychology, we shall now consider how these functions are affected in anxiety and depression. In this chapter, we shall consider how performance is affected with 'neutral' materials, (i.e. those that are of no obvious relevance to the patients' condition). Subsequent chapters will consider the processing of materials relevant to patients' particular emotional preoccupations.

There are two main reasons for considering the performance on 'neutral' tasks as a preliminary to examining tasks with emotional materials. One is theoretical — the interpretation of effects found on tasks involving emotional materials is assisted by knowing what effects obtain with neutral materials. For example, it can be argued that interpretation of the memory performance of depressed patients with positive and negative materials has been impeded by the frequent omission of neutral materials – a point that we return to in Chapter 5. There has also been a failure, until quite recently, to ground theories of memory bias in depression on an understanding of how memory functions are affected by depression. The other reason is practical. Most patients are concerned about their performance on 'neutral' tasks. It is therefore of clinical relevance to understand how and why they have problems with them. In turn, this may have implications for remedial strategies that they could adopt.

The potential scope of a chapter on the cognitive performance of patients with emotional disorders is wide, and some limits will need to be set. Only performance on tasks that lend themselves to analysis in information-processing terms will be considered, though this boundary is not a clear one. For example, studies of the speed of motor performance in emotional disorders will be considered only in as far as they are relevant to information-processing theories. Little or no attention will be given to linguistic or social performance.

It is chiefly the effects of clinical depression and clinical anxiety that will be considered. The literature on the effects of anxiety is extensive, but is mostly not based on research with patients. It will be considered briefly for the implications it may have for the performance of patients with anxiety disorders, but not reviewed in the detail that would otherwise have been appropriate. In any case, good reviews of this non-clinical literature on the effects of anxiety on cognitive performance are available elsewhere (e.g. Eysenck, 1982). Performance deficits in depression have been studied quite extensively and will be a central focus of the chapter. Again, less attention will be given to studies based on mood-induction procedures or on variations in mood within the normal population. A useful review of the early literature on the effects of depression on performance was published by W. Miller (1975). There has been no recent review which is so comprehensive, though reviews which concentrate chiefly on memory deficits have been published by Johnson and Magaro (1987) and Ellis and Ashbrook (in press). Reference will also be made to the growing literature on cognitive performance in obsessional-compulsive neurosis (e.g. Reed, 1985).

There have also been a few studies of cognitive performance in mania which will not be considered here; they have been described by Johnson and Magaro (1987).

Particular interest in experimental abnormal psychology attaches to studies which test for interaction effects (i.e. that emotional disorders affect performance on one task more than another). Such studies contribute a great deal more to the exact specification of the performance deficit in clinical disorders than studies which use a single performance measure. However, there is a methodological problem that besets most studies testing such 'differential deficit hypotheses'. The two tasks may differ in psychometric features, such as discriminating power and reliability, and it may be these differences, rather than substantive differences in the functional demands made by the tasks, that are responsible for groups differing on one task more than another (e.g. Chapman and Chapman, 1973). For example, depressed patients show relatively greater impairment on tests of free recall than of recognition. However, this might not be because of the additional psychological functions required in free recall, such as the generation of retrieval cues, but simply because free recall is better able to differentiate between subjects. In fact, as will be argued in the course of the chapter, the latter explanation is probably not correct in this particular case. Nevertheless, it is a general methodological problem that is serious and pervasive, and raises questions of interpretation that often remain unresolved. It would be tedious to refer to it in connection with every study to which it applies, so it should be taken as a general caveat that applies to many of the studies referred to in this chapter. Unfortunately, there is not yet a consensus about how this problem should be dealt with. The technique of 'matching' tasks advocated by the Chapmans has not been universally endorsed (e.g. Baron and Treiman, 1980; Watts, in press), partly because matching tasks on difficulty may make them different in other ways, producing fresh problems of interpretation. For example, Calev's (1984) matched tests of recall and recognition depend on the recall test being shorter.

It would be premature to present a theoretically integrated review of research on cognitive impairments in emotional disorders. The current data is simply too patchy. However, before reviewing empirical work in detail, it may be helpful to indicate briefly some of the broad explanatory frameworks currently available for explaining performance deficits in emotional disorders, though a more detailed discussion of them will be postponed until later. There are at least three general explanatory frameworks that need to be considered.

The first would be couched in terms of processing resources. It is an assumption of many theories of cognitive performance that capacity is limited. As we shall see in the next chapter, this is particularly the case in tasks requiring conscious awareness. The evidence for capacity limitations comes primarily from studies in which subjects are required to perform two tasks, though there is no consensus about whether the interference effects of one task on another are due to their both requiring *general* cognitive resources, or to their overlapping in specific perceptual-motor requirements (see Chapter 2, section 2.2). A resource allocation theory has been advanced for anxiety by Eysenck (1979a, 1982), and for depression by Ellis and Ashbrook (in press). They will be reviewed in detail later in the chapter.

The next theoretical framework can be seen as a more specific version of the first, in that it involves a specific proposal about *why* resources are depleted. People with emotional disorders are often preoccupied with negative or anxious thoughts, and it can be proposed that these take up cognitive resources that are then not available for other tasks. This is the prevailing view about how anxiety can result in an impairment of test performance (Wine, 1980) and a parallel theory can be advanced for other emotional disorders.

A third perspective that needs to be considered is that at least some of the effects of emotional disorders on cognitive performance are mediated by high levels of physiological arousal. The effects of arousal on performance are complex and depend on the level of arousal and the nature of the task (e.g. Eysenck, 1982); though high arousal is often associated with impaired performance. Many emotional disorders are characterized by high arousal, but there is an important exception. There is good evidence on a range of measures of arousal that 'psychotic' (or 'endogenomorphic') depressives are *under*-aroused (e.g. Byrne, 1975a). If such patients show deficits similar to those found in other emotional disorders characterised by hyper-arousal, the possibility that those deficits are mediated by hyper-arousal can be refuted. Unfortunately, arousal levels are seldom reported, and have to be inferred from the type of depression.

Memory is the aspect of cognitive performance in emotional disorders that is best understood, and it will be reviewed in detail later. First, however, the less extensive research on cognitive speed, attention, thinking and problem-solving will be considered.

3.1 SPEED, ATTENTION AND THINKING

3.1.1 Cognitive and Motor Retardation

Speed of performance is such a basic aspect of performance that it is a good place to begin. There is no doubt that depression results in retarded performance on a wide range of tasks (Payne and Hewlett, 1960; W. Miller, 1975); the interest comes in the details of the effect. Retardation has been reported more consistently for endogenomorphic than for neurotic depressives, but this depends on the task used. A distinction can be made between cognitive and psychomotor facets of retardation, and evidence has begun to accumulate that whereas psychomotor retardation can be found in all depressed patients, cognitive retardation is found only in endogenous depressives.

One operational approach to this distinction is to divide performance times on a task into (a) a preparatory or decision phase, and (b) an execution phase. Byrne (1976a) did this for choice reaction-time performance and found that 'psychotic' depressives were retarded in both phases, whereas 'neurotic' depressives were retarded only on movement time. The relationship between the two phases was also disrupted in depression. In normals, if decision time is artificially extended, there is a compensatory reduction in movement time, but depressives do not show this (Byrne, 1975b). Cornell *et al.* (1984) have confirmed, using a different methodology, that only psychotic depressives are retarded in the cognitive component of a motor task. Three tasks were constructed: (1) a simple reaction-time task, (2) a version involving additional *motor* components, and (3) a version involving additional *cognitive* components. An additional motor component slowed down both groups of depressives significantly more than normals. In contrast, an additional cognitive component slowed down melancholic depressives more than normals, though it affected non-melancholic depressives only slightly (and non-significantly) more than normals.

It is not clear what is the critical feature of endogenous depression that produces cognitive retardation. W. Miller (1975) suggested that cognitive retardation in depression was due to a motivational deficit based on learned helplessness. Even if the motivational deficit is more severe in endogenous depression, it is not clear why this should affect the two types of retardation differentially. Payne and Hewlett's (1960) hypothesis that cognitive retardation is caused by depressive thoughts and worries can be adapted more readily to explain why it occurs chiefly in endogenous depression. We know that ruminative thinking (i.e. the tendency to dwell on the *same* thought or theme repetitively) is more than four times as common in 'melancholic' than in 'non-melancholic' depressives (Nelson and Mazure, 1985), and that the negative thinking of endogenous depressives is less concerned with recent events and their implications (Matussek and Luks, 1981). It is possible that cognitive speed is retarded by processing resources being taken up by the type of ruminative thinking specific to endogenous depression. Another possibility is that cognitive retardation is the result of lowered arousal which, as we have seen, is specific to endogenous depression. Clearly, both these accounts would need to attribute *motor* retardation to some dysfunction found in *all* depressives, possibly the motivational deficit.

3.1.2 Secondary Tasks and Depressive Retardation

There have been several reports that depressive retardation can be *reduced* by adding a secondary task, which is intriguing because it is rather rare for a secondary task to result in improved performance on a primary one. The effect has usually been referred to as the 'distraction' effect, but this terminology will be avoided here because it is not helpful descriptively and it embodies doubtful assumptions about the mechanisms involved. Foulds (1952) showed that a simple secondary task (repeating digits after the experimenter at approximately every 2 seconds) increased the speed of maze performance in depressives, anxiety states and obsessionals, but not in hysterics or psychopaths. Similarly, Campbell (1957) found that the same secondary task (repeating digits), and also letter cancellation, speeded up the maze performance of both depressives and schizophrenics but not normals. Blackburn's (1975) results were more complicated. She found that an 'internal' distraction task (counting upwards at a rate of one digit per 2 seconds) produced a non-significant trend towards faster maze performance in all groups, whereas external distraction (listening to a pre-recorded news item) tended to speed up manics and bipolar depressives, but to slow down unipolar depressives. There was no normal control group.

Foulds' explanation of the facilitating effect of a secondary task was that it disrupted depressive preoccupations and thus left processing capacity available for the primary task. We know from other work (e.g. Fennell *et al.*, 1987) that requiring subjects to do a task that takes up information-processing capacity reduces the frequency of distracting thoughts, and this may be the basis of the effect. However, it is not clear that this can explain why the secondary task does not impair performance as much as the depressive preoccupations which it replaces.

Another problem is that it may not be able to explain the specific form of the effect, as this theory appears to predict a more general improvement in performance as a result of a secondary task than actually occurs. Beneficial effects have been shown only for the *speed* of maze performance, and there is a case for giving this greater prominence in an explanation of the phenomenon. *Errors*, in contrast, tend to be increased by distraction. Foulds (1952), for example, found that the clinical groups whose speed improved most also showed the most substantial increase in 'crossed lines' in the distraction condition. It is plausible that a secondary task produces changes in performance strategies. There may be a tendency for secondary tasks to speed up performance at the expense of level or accuracy of performance, an effect which also occurs when subjects are given incentives (Eysenck, 1982, Chapter 5).

It then remains to be explained why a secondary task should speed up depressives, but not normal controls. This could be the result of depressives and normals adopting different strategies before the addition of a secondary task. Depressives may normally adopt a conservative strategy, maintaining accuracy at the expense of speed, as Glass *et al.* (1981) have suggested. This would leave them more scope to increase speed without conspicuous loss of level of performance. Normals, in contrast, would be more likely to adopt a speed already close to their maximum before the addition of a secondary task.

3.1.3 Attention

Investigations of general attentional dysfunction in depression have been limited, but there are three experiments that are worthy of note.

The first (Byrne, 1976b) distinguished between the dysfunctions in vigilance performance of psychotic and neurotic depressives. As the former are considered to be under-aroused, and the latter over-aroused, it is not surprising that they perform rather differently at a vigilance task. Psychotic depressives showed the poorest overall level of correct detections, and the steepest deterioration over time. Neurotic depressives showed a different pattern. Their overall detection rate was affected less (though still significantly) and their errors mostly took the form of false positives. Byrne argues that these differences are consistent with what might be expected on the basis of differences in arousal, though they have not been replicated (Byrne, 1977).

The second experiment bears on cognitive retardation, but locates it more specifically. Depressives and normals do not differ in the length of exposure necessary for a stimulus to be correctly identified. However, when backward masking is used, depressives show disruption of recognition at longer inter-stimulus intervals (ISI) than normals (Sprock *et al.*, 1983). Extension of the ISI from 60 to 120 ms improved the performance of both depressives and normals, but further extension from 120 to 300 ms helped only depressives. It seems that sensory registration is not retarded in depression, rather it is the subsequent encoding that follows registration that is retarded. It is the latter that backward masking disrupts. Thus Sprock *et al.* suggest that depressives take longer to form a representation of the stimulus, but not to register it.

The third attentional experiment is based on a paradigm developed by Broadbent to test his filtering hypothesis (Broadbent, 1971). He argued that where filtering is possible (i.e. where relevant stimuli can be distinguished from irrelevant ones on the basis of a clear physical cue), pre-stimulus instructions about which stimuli to select should be advantageous. This obtains, for example, if subjects are presented with a list of digits, some of which are spoken in a male and some in a female voice. The performance of normals is improved by telling subjects *before* rather than *after* the series which set of digits they will be required to recall. However, depressives do not show this effect (Hemsley and Zawada, 1976). This has been interpreted as demonstrating a filtering deficit in depression.

3.1.4 Abstracting Ability

The most investigated question regarding general thinking function in depression is whether or not there is a failure of 'abstracting' ability. Most of the available studies indicate that there is. The most commonly used test has required the interpretation of proverbs (Gorham, 1956). Several studies have shown that depressives obtain lower abstraction scores than controls matched for IQ, though scores for concrete interpretations tend not to be affected (Braff and Beck 1974; Sprock *et al.*, 1983;). Donnelly *et al.* (1980) used the Category Test from the Halstead–Reitman battery requiring subjects to abstract features such as orientation from geometric figures, and obtained significantly lower scores in depressives.

The deficit in abstracting ability in depression is a specific one that exceeds that found in general verbal tests such as vocabulary (Braff and Beck, 1974). An unresolved issue is whether abstracting and conceptual functioning are impaired only in depressive episodes or whether they represent a stable trait of people who are vulnerable to depression. Andreasen (1976) failed to find differences between depressives at admission and at discharge in conceptual functioning, but Donnelly *et al.* (1980) found that scores on the Category Test improved with recovery from depression.

3.1.5 Problem-solving

Studies of problem solving in depressed *students* have given inconsistent results (e.g. Gotlib and Asarnow, 1979) but a study of depressed patients (Silberman *et al.*, 1983b) has provided a rich analysis of the nature of the problem-solving deficit in depression. The task, based on a paradigm developed by Levene (1966), involved hypothesis-testing behaviour in a 16-trial, two-choice visual discrimination problem. Feedback was provided on only three trials, which would be sufficient, if problem-solving was perfectly efficient, to narrow down to a single correct hypothesis. A measure of 'focusing' was employed which reflects the extent to which subjects narrowed their hypotheses down, and it was found that depressives showed significantly poorer focusing. All subjects performed the task a second time in which they were required on each trial to list all the hypotheses that they considered might be correct. This improved the performance of all subjects, but helped depressives more than controls. Depressives had no difficulty in listing the four possible hypotheses at the start of the series. Their deficiency seemed entirely attributable to failing to discard invalid hypotheses and thus retaining an over-large set of possible ones. The helpful effect of the requirement to report hypotheses is important from a clinical point of view as it suggests a remedial strategy that could be used clinically.

3.1.6 Attention and Thinking in Obsessional Patients

There have been a number of investigations of attentional dysfunction in obsessionals from which a coherent story is beginning to emerge. Though negative results may be otained if obsessionals and controls are compared on a *single* attentional task (Gordon, 1985), a more interesting picture emerges when the analysis focuses on *differences* in functioning between two paradigms making rather different attentional demands (Broadbent *et al.*, 1986). However, this work has so far been based on 'normal' subjects with high scores on a questionnaire measure of obsessionality, and has not yet been extended to patients.

Broadbent had two similar tasks, one intended as a measure of 'filtering', the other as a measure of 'pigeon-holing'. In filtering, stimuli are selected on the basis of some basic sensory feature, whereas in pigeon-holing they are classified on the basis of meaning or experience. In both cases, choice reaction time to stimuli (A or B) was measured, but only in the filtering task did they know where on the screen the stimulus would appear. Obsessional subjects performed less well on the pigeon-holing task than would be expected on the basis of their performance in a filtering task. If this is replicable with patients, it would provide an account of some aspects of the kind of attentional functioning that obsessional patients display when checking. It is noticeable that they often do not rely on 'scanning' when checking. Rather than assuming that their attention will be captured by something amiss, they try consciously to identify and inspect each object as part of the checking procedure.

The difficulties that obsessionals have with the more complex demands of 'pigeon-holing' is paralleled by their approach to more intellectual tasks. Obsessionals have been shown to operate with *narrow* conceptual categories. Reed (1969a) found that patients with obsessional personality were under-inclusive in a test of features essential to particular categories; and Reed (1969b) similarly found that they sorted blocks into more circumscribed categories. Persons and Foa (1984) also obtained evidence for under-inclusiveness in obsessionals from performance in a card-sorting paradigm. This finding of narrow conceptual categories in obsessionals, which has emerged from studies using different tasks, thus seems reasonably secure.

Regarding problem-solving, Reed (1977) has suggested that obsessionals are impaired in inductive but not in deductive reasoning, and supported this with evidence that patients with obsessional personality perform worse than controls on number-series tasks, but are better at arithmetic. This is an interesting dissociation, but clearly the tasks differ in many ways, and so the results lend themselves to other interpretations. Decision-making is also retarded in obsessionals, primarily due to procrastination and a desire for additional information (Volans, 1976).

Sher has recently approached the study of cognitive function in checking by studying normal subjects with high scores on a checking questionnaire (Sher et al., 1983, 1984). Negative results were obtained on several measures, though checkers were shown to underestimate their performance on a 'reality monitoring' task in which subjects were presented with a series of word pairs (e.g. hot: cold). In some cases the second word was printed in full; in others only the first letter was supplied and subjects generated it themselves. Subjects were subsequently required to distinguish which words were actually presented, and which were self-generated. The actual performance of the 'checkers' was indistinguishable from that of controls (Sher et al., 1983). The under-estimation effect appeared to be specific to obsessional 'checkers' and was not shown by obsessional 'cleaners'; it was also specific to the reality monitoring task and no comparable under-estimation was shown on a recognition task. Perhaps checking is in part a consequence of lack of confidence in the capacity to distinguish whether events actually occurred or were merely thought to occur.

3.2 MEMORY

Memory functions in anxious and depressed people have been investigated quite extensively, though the literature on anxiety is mostly non-clinical. Investigations of clinically depressed subjects have left no doubt that their performance on free recall tasks is poor. The evidence for this, which has been reviewed by McAllister (1981), Johnson and Magaro (1987) and Ellis and Ashbrook (in press) is based on

(a) comparisons of depressed patients with controls matched on intelligence or educational level,
(b) comparisons of the performance of depressed patients when currently depressed and when recovered, and
(c) correlational studies of the association between memory performance and the severity of depression.

The work of Cronholm and Ottosson (1961), which was one of the first clear demonstrations of a memory deficit in depression, remains one of the best studies in the field, and has been substantially replicated by Sternberg and Jarvik (1976). Cronholm and Ottosson (1961) compared a sample of patients with endogenous depression with surgical patients. The groups were matched on educational level (as well as age, sex and area of residence) and were also shown to have comparable vocabulary levels. Three specially devised tests were used, examining memory for word pairs, for simple figures, and for personal data about fictitious people. Subjects were tested immediately, and again after three hours. Significant differences were found on all three tests at both occasions of testing, though there was no evidence of faster forgetting in depressives.

This chapter will not review evidence for the existence of a depressive memory deficit comprehensively, but will focus on qualitative issues about the nature of the deficit.

3.2.1 Responsiveness

The first possibility that needs to be considered is that depressives can access material from memory as well as normals, but perform less well on memory tasks for other reasons. Johnson and Magaro (1987) have argued that the depressive memory deficit is partly due to response bias. There are two related hypotheses that need to be considered, (a) that depressives lack confidence in their memories, and (b) they can't make the effort to report all the memories accessible to them.

Investigation of the first possibility depends on studies of recognition memory, and focuses critically on the level of false alarms. If depressives have low levels of both hits *and* false alarms, it suggests that the low level of hits is due to a cautious-reponse criterion. On a signal-detection analysis, this would result in them differing from controls on β rather than d'. One impediment to investigating this is that tests of recognition memory are often less sensitive to memory problems than tests of free recall, with the result that free recall usually differentiates groups significantly, whereas recognition memory tests may show only a non-significant trend to differentiate groups. This is probably partly just a psychometric artifact due to the different discriminatory power of the two types of rest, and applies just as much to other groups, such as the elderly, as to depressives. However, it is not to be explained wholly in these terms. Even when free recall and recognition tests are matched for difficulty in normals, depressives do less well on free recall than on recognition (Calev and Erwin, 1985). Despite these general problems in demonstrating group differences on tests of recognition, there are several studies that show significant effects of depression on 'hit' rates in recognition memory (e.g. Miller and Lewis, 1977; Silberman *et al.* 1983a; Watts *et al.*, in press c).

Another problem that has beset studies of recognition memory in depression is that the level of false alarms obtained in depression seems to depend on procedural variables. The clearest demonstration of this is in the study of Watts *et al.* (in press c) in which some groups vocalized words on presentation while others did not. Depressed patients showed more false alarms than controls with vocalization, but fewer without vocalization. Consistent with the view that processing conditions are crucial, Zuroff *et al.* (1983), whose subjects performed a self-description task when words were presented, found more false alarms in depression; whereas Miller and Lewis (1977) and Dunbar and Lishman (1984), who used no encoding task, found fewer false alarms. The implication is that, whether or not the lower level of hits characteristic of depression appears to be due to cautious-response criteria, depends on procedural variables. However, it is clear from the study of Watts *et al.* that depression reduces hits even under conditions under which false alarms tend to be increased. The effect on hits cannot therefore be explained entirely in terms of response bias. Overall, Watts *et al.* found that depression affected d' rather than β.

There has been some indirect evidence, from analyses of patterns of errors, to support the hypothesis that depressives' memory performance appears to be deficient only because they do not make the effort to produce all the responses they are capable of. Henry *et al.* (1973) noted that the errors of depressives tend to be of omission rather 'commission'. Similarly, Whitehead (1973, 1974) found that depressives were characterized by high rates of omission errors but low rates of transposition errors in a serial learning task. However, studies which have attempted to control amount of output experimentally suggest that the depressive memory deficit cannot be explained wholly in terms of poverty of output. Watts and Sharrock (1987) tested memory for prose, first by free recall, and then by a form of cued recall that required much less output (i.e. answers of only one word or a short phrase to questions about the passage were sufficient). If the poor performance of depressives on memory tests is due to an output problem, they should have been less impaired on the 'low-output' test, whereas in fact the low-output test differentiated groups slightly better than unaided free recall.

Convergent evidence comes from a study of student volunteers in whom a depressed mood had been induced (Leight and Ellis, 1981). A forced recall paradigm was used in which subjects were required to guess if they did not know the answer, but depressed students nevertheless obtained lower recall scores. This also suggests that the effects of depression on memory are not wholly explicable in terms of poverty of output.

3.2.2 Non-clinical Studies on Level of Encoding

Turning to hypotheses about the effects of anxiety and depression on encoding, one specific hypothesis has been that anxiety biases people *away* from encoding in terms of semantic features and *towards* encoding in terms of more superficial (acoustic or visual) features. This represents a direct application of the 'levels-of-processing' approach to memory (Craik and Lockhart, 1972). There have been a number of relevant experiments on the effects of anxiety in non-clinical samples which have given only weak support to the hypothesis. It is particularly doubtful whether anxiety enhances phonemic encoding, though it may well impair semantic encoding.

An initial finding by Schwartz (1975) that neurotic introverts were adversely affected by phonemically similar response words in paired-associate learning, whereas stable extroverts were adversely affected by semantically similar response words, has not been replicated (Craig *et al.*, 1979). Mueller (e.g. Mueller, 1976, 1977, 1978) has published several tests of the hypothesis that anxious subjects show less *semantic* clustering but more *accoustic* clustering than normals, but has found that they show less clustering of both kinds. Another relevant approach is the false-recognition paradigm. When subjects incorrectly say that a word has appeared before, it is sometimes because it is acoustically confusable with a word that has actually appeared previously and sometimes because it is associated with a previous word. Depressed students show significantly fewer semantic associative errors, but do not show significantly more acoustic errors as might be predicted from the encoding-bias hypothesis (Hasher and Zacks, 1979).

Research with laboratory tasks has been supplemented by analyses of the approaches that students take to studying. A pioneering study was reported by Fransson (1977). In-depth interviews were used to explore the methods students employed in studying textbook passages, on the basis of which they were classified as having used 'deep' or 'surface' methods (see Marton *et al.*, 1984). A strong association was found between high levels of anxiety and use of a surface approach. There was also a negative correlation between state anxiety and performance on a test of factual knowledge for the passage. However, the effects of anxiety only emerged with materials related to the subject the student was studying, which Fransson (1977) interprets as having induced stronger 'intrinsic' motivation. Watts *et al.* (1986a) carried out a related study but, instead of an interview, used Entwistle's questionnaire measures of 'meaning' and 'reproducing' approaches to studying. As would be expected, there were significant positive correlations between the reproducing orientation and several measures of anxiety tension and neuroticism. In contrast, hostility and depression were the emotional states that interfered with (i.e. showed significant negative correlations with) 'meaning' orientation. It thus seemed that different emotional states may bias subjects towards deep processing and bias against surface processing.

3.2.3 Encoding Effort and Structuring of Material

Evidence has also come from a variety of paradigms suggesting that depression and anxiety reduce the level of *effort* expended at encoding, though again, most of the evidence has come from studies of student volunteers. Ellis *et al.* (1984) reported two relevant experiments on normal subjects who had undergone a depressive mood-induction procedure. Both used paradigms designed to manipulate the level of effort involved in encoding. In the first, sentences were presented with a missing target word, together with two possible words to fill the gap. In 'low-effort' sentences it was obvious which was the correct one. In the 'high-effort' sentences it was less obvious. Examples for which the missing word is 'dream' are 'The girl was awakened by the frightening...' (low-effort) and 'The man was alarmed by the frightening...' (high-effort). At recall, subjects were required to write down the target words. Subjects in neutral mood replicated previous work, showing that 'high-effort' words were better recalled, but depressed subjects did not show this. Though there was a main effect of mood, paired comparisons showed that this was almost wholly attributable to poorer performance of depressives on the 'high-effort' sentences.

Another experiment examined the recall of target words that were embedded in sentences at presentation. At test, sentences were presented with the target word omitted. In one condition the original 'base' sentences were used; in the other condition 'elaborated' sentences were used which included an extra phrase that was semantically related to the target word (e.g. 'The hungry child opened the door' and 'The hungry child opened the door of the refrigerator'). Elaborated sentences were better recalled in normals, but the advantage of elaborated sentences was not significant in depressed patients, again suggesting that they are at a relatively severe disadvantage in situations requiring (or at least presenting the opportunity for) elaborated encoded.

Roy-Byrne *et al.* (1986) reported two experiments on depressed patients designed to test the hypothesis that 'effortful' tasks are more impaired than 'automatic' ones. This important distinction was discussed in the previous chapter. In one experiment, subjects heard a word list in which some words were repeated. The effortful task was again to recall the words; the automatic task was to say whether particular words had been heard once or twice. Depressives were impaired on the effortful task, but not impaired at all on the automatic task.

Another experiment that is sometimes cited as showing support for the view that depressed patients are relatively impaired under high-effort conditions is that of Cohen *et al.* (1982). However, the actual data are concerned with the effect of delays on the recall of trigrams; the depressives showed relatively less impairment at zero delays. There are at least two problems with this experiment: one is that the interaction could be due to a ceiling effect in the memory capacity of normals, the other that is it is not obviously concerned with 'effort'.

A specific form of the effortful encoding hypothesis is that anxiety and depression affect people's ability to structure material semantically at encoding. When a list is constructed of words that are capable of being grouped into several semantic categories, but are presented to the subject in random order, normal subjects tend to recall them in semantic clusters. It seems that this may be disrupted in emotional disorders. This has been reported in non-clinical studies of neurotic introverts (Schwartz, 1975), and high-anxiety subjects (Mueller, 1976). The same is true of depressed patients (Koh *et al.*, 1973; Russell and Beekhuis, 1976; Weingartner *et al.*, 1981, Experiment 3; Calev and Erwin, 1985). However, caution must be exercised over assuming that this necessarily represents an explanation of the lower recall scores, as in the studies of Schwartz (1975) and Mueller (1976), lack of clustering was not associated with impairment of recall. It may be that emotional states have separate and independent effects on clustering and level of recall.

Another approach to the investigation of organization processes and memory has been to require subjects to sort words into categories at presentation, though results have been disappointing. Russell and Beekhuis (1976) found that depressed subjects showed no differences from controls in sorting, though they showed lower levels of recall and less clustering at recall. Weingartner *et al.* (1981) found differences in sorting for lists of random words, with depressives using fewer categories. This might be thought to be contrary to the hypothesis of a structuring deficit in depression, though Weingartner *et al.* interpret it, without much discussion, as showing that depressives are impaired in the 'kind of organisation' they impose on material. In any case, level of recall and the number of sorting categories used were uncorrelated in depressives.

A more promising approach to the hypothesized structuring deficit in emotional disorders is to vary the amount of structure in the material, and to see how this interacts with anxiety or depression. Ellis *et al.* (1985) and Ellis and Ashbrook (in press) have argued that highly structured materials make fewer encoding demands and are therefore less vulnerable to the disruptive effects of emotional disorders. Ellis and Ashbrook (in press) cite a number of non-clinical studies, especially those based on mood induction, which have failed to show effects of depressed mood on prose and other highly organized materials. However, caution needs to be exercised over assuming that this will also be true of clinical depression. Among clinical studies, Weingartner *et al.* (1981, Experiment 3), used lists composed of words from various different semantic categories, and found the effect of depression on performance was relatively slight when words from the same category were grouped together at presentation. In contrast, Levy and Maxwell (1968) varied structure by varying the approximation to text of word lists, and found that depressives benefited *less* than normals from increasing structure. These two kinds of structure differ in many ways, but to explore the apparent discrepancy, Watts (unpublished) varied both clustering into semantic categories and approximation to text in the same experiment, and found that in *both* cases depressed patients benefited less than controls from increasing structure in the material. Clearly, the discrepancies between the results of these experiments require investigation.

Memory for prose in clinical depression is of considerable interest, not only for its relevance to the hypothesis of a structuring deficit at encoding, but also because of its greater relevance to everyday life. Watts and Sharrock (1987) studied memory for a passage of prose in depressed patients, though the passage chosen, the 'Circle Island' story (Dawes, 1964), can itself be criticized for its artificiality. Subsequent analyses have focused on whether a structuring deficit could be demonstrated for prose that paralleled that already described for word lists. With prose passages, selectivity of recall provides a useful index of the degree of organisation imposed on the passage. The units of a prose passage vary in how central they are to its structure, and it can be inferred that subjects who show a strong bias towards recalling central units have performed more structuring than those who recall a more random selection of units. Depressed patients showed significantly less bias towards recall of central units than did controls, whether centrality was identified on the basis of a story grammar analysis or on ratings of centrality to the gist of the passage made by a separate group of subjects. However, depressives showed as strong a bias as controls towards selective memory for highly imageable units, a non-structural variable used as a control.

At present, there is thus considerable support for the view that structuring of materials is deficient in the memory processes of depressives. This may be a specific example of a general deficiency in 'effortful' cognitive processes (Johnson and Magaro, 1987).

Evidence from mood induction studies has a unique value in disentangling effects of mood at encoding and retrieval, and indicates that both encoding (Ellis *et al.*, 1984) and retrieval (Ellis *et al.*, 1985) are affected, though the encoding affect is probably more powerful (Leight and Ellis, 1981). This is readily compatible with the hypothesis of a structuring deficiency, as analogous structuring processes can be assumed to operate at both encoding and retrieval.

3.3 GENERAL ISSUES

The final section of this chapter will be concerned with three general issues: formulations of cognitive impairments in emotional disorders in terms of processing resources, the role of worry and ruminations in impairing performance, and the possibility of using remedial strategies to improve performance.

3.3.1 Processing Resources

As suggested at the outset, an account of the performance deficits found in depressed patients can be offered in terms of depleted cognitive resources. Ellis and Ashbrook (in press) have recently set out the assumptions of such an account. (1) Depression can affect the amount of capacity that can be allocated to a given task, through some capacity being tied up in thinking about one's sad state (extra-task processing), and perhaps also because processing capacity is directed towards task-irrelevant features (task-irrelevant processing). (2) The encoding of information, both in everyday and laboratory tasks, normally requires allocation of capacity (i.e. 'cognitive effort') and performance will be positively correlated with the effort allocated. (3) Where depression is mild, or where the capacity required by a task is only moderate, the task performance may be unimpaired; where depression is severe and the task is demanding, performance will be affected by depression. Krames and McDonald (1985) have advanced a similar hypothesis, and shown that the performance deficits found in depression are comparable to those produced in normal subjects by adding a secondary task.

Eysenck (1979) has advanced a capacity theory of the effects of anxiety but, following Kahneman (1973), uses the concept of effort somewhat differently. Eysenck starts with the parallel assumption that capacity is taken up with extra-task processing (e.g. worry), an assumption shared by other theorists (Wine, 1980), and he assumes that this reduces the capacity available for task performance. However, he also assumes that potential adverse effects on performance may be compensated for by *increased* effort. This contrasts with the implict assumption of Ellis and Ashbrook (in press) that in depression the reduction in the capacity available is paralleled by a reduction in the capacity allocated to the criterion task. Eysenck's position leads him to locate the primary effect of anxiety, not on the quality of performance, but on 'effectiveness', which is the ratio of performance to effort.

Eysenck's distinction raises the question of whether the more appropriate capacity theory explanation of the effects of depression on performance should be that fewer resources are available (perhaps because of depressive ruminations) or that fewer resources are deployed (perhaps because of a motivational deficit). Capacity theory has difficulty in satisfactorily measuring or operationalizing resource allocation with sufficient precision to resolve this point. As Navon (1984) has pointed out, most of the current paradigms from which inferences about processing resources are made are capable of alternative explanations.

It is significant that the different formulations of Eysenck (1979) and Ellis and Ashbrook (1987) were concerned respectively with anxiety and depression, and it seems plausible that cognitive effort is affected differently in these two states. Eysenck (1982) has assembled a variety of evidence that is consistent with the hypothesis that anxiety is associated with increased effort, and that anxious people have fewer undeployed resources in reserve. First, and perhaps most compelling, are dual-task studies showing that secondary tasks are adversely affected by anxiety more than primary ones (e.g. Hamilton,

1983). Also relevant are studies using self-report indices of subjective effort (e.g. Dornic, 1977, cited by Eysenck, 1982). Thirdly, there is the fact that, though ego-involving instructions tend to improve the performance of less anxious people, they have little effect on the more anxious subjects (e.g. Nicholson, 1958), suggesting that they are already making cognitive effort close to their maximum. Finally, the suggestion that anxiety is associated with greater effort can also form part of an explanation of the intriguing finding that anxiety is often associated with poor performance on hard tasks, but with *better* performance on easy tasks.

Though the evidence suggesting that anxiety leads to enhanced effort is not conclusive, the case is a plausible one and the conclusion probably correct. Because of increased effort, anxiety may often not bring about an immediate reduction in cognitive performance. However, there may be longer costs in terms of the strain of having to maintain performance on the basis of high effort. Hockey (1986) has presented a similar theory of the effects of stress on performance in terms of increased effort to preserve performance levels in the short term, but with longer-term physiological costs.

Increased effort seems much less likely to apply in depression. Indeed, the motivational deficit often assumed to be associated with depression would lead to the view that reductions in available capacity are exacerbated by poor allocation of even such resources as are available. Though direct assessments of this are difficult, the prediction would be that the kind of evidence Eysenck cites for increased effort in anxiety could not be paralleled in depression.

However, a commonality between anxiety and depression may be that both chronicaly overestimate the difficulty levels of tasks (see Kukla, 1972). The likely effect of this is that they overestimate the amount of effort that will be required to achieve any given level of success. Such an account has been successfully used by Williams and Teasdale (1982) to account for some laboratory helplessness deficits, and this is a matter that, may repay further investigation.

3.3.2 Experiential Correlates of Performance Deficits

It has been noted that current theories of the effects of anxiety and depression on performance assume that these states lead to ruminations and worries that occupy cognitive resources, leaving less for task performance. There is general agreement that anxiety and depression are associated with an increased incidence of task-irrelevant thoughts. Some of the studies claiming to support this have used rather indirect measures of task irrelevant thoughts, but it has also been supported by studies using more direct measures (e.g. Ganzer, 1968). The evidence is stronger for anxiety than for depression, and for non-clinical than clinical studies, though Watts and Sharrock (1985) reported that depressed patients showed considerably more mind-wandering than normal controls. What is less clear is whether these task-irrelevant thoughts mediate the deleterious effects of anxiety and depression on performance.

Support for this idea came initially from evidence that scores on a questionnaire measure of worry correlated negatively with task performance, whereas other aspects of emotionality did not so correlate (Doctor and Altman, 1969). However, there are now sufficient studies finding a lack of correlation between task-irrelevant thoughts and task performance to justify a reconsideration (e.g. Galassi et al., 1981a, 1981b, 1984; Bruch et al., 1983). A recent study by Bruch et al. (1986) suggested that what correlated with test performance was not the *frequency* with which task-irrelevant thoughts occurred, but the subjective meaning attached to them. The 'worry' scale used in most of the early studies did not make this distinction. This suggests a reformulation of the hypothesis in terms of the meaning rather than the frequency of emotional thoughts. However, it remains to be seen how well this reformulation theory will stand up to empirical test.

So far, there has been very little investigation of whether there is a correlation between task-irrelevant thought and objective performance in clinical groups, but Watts et al. (in press a) examined this for depressed patients. The results indicated that it may be important to distinguish between tasks. Poor performance on some tasks was correlated with task-irrelevant thoughts and may well be mediated by it, but other tasks showed different phenomenal correlates. Watts et al. distinguished between two phenomenally distinct forms of lapse of concentration: (a) mind-wandering, and (b) going 'blank', which were uncorrelated with each other. Subjects who reported high levels of mind-wandering had poor performance on memory for prose, as might be expected if Wine's (1980) theory of test anxiety were extended to depression. However, performance on a planning task, the 'Tower of London' (Shallice, 1982), showed no correlation with mind-wandering but was instead related to patients' reports of going 'blank'. The different phenomenal correlates of the two tasks could have been partly due to their having different structural characteristics (such as more 'sub-routines' in the planning task). However, they could also have been due to the differences in the amount of effort required. When memory for prose was made more effortful by adding a requirement to form imagery, it showed a tendency to correlate with 'blanking' rather than 'mind-wandering'. Possibly, people who are vulnerable to 'blanking' have particular difficulty with effortful cognitive tasks; they may try to avoid them because attempting to apply effort tends to result in their going 'blank'.

Whatever the truth in such speculations, it is clear that, though the assumption that performance deficits are associated with the presence of task-irrelevant thoughts may be correct for some tasks, it is not correct for all. This is a conclusion that is readily consistent with recent trends in evidence regarding dual-task performance. It has become clear that the extent to which one task interferes with another depends not just on the amount of general resources they both require, but in large measure on the extent to which they overlap in the *specific* resources required (Allport, 1980). It is therefore not at all surprising that mind-wandering should be more incompatible with some tasks than others, depending on their specific properties.

3.3.3 Remedial Effects of Processing Strategies

Finally, we shall consider the use of strategies to remedy the cognitive impairments found in emotional disorders. Even where other treatments for general mood state are being used, there may be a case for using cognitive remedial strategies where problems of cognitive performance are a particular concern. For example, treating examination anxiety in students generally only lowers subjective anxiety but does not also combat the poor academic performance associated with anxiety (Finger and Galassi, 1977). Separate cognitive interventions are needed for that. Similarly, there may be depressed patients in whom memory problems are unresponsive to more general treatments, so that specific remedial strategies will be of practical importance for the patient. Reducing cognitive deficits may thus contribute to patients' general clinical improvement. Concentration problems are pervasive in depression and cause considerable frustration (Watts and Sharrock, 1985). Reducing them may thus cut out one of the factors that maintain negative mood state, just as treating negative thoughts cuts out another such factor.

There have been numerous demonstrations (e.g. Cermak and Craig, 1979) that strategies designed to promote 'deeper' processing improve memory in normals, and it seems that they may also do so in subjects who are anxious or depressed. The characteristic description that depressed patients give of their difficulties in reading is that they can't 'take in' what they are reading, with the result that when they get to the bottom of a page they have no idea what they have just read. This seems to be a phenomenological account of poor semantic processing. However, the application of processing strategies to help depressed patients concentrate differs from their standard laboratory application. For example, most laboratory research has examined the effects of processing strategies on incidental rather than intentional learning. In normal subjects incidental learning is probably more sensitive to the effects of processing, though the incremental benefit of processing strategies in intentional learning may be more marked for depressed than non-depressed subjects. When required to learn, most non-depressed subjects may spontaneously adopt good processing strategies while depressed patients fail to do so.

Though there is a good deal of *clinical* interest in such studies, it seems unlikely that comparisons of the effectiveness of such strategies in normals and emotional groups will not contribute much to a *theoretical* understanding of the nature of the processing deficit associated with emotional states. The reason for this is that, as with structure in materials, it is unclear what prediction ought to be made from the hypothesis of a processing deficit in emotional groups. On the one hand, depressives might benefit *more* from processing instructions because such instructions would remedy a natural processing deficiency. On the other, it might be predicted that depressives would benefit *less* because of their inability to do deep processing.

In general, the evidence confirms that processing instructions improve the memory performance of anxious and depressed subjects. Two experiments have investigated the effects of imagery instructions in high-anxiety students. Edmunson and Nelson (1976) found that all subjects performed better at paired associate learning with instructions to form images than with instructions to repeat the word pairs. However, puzzlingly, Scott and Nelson (1979) failed to replicate this. Conflicting results have also been found in experiments on depressed subjects. Ellis *et al.* (1984) carried out a similar study using a group of normal subjects who had been given a depressive mood induction and found that semantic processing instructions helped subjects in sad mood as much as subjects in normal mood. However, Weingartner *et al.* (1981, Experiment 1) in a study on depressed patients cast doubt on this conclusion. Their results are incompletely reported, but it appears that, with cued recall, semantic processing instructions helped both depressives and controls, whereas, with free recall, they helped normals but not depressives. However, the latter seems likely to have been due to a floor effect. Watts *et al.* (in press b) have recently examined the effects of imagery instructions in memory for prose (descriptions of a department store) in relatively severely depressed patients. Imagery instructions substantially improved memory performance, especially in non-endogenous depressives, though it did not affect the number of times patients actually reported losing concentration while listening to the passage, or their later ratings of the concentration problems they had experienced while listening to it.

None of these studies has looked at anything more than immediate effects of processing instructions, and much more work needs to be done to investigate whether they have any clinically useful long-term effects. One key issue here will be the potential applicability of the processing strategies concerned to everyday situations. Clearly, many commonly used 'semantic' processing instructions, such as rating the meaningfulness of words, have very limited application. However, imagery is more flexible. For example, a patient who was finding it difficult to concentrate on job instructions at work might find it helpful to imagine the operations while they were being described to him. The evidence that depressed patients are deficient in structuring material at encoding, which was reviewed earlier, suggests that they might benefit from strategies designed to ensure adequate structuring. Structuring strategies can be applied to a variety of intellectual tasks, and Watts (1985) has discussed their application to study counselling.

The main practical issue is the extent to which people who are anxious or depressed will actually apply remedial strategies in everyday life, a problem that is analogous to extending the effects of social skills training outside the training situation. It can hardly be expected that depressed patients will make consistent use of relatively effortful strategies such as imagery formation. Perhaps the best that can be hoped for is that they will find it useful to have strategies available to lift their performance in situations in which poor performance would be particularly frustrating.

Chapter 4

Attention to Emotional Stimuli

One of the themes emerging from both Chapters 1 and 2 was the extent to which the cognitive system demands selectivity in processing. In Chapter 3 we reviewed evidence that one effect of emotional disturbance was to bring about a general impairment in cognitive performance, for example, concentration and memory deficits, even on neutral materials. Part of that effect could be explained by the task-irrelevant processing being done by the patient concurrently with the 'primary' task. It was not simply the amount of such secondary processing but its affective meaning and valence which explained impaired performance on neutral tasks. In this chapter, we concentrate on this tendency of emotionally disturbed people to find their attention drawn towards emotional stimuli.

Consider the cases of two patients referred to a clinical psychology department for treatment of their anxieties. MM had a phobia of birds. She had lived with this fear for some years, but lately it was inhibiting her work. She was employed by a government department in a converted small aircraft hangar, and birds occasionally flew in and became trapped inside the building. She could no longer disguise her fear, and became extremely upset and tearful. On assessment it was found that her fear extended to both live and dead birds, her fear of dead birds inhibiting her from walking through markets or past butchers' shops where there might be poultry hanging for sale. The more that butchers' poultry looked like a dead bird (e.g. neck and head with feathers remaining) the more fearful she was. For our present purposes the interesting aspect of her fear was her extreme sensitivity to bird-type stimuli in her environment. When walking down the street, she would notice a dark, flapping shape on the road many metres away and avoid it lest it should turn out to be a dead bird. She would notice live and dead birds more frequently than any of her family and friends, though sometimes she would be wrong, and a shape would turn out to be pieces of black plastic flapping in the wind.

TS was a welder in a shipyard who had been off work for a considerable time owing to a chronic anxiety state. This would manifest itself in tremors and sweating when in the company of co-workers. Coffee-breaks and lunchtime in the canteen were a special problem. The anxiety symptoms also affected his work as a skilled welder. As this began to deteriorate, it had an inevitable vicious circle effect on his mood and then again on his work performance. Of all his symptoms, what was particularly distressing for himself and his wife was the way in which he noticed bad news in the newspaper. Only a brief scan of a page would make his eye rest on the stories of muggings, assault and suicide. These were occasionally small articles at the bottom of the page, but his eyes would find them first, setting up a long ruminative anxiety about harm possibly coming to himself or his wife. He would discuss these issues with his wife who, though patient at first, began to tire of his constant worrying. This only served to make him more anxious.

A feature shared by these two patients is their sensitivity to stimuli in their environment which represent their fear. We shall examine this phenomenon of 'attentional bias' in this chapter, first outlining some of our basic assumptions, then by examining how investigators have sought to bring the phenomenon under experimental control in clinical and subclinical groups. In the case of each experimental investigation of the clinical phenomenon, we shall see if there exist parallel experiments on non-clinical groups in the cognitive psychological literature which might help to explain what the underlying processes are.

4.1 THE NATURE OF ATTENTIONAL BIAS

First let us outline our assumptions. *We assume that attentional bias can be said to have occurred when there is a discrete change in the direction in which a person's attention is focused so that he/she becomes aware of a particular part or aspect of his/her stimulus environment. We also assume that such a change (a) may take place in any sense modality; (b) is perceived as being passive or involuntary but can operate voluntarily; and (c) is normally perceived to be contingent upon a discrete change (onset or offset) in the 'internal' or 'external' environment of the person.* These assumptions serve only to begin the process of studying the phenomenon in greater detail. They beg many questions. For example, what is 'direction of attention'? Is it always 'passive and involuntary'? Does there always have to be a discrete change in the perceptual environment, or can an individual suddenly become aware of something that was there all along? Nevertheless, they do highlight three aspects that we assume (at least at the outset of this chapter) are present. First, that the 'attentional bias' with which we shall be concerned is something of which the person is aware.* There may be other sources of disruption to the person which are related to such attentional bias and which indeed may share common mechanisms. For example, one's

---

*Although we are concerned to explain a phenomenon of which individuals are *aware*, some of the psychological research which may elucidate the processes underlying the phenomenon do not themselves involve subjects being aware of what is distracting their attention. Where this research is relevant, it is reviewed despite its apparent breach of our assumptions.

mind may go blank while trying to read, a phenomenon which might be explicable in terms of one's attention being caught by something of which one is not aware. However we reserve 'attentional bias' to refer to an aspect of phenomenal awareness. The individual *notices* something, and he/she knows he/she has noticed it. Second, the 'environment' from which the stimuli are 'picked up' may be internal or external. This simply allows that one may be particularly sensitive to some sorts of pain in the body, as well as shapes in the external environment. Third, although vision and audition have been the most studied, we should allow that similar phenomena may occur in any sense modality. So we may be sensitive to the smell of gas, the taste of cooked tomatoes, the sight of a dead bird, the sound of a spouse's car, or the bodily sensation of chest pain. Notice that examples of 'attention to salient material' may be drawn from everyday life and not just psychopathology. If one is buying a house, one seems to notice 'For Sale' signs. If one buys a new car, the number of people driving just that type of car suddenly seems to increase.

The most natural analogy for such shifts in attention has been to liken attention to a beam of light, narrowly focused on one aspect of the world. The narrower the attention, the more 'concentrated' or 'brighter' the light. The broader the attention, the less concentrated or 'dimmer' the light. Some monitoring also takes place outside the bright 'focus' (a dim illumination – a sort of 'night light'!) If any stimulus related to one's current concern occurs in this dim light, this peripheral light is brightened slightly at the expense of the 'focused' beam, or the entire focus may shift, so that what *was* once peripheral is now central. This latter shift is the attentional switch towards salience with which we are concerned. Such a spatial analogy has many ambiguities and there may be other better analogies (discussed by Broadbent, 1982), but it does suggest at least two ways in which individuals may differ from each other (or in which a single individual may vary over time). First, the degree of threat of the current concern represented in the periphery may vary. Second, the strength of resistance to switching may vary – how flexible or rigid, how easily distracted the system is. These two characteristics may not be mutually exclusive, but each needs to be borne in mind. For example, overtiredness may make concerns *seem* more distracting because they become more salient, and/or because switching becomes more probable even in the absence of concern-related stimuli.

There is one more point that needs to be made before considering the experimental work. We have defined attentional bias partly in terms of the phenomenal awareness of the individual. But phenomenal awareness may involve both perceptual and response aspects of processing. Consider the stimulus array in Figure 4.1. In each of the three arrays, the word 'dead' appears in the same location. One can vary the discriminability of the word by varying the number and type of different irrelevant letters surrounding the target stimulus. One might expect a patient, such as TS, mentioned above, to be quicker than average at spotting the word 'dead' even when others find it relatively difficult (such as in array (a)). Phenomenally, it appears that the 'perceptual' side of the cognitive system is 'tuning in' more quickly. However, the response demanded in such an experiment (saying the embedded word) allows an alternative explanation. That is, TS may have a 'response set' or 'response bias' towards particular words such as 'dead', 'suicide', 'accident'. His perceptual system may extract no more or less information from the stimulus array, but the output mechanisms may be biased to respond to a wide variety of stimuli with the concern-related word. We shall see later how some experiments have been unable to disambiguate the perceptual-bias from response-bias explanations.

```
D B A E D A E        B F G Y S H S        S S S S S S S
B D B A D A D        D A S T F C G        S S S S S S S
B E D E A D E        B T D E A D F        S S D E A D S
B B D A D E D        F A C T P T C        S S S S S S S

     (a)                  (b)                  (c)
```

Figure 4.1   Stimulus arrays varying in discriminability of the negative word 'dead' (see text).

Two broad strategies for investigating attention bias have been used in experimental investigations. The first is to show how the tendency to attend to salient stimuli may *facilitate* performance. The second has been to show how the same tendency may *debilitate* performance. So, for example, TS might pick out salient stimuli more quickly if offered stimulus arrays such as those in Figure 4.1. But an alternative would be to ask him to pick out an alternative word (for example, a word containing a letter 't' — 'fact' in array (b)). In this case we might expect TS to show debilitated performance because, the assumption will be, his attention has been drawn towards the concern-related stimulus 'dead'.

4.2 ATTENTIONAL BIAS AND FACILITATED PERFORMANCE

4.2.1 Attentional Bias and Lowered Auditory Thresholds

Parkinson and Rachman (1981) used a task in which subjects listened to taped music within which were embedded words related to a major current concern. Two groups of mothers were used in the experiment, matched for age. Mothers in the experimental group each had a child who had been admitted to hospital for tonsillectomy on the day of testing. Control mothers had a child the same age but their child was not being admitted. The two groups each listened to music in which three types of word (ten of each) were embedded at random — concern-related (e.g. bleeding, injection, operation, pain); auditorily confusable neutral words (e.g. breeding, inflection, operatic, pine); and dissimilar words (e.g. newspapers, bird, pass, uniform). Subjects were asked to repeat each word as they heard it, the entire list of 30 words being played five times, starting at a low volume, and gradually increasing in volume until all words were clearly audible. Results showed that the experimental mothers, whose children were having operations, reported more concern-related words than controls at Times 1, 2, 3 and 4 but in the fifth (loudest) presentation of the words this difference disappeared. However, the two groups did not differ on how many auditorily dissimilar neutral words they were able to report. An interesting aspect of the data is whether auditorily confusable neutral words (e.g. breeding) would behave like the concern-related words or like the neutral words. Results showed that these words fell between the two. At the lowest volumes (Times 1 and 2) the experimental group reported more of these words, but as the words were played more loudly — Times 3, 4, 5 — this difference disappeared.

This result is reminiscent of the patient who feared birds and would confuse any black, flapping material on the road with a dead bird when at a distance. Unfortunately, information about the experimental procedure given by Parkinson and Rachman is not very detailed. They do not, for example, report whether a response to an auditorily confusable item was counted only if the subject was accurate or if the subject merely heard anything. There are other unsatisfactory aspects of this experiment, such as the apparent non-matching of frequency of stimulus words. A further problem is that subjects were allowed to set the volume of music to their own comfortable level. It is possible that the more anxious mothers set themselves a lower volume, which would, of course, allow them to hear more words. Fortunately for the investigators, the fact that the experimental and control mothers did not differ in perception of neutral words allows them to escape some of these criticisms.

There is one further problem with this paradigm, however, which has been alluded to in relation to Figure 4.1, and to which we shall return — the task demanded of the subjects that they respond by giving the word they had heard, so the data are consistent with a response bias interpretation.

Klinger et al. (1981) report a number of experiments examining subjects' sensitivity to material related to current concerns. In one experiment, college students completed a Thought Sampling Questionnaire which had been found to reflect an individual's concerns. Some days later the subjects were given a 15-minute dichotic listening task. During the 15 minutes, twelve 25-second sections were inserted such that the material within the section would refer to the current concern of the individual. Subjects did not have to shadow either message, but were asked to move a toggle switch to indicate which message they were listening to at any moment. At intervals during the tape, a tone sounded and the subjects reported on their thoughts of the moment. Results showed that subjects spent more time listening to concern-related material than would be predicted by chance, and were more likely to report that they were thinking about their current concern when the tone had called for a thought report after the concern had been alluded to on the tape. The implication of this experiment was that something in a channel not currently being attended to was being 'noticed' and causing a switching of attention to that channel.

The perception of concern-relevant target words embedded in either message in a dichotic listening task has been studied by Burgess *et al.* (1981). Six socially anxious and agoraphobic patients were compared with six control subjects and twelve highly fearful non-patients (i.e. people who identified having significant fears on the Fear Survey Schedule, six of whom were extraverts and six introverts). Both shadowed and non-shadowed messages contained ten occurrences of the neutral word *pick*. On another tape, shadowed and non-shadowed messages contained ten occurrences of a word or a phrase chosen to be personally relevant for each subject (e.g. *seminar, failure, shopping alone*) on each channel. All target stimuli were embedded out of context. After some initial practice at shadowing, subjects were instructed to tap whenever they heard the specified target on either channel. They were told not to switch attention between ears but rather to tap 'if (s)he should happen to hear the target word'. The results showed that fearful subjects and patients differed from controls in their response to the targets in the shadowed message. The main hypothesis of the authors was confirmed; individuals were able to perceive and respond to concern-related stimuli in the non-shadowed message without any loss of performance on responding to targets in the shadowed message. A problem with interpreting this result is that the stimuli that were chosen were likely to be words that are frequently in use by the subjects and patients. Thus frequency (which can itself be responsible for distracting attention) and emotional salience are confounded in this experiment.

The issue of fearfulness vs. familiarity of stimuli was examined by Foa and McNally (1986) who repeated Burgess *et al.*'s design with 11 obsessional-compulsive patients undergoing a three-week exposure and response-prevention treatment. Patients showed greater sensitivity on a behavioural (button-pressing) and skin conductance response to salient stimuli (e.g. urine, cancer, rabies) embedded in the unattended channel, than to neutral stimuli in that channel. The authors reasoned that the treatment would make these stimuli more familiar but less feared, so that the fear hypothesis would predict less and the familiarity hypothesis greater difference in response to salient and neutral stimuli, respectively. Following treatment the difference between response to salient and neutral stimuli did not reach significance, which the authors took to be confirmation of the fear hypothesis. In fact, the proportionate differences between responses to salient and neutral stimuli were almost identical before and after treatment, and the appropriate statistics to test directly pre-to-post treatment changes were not performed. Their results are somewhat ambiguous, therefore. However, since a familiarity hypothesis may have predicted greater sensitivity to the salient stimuli, and this was not evident, the conclusion that it is the fear of the stimuli which renders it salient seems relatively safe. A similar issue regarding fear vs. familiarity will arise in relation to Stroop effects, to be discussed later.

More evidence on the nature of the attention switch comes from shadowing experiments in which there are no targets to be responded to in the non-shadowed message and in which there is an independent way of assessing attentional focus. If an individual is constantly monitoring stimuli in the non-shadowed message, and if when this monitor picks up threatening or concern-related material that attention tends to shift, then there may exist an attentional 'draining' phenomenon in which attention to focal stimuli is impoverished, though not yet shifted away completely. How should such subtle attention shifts be measured?

A paradigm incorporating a secondary 'probe' stimulus (Posner and Boies, 1971; Bargh and Pietromonaco, 1982) was used by Mathews and MacLeod (1986) to examine attentional 'draining'. They compared the performance of anxious patients and matched normal controls on a dichotic listening task where one message was shadowed. The other, unattended channel was made up of lists of words which were either neutral or threatening. In addition to assessing the effects of type of unattended material or shadowing performance, subjects' RT to a visual probe on a VDU screen in front of them was measured. Results showed that subjects were unaware of the identity of the words in the unattended channel as assessed both by random interruptions of the tape with instructions to recall the non-shadowed words, and by a surprise recognition test following the tape. Despite this, anxious patients were slower to respond to the tone when the words on the unattended channel were threatening, though not when they were neutral. What is the relevance of such phenomena for the sort of attention to salient stimuli we have been considering?

It has been known for some time that unattended material is processed semantically. Lewis (1970) showed that when an unattended word is a synonym of a simultaneously presented word in the shadowed ear, shadowing slows down. Further work by Underwood (1977) showed that a context presented in the unattended ear facilitates shadowing of target words which mesh with the context. There have been many interpretations of these sorts of result (see Laberge (1981) for a review). One possibility is that the meaning of stimuli are processed without drawing on attentional capacity, but that perceptual identification of the source of location of that information demands follow-up by attentional processing. This suggests that the means of distributing attentional resources within the cognitive system, though normally under voluntary control, can be overridden by the occurrence of salient stimuli. If the salient stimuli are under current attentional focus, voluntary attempts to switch *away* will tend to fail. By contrast, if the salient stimuli are outside current attentional focus, voluntary attempts to *remain* focused will tend to fail. This analysis shows up an ambiguity in paradigms which use dichotic listening tasks. For maintaining attention in the light of distraction may require greater effort, which in turn affects shadowing and RT performance, rather than these being affected by depleted attentional resources themselves. It may, of course, amount to the same thing in the case of 'attentional draining', but we should be aware of the ambiguity lest it has implications for other experiments or for possible remedial strategies.

4.2.2 Attentional Bias and Lowered Visual Thresholds

In reviewing the studies of perceptual pick-up of concern-related stimuli in the auditory system, we saw how a threshold paradigm (Parkinson and Rachman's (1981) experiment on mothers whose children were having tonsillectomies) suffered from not being able to distinguish between perceptual and response-bias explanations. Equivalent experimental paradigms on visual modality have been used under the 'perceptual defence' rubric, though most tend to share the same interpretive problems. In the next section we shall review some attempts to use experiments in the visual system which overcome these ambiguities, but first we shall consider the question to what extent the visual perceptual defence literature is relevant.

In the typical visual perceptual defence experiment, threatening or non-threatening words are presented for successively longer and longer intervals in a tachistoscope until they are successfully identified. Typically, taboo words or threatening words have been used, and 'defence' is said to have occurred when a threat word has a higher recognition threshold. (See extensive reviews by Erdelyi (1974) and Dixon (1981).) A variety of arguments has been proposed which attempt to attribute this perceptual defence phenomena to factors other than the emotionality of the stimuli, but most such criticisms have proven difficult to sustain. One early suggestion was that frequency differences between taboo and non-taboo material may account for the findings (e.g. Howie, 1952; Solomon and Postman, 1952; Postman, 1953; Howes, 1954). However, this argument was largely based on comparisons of frequency counts for such items in standard word-frequency texts, such as the Thorndike–Lorge (1944), which has subsequently been shown grossly to underestimate the frequency of taboo items (e.g. Eriksen, 1963). Furthermore, many studies which specifically controlled for frequency or eliminated potential frequency confounds by conditioning affect to novel meaningless stimuli, have reported a significant influence of negative affective tone on perceptual threshold (e.g. Dulany, 1957; Levy, 1958; Sales and Haber, 1968).

An alternative explanation for the perceptual defence phenomenon was that it simply reflects a subject's relative expectancies for encountering taboo and neutral stimuli, rather than representing a specific perceptual reaction to affective tone (e.g. Postman *et al.*, 1953; Freeman, 1954). Again, however, many studies find a relationship between affective tone and perceptual threshold when differential expectations are directly controlled, or made unlikely (e.g. Bootzin and Natsoulas, 1965; Dorfman, Grosberg and Kroecker, 1965).

The most influential, and initially compelling, criticism of the perceptual defence hypothesis has been based on the argument that the disproportionately low correct report rates found for emotionally threatening stimuli arise because subjects are less willing to *report* perceiving such stimuli until they are very sure they actually occurred. Thus the anxiety-provoking nature of the stimuli may produce a response bias rather than a perceptual bias (e.g. Goldiamond, 1958; 1962; Eriksen, 1963; Minard, 1965). While such a response bias may indeed exist, appropriate experimental and statistical techniques have confirmed that perceptual sensitivity appears to be genuinely influenced by the affective tone of the stimulus (e.g. Broadbent and Gregory, 1967; Dorfman, 1967; Bootzin and Stephens, 1967).

It has been suggested that the degree to which such defence actually occurs may be subject to individual differences, with various writers proposing specific personality dimensions which are supposed to underlie such variations (e.g. repression–sensitisation, Byrne, 1961, 1964; deniers–non-deniers, Silverman and Silverman, 1964; blunters–monitors, Miller, 1987a, 1987b). Of particular clinical interest is the potential relationship between this personality dimension and manifestations of anxiety. Miller (1987a), for example, specifically argues that blunters, who engage in cognitive avoidance of threat-related cues, will show less stress and arousal than monitors. Indeed the correlation between Byrne's repression-sensitisation scale, and the Spielberger Trait Anxiety Inventory has been found to be 0.80 (Wason and Clark, 1984), which has led to the suggestion that this scale is probably simply a measure of anxiety (Cromwell and Levenkron, 1984). This would imply that anxiety may be associated with a weakening or reversal of perceptual defence, and there is indeed recent evidence that this is so in anxious patients (e.g. Mathews and MacLeod, 1985) though the data for depressed patients remain ambiguous (Powell and Hemsley, 1984).

4.3 ATTENTIONAL BIAS AND DEBILITATED PERFORMANCE — THE STROOP TEST

So far we have considered experiments in which the dependent variable was chosen so that attentional bias would facilitate performance. In this section we consider the alternative strategy — where performance on the dependent variable suffers as a result of the allocation of attention to alternative, more salient aspects of the stimulus array. We shall concentrate on one experimental paradigm here — the Stroop test.

The Stroop task (Stroop, 1935) has long been used by experimental psychologists to study attentional processes. In the original version of this task, a subject is asked to name the colour of ink in which an item is printed while attempting to ignore the item itself. The items in question are meaningless stimuli such as rows of 'X's, or actual names of colours. In the latter case, a word such as 'red' would appear in green ink, the word 'brown' in red ink, and so on. Stroop (1935) found, as all investigators have found since (see Jensen and Rohwer 1966), that it takes subjects longer to name the colours when the base items are antagonistic colour names than when they are rows of meaningless stimuli. But it is not only antagonistic colour names which cause interference. Subsequent research has found that any common word produces some interference (Klein, 1964) especially if the word itself tends to be associated with a colour (e.g. sky, grass) (Scheibe et al., 1967). Warren (1972, 1974) found that more interference was produced in naming the colour of a word if it or its associate had recently been presented auditorily to the subject. Geller and Shaver (1976) found that more interference was produced in the colour naming of self-referent words if a subject had to perform the task in front of a camera and mirror which acted to increase self-awareness.

More recently, several investigators have attempted to use Stroop-like tasks to examine cognitive processing associated with emotional disturbance. Although the conceptual structure within which the research is carried out has varied, the Stroop being used to measure 'construct accessibility' (Gotlib and McCann 1984; Williams and Nulty, 1986), 'activation of danger schemata' (Mathews and MacLeod, 1985) the 'emotional salience of words' (Watts et al., 1986b), or simply 'distraction by emotional stimuli' (Ray, 1979; Williams and Broadbent, 1986), the different studies have in common the measurement of latency to name colours of negative affect words (either series of individual words presented in a tachistoscope or columns of words presented on a single card). Studies have used both neutral and positive words as control stimuli, have compared performance in 'disturbed' groups with non-disturbed controls, and have selected emotional words which are specific to the psychopathology under study.

Gotlib and McCann (1984) selected depressive words for their study of mildly depressed students. High or low scorers on the Beck Depression Inventory named the colours of either neutral, depressive or positive words. Results showed that the valence of the word made little difference to the non-depressed subjects' speed of colour naming. However, the mildly depressed subjects were significantly slower to name the colours of the negative words than the positive or neutral words. Similar results were found by Mathews and MacLeod (1985) using threatening words with anxious patients. In their experiment, 24 patients were grouped on the basis of whether their worries were predominantly social (e.g. patients who found it embarrassing to talk to new people) or physical (e.g. patients who thought it was likely they would have a heart attack). The patients were tested on four Stroop cards each containing 96 stimuli (twelve words repeated eight times). The words on the first card represented physical threat (e.g. disease, cancer) the second represented social threat (e.g. failure, pathetic) and the two other cards contained matched positive words. Control subjects (n = 24) showed no difference in colour naming latency between the threat and no-threat cards. By contrast, not only did anxious patients show slower colour naming for the threat words, but there was a relationship between the type of threat word that most disrupted colour naming and the type of anxiety that predominated in the patient. Whereas all anxious patients were disrupted on social threat words, only physical worriers were disrupted on the physical threat words. The degree of disruption was significantly associated with depression (Beck Depression Inventory), trait and state anxiety, but partial correlation coefficients showed that the main predictor of degree of colour naming disruption was state anxiety. The authors suggest that interference must thus reflect *current* level of activity in danger schemata (though it must be noted that the State Anxiety Inventory is not a test of the current state of anxiety specifically about physical condition).

Watts *et al.* (1986b) used both a general emotional Stroop test (containing words such as fear, death, grief) and a test containing stimuli specifically related to psychopathology – spider words (e.g. hairy, crawl) in a study of spider-avoidant subjects. They found that these subjects showed little disruption on general emotional words compared to control subjects, but a very large disruption in colour-naming spider words. Indeed, the extent of the disruption was almost as great as the disruption in naming antagonistic coloured stimuli (the original Stroop phenomenon). Furthermore, desensitization treatment reduced the amount of disruption to a greater extent than a waiting list control group.

Williams and Broadbent (1986) used a similar emotional Stroop test in patients who had recently taken an overdose. They found greater disruption in naming words which were more specifically related to psychopathology (e.g. overdose, drug) than in more general emotion words (e.g. immature, helpless). Unlike Mathews and MacLeod (1985) the extent of disruption correlated with levels of current depressed mood (assessed with the Profile of Mood Scale; McNair *et al.*, 1981) rather than current anxiety, but this could have been due either to the different word stimuli used or to the different patient group studied.

There is thus a considerable body of evidence suggesting that emotionally disturbed patients' performance on colour naming is particularly disrupted when the words they have to name relate to their specific current concern. This disruption is greater than that shown in relation to generally negative stimuli. What is it about the specific Stroop words that causes greater colour naming interference? In the spider phobic study of Watts *et al.*, the spider Stroop words were more imageable and more concrete (e.g. hairy, legs, spider) than the general emotional words (e.g. fear, death grief). But differences in imageability and concreteness between the general emotional and specific overdose words were not so marked in the overdose study of Williams and Broadbent (1986).

An alternative (or perhaps supplementary) explanation may be that the general and specific words differ in their frequency of usage by the patients/subjects tested in the experiments. Klein (1964) found that words which were more frequent in common usage produced greater interference in colour naming. Frequency norms such as Thorndike–Lorge may be a useful guide to overall frequency for neutral words in general language usage but provide a poor assessment of frequency within the domain of words representing that individual's current concerns. Any event or emotional state which increases the frequency with which an individual thinks or uses a word will, if Klein's (1964) result can be generalized, increase the amount of colour-naming interference for that word. The interference effects are then likely to spread to high-frequency associates of these recently used words (Warren, 1974). However, a frequency explanation of these effects is rendered less likely by the findings of Watts *et al.* (1986a) that desensitization treatment differentially reduced Stroop interference, and those of Foa and McNally (1986) that exposure and response prevention treatment of obsessions did not increase behavioural and physiological sensitivity to fear-relevant stimuli in a non-shadowed message. These treatments were likely to have exposed subjects to fear stimuli far more recently than the waiting list control condition. Yet attention to salient stimuli appeared to lessen following treatment.

To what extent does emotional Stroop disruption reflect current mood level, or more permanent trait mood level? Williams and Nulty (1986) tested 40 subjects one year apart on the Beck Depression Inventory (Short-Form), and were thus able to identify a stable depressed group (high BDI at Times 1 and 2) and a stable non-depressed group (low BDI at Times 1 and 2). In addition, although very few (N = 2) had become more depressed over the year, a moderate number (N = 9) had become non-depressed between Times 1 and 2. All subjects were given a general emotional Stroop (together with control word stimuli) at Time 2. The biggest disruption was shown by the stable depressed group and the smallest by the stable non-depressed group. However, the extent of disruption was more clearly predictable from the Time 1 depression measure than the Time 2 (concurrent) measure. This impression was confirmed by examining the few 'unstably' depressed subjects who had reduced depression over the year. The extent of these subjects' disruption in colour naming was predictable on the basis of their *initial* mood level, rather than their current lower level. These results suggest that under some circumstances the emotional Stroop may be assessing residual effects of previous depression, which contrasts with Mathews and MacLeod's (1985) findings that disruption is predicted best by current state mood levels.

Perhaps there are some circumstances in which Stroop disruption is sensitive to trait mood rather than state mood, and other circumstances in which the reverse is the case. Taken together, the research suggests that both the degree of disturbance and the stability of the disturbance may depend on an interaction between type of emotional disturbance (e.g. anxiety vs. depression) and types of word used in the Stroop task. To establish this result, however, this interaction would have to be demonstrated in the same experiment, rather than be inferred from different experiments using different populations with slightly differing procedures.

The exact locus of the interference effect on these 'emotional' Stroop tasks remains for further research to determine. Within experimental cognitive psychology the original colour-word version of the task produces such a robust phenomenon (Jensen and Rohwer (1966) could find no instance of anything other than interference having been demonstrated) that it has been possible to examine the parameters of the effect much more minutely. Research, such as that which has examined the time course of each subcomponent of the effect (e.g. Glaser and Glaser, 1982; Naish, 1985), has concluded that neither a perceptual nor response interference model is sufficient to account for the effect. Rather, interference seems to occur at an intermediate processing stage where the stimulus components are semantically evaluated. Whether the same model applies to emotional Stroop phenomena, further research will need to determine. Some explanations of the Stroop effect which emphasise competition between incompatible colour stimuli, meanings or responses are likely to be inappropriate in accounting for the emotional Stroop in which there is no such direct competition between the word's meaning and its colour.

In analysing the locus of the Stroop effect, it is of interest to note the specificity of the effect. As we shall see, this specificity is not a universal characteristic of experiments demonstrating disruption. In the next section we examine an experiment in which both facilitation and disruption due to threat material are demonstrated in the same paradigm.

4.4 DISRUPTION AND FACILITATION: THE VISUAL PROBE EXPERIMENT

In the research using the Stroop phenomenon, it is difficult to separate perceptual from response explanations. The data are consistent with the notion that the cognitive systems of emotionally disturbed people are 'set' to respond to stimuli related to their psychopathology, and that this bias accounts for the disruption in colour naming (that is, it takes time to inhibit this response tendency and name the colour). In such a case a response-bias effect would be masquerading as a 'perceptual' effect.

Much of the literature on perceptual defence, as we have seen earlier, is open to the same objection. What is clearly required is a paradigm which examines the effects of attentional bias on *responses* (which are not themselves affectively toned), to *stimuli* which are not themselves affectively toned. Such a paradigm was used by MacLeod, Mathews and Tata (1986). They presented 16 'generally anxious' patients and 16 matched controls with pairs of words appearing simultaneously towards the top or bottom of a VDU screen (3 cm apart). The words appeared for 0.5 second and the subjects' task was to name the top word each time out loud. On some randomly specified trials, a small dot appeared in the place where the word had been, and when this occurred, subjects were to press a button as fast as possible. On half the trials on which the dot-probe appeared, it replaced the top word, and on half it replaced the bottom word. (Navon and Margalit (1983) have confirmed that detection latency for such a probe is a sensitive measure of visual attention. Subjects take longer to respond to a probe if their attention has been drawn elsewhere.) The interesting question that this paradigm can answer is whether anxious patients differ from controls in this measure of visual attention when threat words occur at the top or bottom location.

The results showed that anxious patients and control subjects showed a very different pattern of response, depending on whether the threat word was at the top or bottom, and whether the probe replaced the word at the top or bottom. If the probe replaced a threat word at the top, anxious subjects responded quickly relative to their response if the probe replaced a neutral word at the top and a threat word had occurred at the bottom. If however the probe occurred at the bottom after a threat word had occurred at the top, anxious patients were relatively slower to detect and/or respond to it. This pattern of results for the anxious patients suggests that they orient *towards* the location at which threat has occurred. Control subjects tend to show the opposite pattern, suggesting that they orient *away* from the location at which threat has occurred. Thus this experiment has been able to demonstrate individual differences in response to threat stimuli, using a neutral response to a neutral probe stimulus.

In order to investigate the specificity of these effects, the patients were divided into two groups on the basis of whether their concerns were predominantly physical or social in nature. The responses of these patients to threat words showed *no* tendency for different degrees of facilitation or disruption by stimulus components with different predominant concerns.

What can we conclude from this experiment? It is important to realize what it does *not* show. It does not show that anxious people are any more 'sensitive' to threatening material at the most peripheral level. Controls may have been 'picking up' the threat stimuli as early as the anxious patients. What differed was the attentional allocation pattern in response to these inputs.

This experiment is one of the first to demonstrate that allocation of attention towards threatening stimuli found in attentional bias may be explicable without involving response bias. It would be entirely un-parsimonious to suggest that the anxious subjects in this experiment had 'output logogens' for threat words which were nearer threshold, the 'firing' of which then activated an attentional response which could account for the differences in response latency to a neutral dot-probe. Rather, we need to assume the existence of a decision mechanism which is (a) at a pre-attentive level, (b) sensitive to general differences in threat, (c) allocates attention to different parts or aspects of the environment, and (d) is independent of response bias.

4.5 ACCOUNTING FOR ATTENTIONAL BIAS

Perhaps it will be most helpful to set these results within a wider cognitive psychology framework. Some closely related work is that on perceptual memory reviewed by Jacoby and Witherspoon (1982) and Graf and Mandler (1984).

In this research, memory which is based on awareness is contrasted with memory which appears not to depend on awareness. The need to make such distinctions is often traced back to the nineteenth century neurologist Claparede. As part of an experiment to discover what an amnesic patient could remember, he shook hands with such a patient while holding a pin in the palm of his hand. The next day, the patient was, as usual, unable to recall ever having met Dr Claparede. However, he showed an 'inexplicable' reluctance to shake hands. The patient clearly 'remembered' something, but was not aware of any memory. Similarly, research by Warrington and Weiskrantz (1974) shows how the advantage of previous cueing on a figure identification task or facilitated performance due to previous practice on jigsaw puzzles is retained in amnesics despite their having forgotten ever doing the tasks. Procedural memory appears relatively intact; declarative memory is by contrast very impaired. Discussion of the procedural–declarative distinction is beyond the scope of this chapter. It is how such distinctions are elucidated by perceptual memory research that is relevant for our present purposes.

In perceptual memory experiments the presentation of words as part of the first phase of an experiment makes them more likely to be identified when presented for very brief (e.g. 35msec) intervals in phase two of the experiment. The important aspect of this work, however, is that this perceptual facilitation can be shown to be independent of more awareness-based recollection procedures. That is, after learning a list of words, some will be recognized later in a memory task; some will be identified more easily in a tachistoscope; but these will not necessarily be the same words. Graf and Mandler (1984) used a depth-of-processing paradigm in which different questions were asked of the to-be-encoded words, emphasising either structural features (how many 'T' junctions in this word?) or semantic features (e.g. is this a pleasant word?). In this paradigm one would expect better memory for the words encoded under semantic conditions because the encoding and retrieval procedures involve more awareness-based strategies of elaboration. (Though see Klein and Kihlstrom (1986) for an alternative explanation of such depth of processing effects. The explanation for these phenomena does not concern us here.) Graf and Mandler's results confirmed the superior recall and recognition of semantically encoded items, but also showed that depth of processing made no difference to a task chosen to assess perceptual memory (word-stem completion in which subjects are given three letters of a six-letter word and asked to complete the word; e.g. FOR---: forbid, forget, forest, etc.). The numbers of stem completions of previously presented words in the semantic condition was only 1.2 times the number of such stem completions following structural encoding. This figure can be compared to a semantic:structural ratio of 2.7:1 for recognition performance and 4.0:1 for recall performance.

Graf and Mandler's account of their results may have significant bearings on the interpretation of attentional bias phenomena in clinical conditions. They distinguish two processes which operate on mental representations: *integration* and *elaboration*.

Integration is the mutual activation among different components of a single schema (defined for their purposes as a cluster of perceptual and semantic variables which represents a word or concept in the cognitive system). Integration makes a word more accessible — that is, the word will be more likely to come to mind, be noticed or identified when only some of its features or components are presented to the subject. This clearly closely resembles attentional bias as we have defined it.

Elaboration occurs when schemata are activated in the presence of *other* mental events, making further new relationships with those events or reactivating previously established relationships. Such elaboration is required for a subject to become aware of relations among sets of previously unrelated words (e.g. clustering in free recall), and to relate a word to its context (e.g. encoding specificity phenomena, and the depth of processing effects on free recall and recognition noted by many investigators). Graf and Mandler (1984) use the term 'retrievability' to describe the better recall of material mediated by the activation of relationships between schemata, that is, by the generation of new, and reinstatement of old, paths for retrieving the words.

If these authors are correct in postulating two distinct processes underlying recall performance and perceptual memory performance, then it is possible that different types of emotional disturbance may be associated with disruption of only one or other aspect of processing. Some patients may show facilitated performance on a perceptual memory task because the underlying mental representations have been active recently and are therefore in a more integrated state (the internal components are mutually activating each other). Others may show facilitated recall of negative words or personal memories because their mood has caused the underlying mental representation to form new, or reactivate old, links. Let us consider how these formulations may help in elucidating the examples of attentional bias considered in this chapter.

Eysenck *et al.* (in press) discuss the nonspecificity of the dot-probe results and suggest that it is consistent with the notion that the bias is 'pre-attentive'. The bias is general, because it 'operates on rapidly available information concerning affective tone or threat value of stimuli rather than on detailed semantic information.' Our review suggests that it may be possible to be more specific. If we suppose that an individual's cognitive system allocates attention initially to any stimuli that are better 'integrated' in Graf and Mandler's sense (but not necessarily better elaborated), then the greater perceptibility of threat words in perceptual defence experiments is more understandable. A threat stimulus or recently presented stimulus may cause similar effects, and it is possible that at this level differences in elaboration between stimuli are ignored. We can perhaps tentatively suggest that the visual dot-probe task has more in common with the perceptual memory tasks of Jacoby and Witherspoon (1982) and Graf and Mandler (1984) — that is, it is concerned with *integration* of subcomponents of *individual* schemata. These possibilities are discussed further in the final chapter.

4.6 BIASED ATTENTION AND COGNITIVE AVOIDANCE

It is clear from the evidence reviewed that people orient attention towards words related to their emotional concerns, and that such words disrupt performance on tasks such as colour naming. However, emotional stimuli are not always well processed. Indeed, if they arouse too much anxiety, the processing of emotional stimuli may be unusually poor. Foa and Kozak (1986) see this as the result of 'cognitive avoidance' and suggest, on the basis of their clinical observations, that it may result from strategies of distraction (pretending it is something it isn't). Also relevant is psychophysiological evidence that phobics are likely to give defensive rather than orienting responses to phobic stimuli (Hare and Blevings, 1975).

It seems that such strategies of cognitive avoidance can be invoked quickly and involuntarily once an emotional stimulus is identified as such. Of course, for this identification to occur, the stimulus must be processed to a reasonably advanced stage. We have seen from the visual-probe experiment how anxious people initially orient towards threat. However, there are other aspects of processing which may be aborted once the stimulus has been identified as an emotional one. It may be that elaboration and further inspection of detailed stimulus features are not carried through if a stimulus is identified as sufficiently emotional.

There may indeed be a degree of *mutual* antagonism between elaborate processing of neutral features and the identification of the stimulus as an emotional one. Leventhal and Cupchik (1976) have shown, for example, that emotional experience in focal awareness can be reduced by attending to detailed features of emotional cartoons. Similarly Leyens *et al.* (1976) found aggressive responses were reduced by requiring subjects to analyse the aesthetic properties of slides designed to stimulate aggression.

If subjects do not elaborate details of emotional stimuli, then it can be predicted that memory for them would be poorer. Without detailed attention it will be more difficult, for example, to distinguish emotional stimuli that have been presented from those that have not. Watts *et al.* (1986d) tested this with spider phobics, the prediction being that the emotional properties of spiders for spider phobics would result in poorer recognition memory for them. Dead spiders mounted on cards were used. It transpired that the effect depended on the size of the spiders, being found only with the larger ones – presumably because they aroused more anxiety. Because of this unpredicted moderator variable, a second study was undertaken which again found that phobics' recognition of spiders tended to be poorer only for the larger ones. In this study, a processing manipulation was introduced in which subjects were required to describe the spiders while they were looking at them. The effect reached significance with this manipulation, but fell short of significance without it. This is relevant to the interpretation of the effect; if it can occur when subjects have to describe the spiders, the nature of the cognitive avoidance involved is clearly more subtle than simply not looking at the spiders. The second study also showed clearly that the effect of phobic status on memory for spiders was not mediated by differences in response criteria.

The boundary conditions of this phenomenon are not yet known; we do not know which emotions produce it and in what range of intensities. However, it seems unlikely, for example, that positive emotional responses would produce it in the way that anxiety does. It also seems likely that it is only produced by stimuli that produce more intense emotional responses than the *words* used in most of the studies reported in this chapter. The clinical significance of cognitive avoidance is that it may disrupt the beneficial effects of exposure treatments, especially long-term benefit. Evidence is accumulating that distraction strategies interfere with the efficacy of exposure treatments (e.g. Grayson *et al.*, 1982; Sartory *et al.*, 1982), whereas instructing patients to give more detailed attention to the stimulus improves it (Watts, 1974).

If the visual dot-probe results are to be explained in terms of the integration process, and cognitive avoidance, which impairs recall of threat stimuli, is to be explained in terms of the elaboration process, what explains deficient performance on the emotional Stroop? We suggest that the Stroop occupies an intermediate position, sharing characteristics of both processes. Mathews and MacLeod (1985) found that Stroop debilitation was independent of the ability to recognise which words had been causing the interference. This suggests an 'integration' component. But note that non-emotional Stroop interference is shown on coloured words that are the *associates* of those recently presented (Warren, 1972) and that Stroop interference is sensitive to depth-of-processing manipulations, and indeed has been used as one of the few independent measures of 'depth' to which stimuli have been processed. Recall that Graf and Mandler (1984) found no evidence that the depth to which words had been processed made a difference to their 'perceptual memory'-dependent variable (word completion), but did make a difference to recognition and recall performance. Jacoby and Witherspoon (1982) also report that depth of processing made no difference to a perceptual memory task (tachistoscopic identification). It is possible, then, that the Stroop task as used in the experiments on emotion reviewed here includes an 'elaboration' component. We are currently carrying out experiments using a 'subliminal' Stroop which should help to clarify the extent to which each type of processing is involved.

4.7 CONCLUSIONS

At the outset we defined attentional bias as an aspect of phenomenal experience — as a process in which people are aware of something novel, threatening or related to their current concern. What are the clinical implications of the experiments we have examined? Let us look again at the bird phobic MM, and the generally anxious TS. Both found their attention being caught by concern-related, threatening material; dead birds or similar shapes on the one hand; suicide stories on the other. First, we have seen that this tendency probably occurs at an early stage in cognitive processing, at a point where the significance of the stimuli has been assessed but its perceptual characteristics have not yet been analysed by the allocation of focal attention. At this point, whereas a non-anxious person's attention might orient *away* from the suicide story in the newspaper, the anxious person's attention tends to switch towards the unpleasant story. (This apparent paradox of meaning extraction occurring prior to full perceptual analysis will be more fully explored in Chapter 9, and its clinical implications in Chapter 10.)

The two patients referred to above were similar in their 'noticing', but very different in how much they subsequently ruminated about the stimuli. This difference may have been due to the difference in how circumscribed the stimuli were - a bird is a fairly concrete, well-circumscribed stimulus, whereas an overdose story is less so. Or the difference could be due to the comparative self-relevance of the stimuli. A bird stimulus has arguably less personal implications than do stories about suicide, muggings and murder - the former less likely to be encodable along many self-schema dimensions, the latter is more likely to be so encodable. Nevertheless, it is important that the same amount of attention to emotional stimuli should have different consequences.

Further corroboration for the distinction between the 'noticing' and 'ruminative' aspects of attentional bias comes from some research reported by Klinger *et al.* (1981). They have derived a Concern Dimension Questionnaire in which subjects begin by listing a number of 'things they had thought about most today and yesterday', followed by listing a number of things which were significant in their lives which they had not thought about (or very little) during the same period. Subjects then rank-order all items according to how much they have been thought about, and characterize them on a number of scales assessing value, expectancy and time-course of the concern.

Analysis of the questionnaire has revealed four dimensions: the valence of the goal (positive or negative), the time available before something has to be done, the intensity of valence (*how* positive or negative), and the probability of success in the goal being achieved. The valence of the goal was in general a weak predictor of the amount of time people report thinking about things (confirmed by time-sampling methods in subjects' daily lives). The time available for action, intensity and expectancy of success were better predictors of time spent thinking about the goal, but were predictive only in natural settings. They did *not* predict 'switching' in the dichotic listening task reported earlier in this chapter. This is consistent with the possibility that subjects' tendency to notice concern-related stimuli were not mediated by the same processes that determine whether they spend further time on thinking about the concern. Although these may be independent, the evidence reviewed in this chapter has shown how orientation towards sources of threat may disrupt performance whether or not subjects are consciously aware of the threat stimuli. How much this attentional bias contributes to 'noticing' and to 'rumination' remains for further research to determine.

Chapter 5

Mood and Memory

It seems an inevitable outcome of the biases in attention reviewed in the previous chapter is that more negative material will be encoded in memory. If the bird phobic MM sees more birds today, surely she will, tomorrow, remember having seen more birds. Similarly, TS ought to remember having read more suicide stories in yesterday's newspaper. However the picture may not be as straightforward as this. First, there was some evidence that enhanced 'noticing' of an item may in some instances be followed by 'cognitive avoidance' in which the information-processing system aborts further elaboration of the salient stimulus. The result may be that only an impoverished record of the event is encoded in memory, compensating for the increased 'noticing'. Second, even if the stimulus events were encoded, their later recall will depend on ready availability of mnemonic cues to help the recollection process. Different emotions may vary in the extent to which they facilitate or inhibit the utilization of such cues at encoding or retrieval.

In September 1980, Gordon Bower began an address to the American Psychological Association on 'Mood and Memory' with a stark example of the way memory may be affected by mood. He referred to the findings of Diamond, the forensic psychiatrist who had examined Sirhan Sirhan, the assassin of Senator Robert Kennedy in 1968. Apparently Sirhan had carried out the deed in a greatly agitated state and afterwards remembered nothing of the event. Diamond hypnotized Sirhan and helped him to reconstruct from memory the events that had occurred in the kitchen of the Ambassador Hotel in Los Angeles:

> Under hypnosis, as Sirhan became more worked up and excited, he recalled progressively more, the memories tumbling out whilst his excitement built to crescendo leading to the shooting. At that point Sirhan would scream out the death curses, 'fire' the shots, and then choke as he re-experienced the secret service body guard nearly throttling him after he was caught.

Despite the fact that Sirhan would have liked to have felt that he did the deed (in the cause of Arab nationalism) he was never able, through conscious effort in a non-hypnotized state, to remember doing so.

The point that Bower wished to make by quoting this episode is that mood can act as a distinctive 'state' or 'context' which can have powerful effects on memory. Once one has changed the state or context it will be harder to remember things that were learned in the original state. However, if the context is reinstated, the material again becomes available to normal memory.

 There are two issues raised by this example. The first is whether context-dependent memory is a reliable phenomenon; the second is whether, even if it is, mood states can act as such contexts. If we find that they can, we need to ask some further questions about when they are most likely to do so, and what clinical implications, if any, result.

 The first question is more easily answered. Ability to successfully retrieve from memory appears to be facilitated if one can reinstate the conditions which prevailed when the material was encoded. One demonstration of this comes from the experiments on diving and memory by Alan Baddeley and colleagues. For example, Godden and Baddeley (1975) had divers learn lists of words either on the beach or under approximately 4.5 metres of water. They were asked to try to recall the list learned in one context while in the same context on some cccasions and while in the changed context on other occasions. Godden and Baddeley found a decrement in recall of words of over 30 per cent if the context was changed in this way between learning and recall. Other examples of context-dependent learning are reviewed by Bower (1981).

The second question – can mood states act as such a context? – will be the main subject of this chapter. On the face of it there appears to be enough *prima facie* evidence to suppose that it can. There appear to be many clinical examples which could be accounted for in such a way. Williams (1984, p. 195) quotes the case of a patient whose experience of going swimming was reinterpreted later in the light of subsequent bad events. At one therapy session when she was in a good mood she recalled the swimming event as having been a good experience. On a subsequent session when she was in a more depressed mood she remembered various aspects of the swimming event which made it seem much less good, for example that it had been a struggle to get to the pool for fear of making herself look ridiculous, and that it had been embarrassing to see herself in a swimsuit because of her weight problem. On the basis of this 'recoding' of the swimming experience, she felt that bad experiences in the future were entirely predictable. If we assume in this example that the original mood was neutral, note that a strict state-dependent explanation (in which positive, negative or neutral material is better recalled if the original context is reinstated) is inappropriate. Rather, this patient would have been showing *mood-congruent recall* – remembering better the unpleasant aspects now she was in a low mood, having remembered the pleasant aspects when in a good mood. She would have been showing a different phenomenon if the original mood had been distinctively bad rather than neutral. In that case all the bad aspects would have been encoded and even if later retrieval mood was neutral it would have been the bad aspects which would have been recalled. In this case she would have been showing evidence of *mood congruent encoding*. The distinction between strict context/state-dependent learning on the one hand, and mood-congruent encoding and recall on the other, should be kept in mind in the discussion which follows. To anticipate slightly, mood-congruent encoding and retrieval has been much easier to demonstrate experimentally than has mood state-dependent learning. Much of the research on mood and memory has been done within associative semantic network theory (Anderson and Bower, 1973). We shall leave detailed comment on this theory until later in the chapter. However, it may be helpful at this point to give a broad outline of network models to understand better how Bower has adapted them to explain mood memory phenomena.

5.1 ASSOCIATIVE NETWORK MODELS

There are several different semantic network models (reviewed by Johnson-Laird *et al.*, 1984). Most are derived from the early theories of Quillian (1968) who made the distinction between concepts (type nodes) and instances of concepts (token nodes). The meaning of a word can be defined in terms of a certain configuration of token nodes linked to the type node (representing the word). Each token node (instance) in the configuration would itself be linked to its respective type (concept) node. The model assumed that when people evaluate the relation between two concepts (e.g. brick-house) or form an association between them, a search is made along links radiating out from the two type nodes (one for 'brick', another for 'house') which will have been activated by the presentation of the two words. The search moves outwards in a *spread of activation*, passing intermediary type nodes *en route*, and leaving at each such node a tag specifying the immediately preceding node and the node from which the search started.

Two processes then operate: *intersection* and *evaluation*. *Intersection* occurs when search from one starting-point (e.g. type node for 'brick') encounters a node with a tag from the other starting-point (type node for 'house'). The system then *evaluates* the pathway that has been created between the two nodes. The result of this evaluation gives the nature of the *semantic* relationship between the two originally presented words. In early experiments, this model was used to predict the latency with which people could verify statements such as 'A canary is a bird' or 'A canary has wings' involving different combinations of superordinate and subordinate 'type' and 'token' nodes. These early experiments and the problems in interpreting them are reviewed by Johnson-Laird *et al.* (1984), and are beyond the scope of this chapter.

The network model that has been most used as a framework for mood effects on memory has been the Human Associative Memory (HAM) Network of Anderson and Bower (1973). Bower (1981) describes the way in which

HAM may explain mood and memory effects. Events are represented in memory by descriptive propositions, configurations made up of associative connections (pathways) between different instances of the concept (token nodes) used to describe the event. Activation spreading from one node to another creates the novel pathway, and recall consists of using cues to probe locations in memory until the correct pathway is identified. The crucial assumption of Bower's model is that each distinct emotion has a specific node in memory which 'collects together many other aspects of the emotion that are connected to it by associative pointers'.

In this framework, free recall is the output of the network of tagged pathways which have been formed between the concepts/words subjects think of as they study lists or stories. Recall makes use of connections which have been tagged during learning. Mood at encoding biases the way in which connections are formed, favouring mood-congruent material rather than mood-incongruent material. More 'elaborated' associations (more alternative tagged pathways) will be set up for those items congruent with mood. Mood at recall acts as a 'constant cognitive element' in working memory. If the mood at recall is congruent with mood at encoding, the search is biased to proceed along the same associative pathways.

The combination of the activity of individual 'emotion nodes' and activation of other associative nodes, together with a biased search that such activation produces is said to account for state-dependent learning and mood-congruent encoding and retrieval effects. Blaney (1986) has recently made a comprehensive review of this literature, and so we shall not attempt to reproduce such detail here. However the main studies will be mentioned to serve as the basis for a discussion of key issues relating to network theory. We shall attempt to show how the laboratory studies have raised questions concerning (a) different processes underlying the biases in depressive and anxiety related material; (b) the nature of the relationship between positive and negative material in memory, and between positive and negative moods; and (c) possible deficits in retrieval processes in negative mood states.

5.2 THE EVIDENCE

5.2.1 Recall of Personal Memories

Since a characteristic of depression is the predominance of negative aspects of the past, it is appropriate to examine first whether this phenomenon can actually be observed under controlled conditions.

Lloyd and Lishman (1975) used a list of neutral words as stimuli to cue memories in clinically depressed patients attending the Maudsley Hospital in London. Patients were instructed to think of either a pleasant or unpleasant memory, and to signal to the experimenter by tapping on the table when a suitable memory came to mind. The time taken to retrieve memories to each cue word was recorded by stopwatch. They found that the more severe the depression, measured by the Beck Depression Inventory, the quicker the patient was to retrieve an unpleasant memory, thus reversing an often reported tendency for non-depressed people to be faster at retrieving pleasant memories than they are at retrieving unpleasant memories.

Two major problems in interpreting these results occur. First, the more severely depressed patients may have had more genuinely depressing experiences, so may find it easier to retrieve any one of them. Secondly, the more severely depressed may simply be evaluating more of their neutral or ambiguous experiences as more depressive, thus spuriously inflating the number of memories from which to choose. Both of these have been taken account of in two separate research strategies employed by John Teasdale and co-workers at Oxford. The first uses non-depressed volunteers whose mood has been experimentally manipulated using Velten's (1968) self-statements (Teasdale and Fogarty, 1979). In this case, where subjects are randomly allocated to 'elation' or 'depression' conditions so that the amount of actual depressive experiences can be assumed to be equal prior to mood induction, latencies to remember positive or negative personal events are biased (though most of this is due to slowed recall of positive material in depressed mood rather than speeded recall of negative material). Both this and later experiments have shown that the memories recalled are actually pleasant or unpleasant (when rated in neutral mood), and so the bias cannot simply be explained in terms of the over-inclusive effects of depressed mood (Teasdale *et al.*, 1980).

The second strategy has used clinically depressed individuals selected for the presence of diurnal variation of mood (Clark and Teasdale, 1982). Patients were given words as cues and asked to respond with the first personal memory which came to mind. These were later rated for pleasantness/happiness. Two independent though complementary effects could be observed. First, happy memories were less probable (and depressing memories more probable) when patients were more depressed. When the same patients were at the less depressed point in their cycle, this picture was reversed. These within-subject results clearly cannot be explained with reference to different frequencies of actual depressive experiences. Secondly, negativity ratings of the experiences were also mood-dependent, the more depressed ratings being given the more depressive the current mood. This effect was not by itself sufficient to explain the memory biasing, however.

Results consistent with the above have been found using mood-induction procedures other than the Velten technique (e.g. hypnosis, Gilligan and Bower, 1980; Autobiographical Recollections Method, Salavoy and Singer, 1985). Gilligan and Bower (1984) report an experiment in which subjects kept diaries for one week, noting down any positive or negative events (time, place, gist), and giving an intensity rating. One week after handing in the diary, subjects were randomly allocated to two groups. Subjects were hypnotized and either a happy or depressed mood suggested. Percentage recall of happy incidents averaged 32 per cent for both types of recall mood. However, this figure fell to 23 per cent for those subjects recalling negative events in happy mood, and rose to 38 per cent for those subjects recalling negative events in sad mood. In another study, subjects spent 10 minutes generating memories from childhood, giving details of the gist, time and place while either in hypnotically-induced happy or sad mood. Next day they returned and rated the memories (in neutral mood) for how positive or negative they were. Ninety-two per cent of memories recalled by 'happy' subjects were positive, compared with 45 per cent for the 'sad' subjects.

How reliable are these findings of mood biasing in personal memory? The answer seems to be that the effect is robust. Bias occurs whether naturally occurring depression or mood induction is used. Methods of cueing personal memory have also been varied without affecting the nature of the results: Lloyd and Lishman (1975) and Teasdale and Fogarty (1979) used neutral words and told subjects whether to retrieve a pleasant or unpleasant memory to each cue. Teasdale *et al.*, (1980) and Clark and Teasdale (1982) used neutral words but allowed subjects to retrieve any personal memory which was later rated for its hedonic valence. Gilligan and Bower (1984) did not use any specific cues, allowing subjects to recall anything that came to mind from their diary or their childhood. Only in the case of this latter finding has some doubt on replicability been cast by Salavoy and Singer (1985). Using a guided imagery (autobiographical recollections) method as well as a taped depressing story (see Goodwin and Williams, 1982; Williams, 1984, p. 168 for details of this method) they found no effect of elated or depressed mood on recall of early childhood memories, though they did find the usual bias effect when memories from the previous week were asked for. The non-replication of the childhood memory bias could have been due to a less effective mood induction being used than that of Gilligan and Bower (1984). It was more probably due to the fact that only five childhood memories were elicited. Subjects may produce highly over-rehearsed memories at the outset of such a task. Mood may only be an effective extra cue in the search for memories that do not so readily come to mind.

Finally, mood biasing appears to occur in other types of emotional disturbance. Recent experiments have shown that large biases in latencies to retrieve personal memories exist in people who have recently attempted suicide (Williams and Broadbent, 1986). These people are more emotionally disturbed than control patients on a number of scales—more confused, tense, depressed, fatigued, angry and have less vigour. Which of these moods contributes to the memory bias is difficult to determine. We shall see later that not all moods appear to be so potent as depression in acting as a 'context'. It is also worth noting at this point that none of the research to date has directly addressed the question of whether the mood is more powerful as a 'state' or 'trait' effect. The fact that Teasdale and Fogarty (1979) were able to demonstrate mood-congruent recall on normals using mood induction shows that it can be a state effect, but that does not preclude the possibility that in clinical groups mood memory bias can also be a relatively enduring characteristic. Martin's (1985) demonstration of such biases in subjects scoring highly in neuroticism supports this possibility.

5.2.2 Word-list Learning

Although the experiments reviewed above examined phenomena which bear a close relationship to clinical aspects of mood, they do not allow us to specify very exactly which factors underlie the bias. A number of experiments have therefore used lists containing some positive and negative words to examine memory biases in more detail. The use of word-lists allows one to control the affective tone of the encoding material so that strict state-dependent learning may be experimentally distinguished from mood congruent encoding and retrieval effects. This is not possible using autobiographical recall as one can never be sure what the original situation was — neither what the original mood was nor what the original material was, which is being recollected.

Do depressed and anxious patients selectively learn negative words? Several studies have investigated selective learning in depression. Breslow et al. (1981) found that depressed patients were less good than non-depressed at remembering positive material, but were no better than non-depressed at remembering negative material. McDowell (1984) gave positive and negative words to depressed patients to learn, either in separate lists (one containing positive, the other negative words) or mixed together in the same lists. He found that patients were biased in their recall, but only in the 'mixed list' condition—possibly because this condition involves competition at encoding and retrieval between positive and negative items. Zuroff et al. (1983) used high or low scorers on the Beck Depression Inventory (Short-Form), and presented them with 40 words (20 likeable, 20 dislikeable), asking them to make judgements as to how much the adjectives described themselves. They were all given recall tests after one hour, two days and seven days. Results showed that the more depressed group correctly recalled more negative items, but also showed more negative intrusions. Zuroff also included a recognition test following the final recall test. This showed that depressed subjects, although recognizing correctly more negative items, also gave more false positive responses. A signal detection analysis confirmed that depressed subjects were more lenient in their response criteria (lower value of β), but were not more able to discriminate old from new negative items (no difference in d').

This result is important in two respects. First, it is a reminder that increased recall of negative material in other experiments may be due to response biases. This would be consistent with some aspects of a study of memory in depressed patients by Dunbar and Lishman (1984) (though see Clark and Martin's (1986) critique of these investigations).

The second respect in which Zuroff et al.'s result is important is that a similar negative bias to that shown by the depressed subjects was found in a third group of subjects who were not currently depressed (mean BDI-SF = 1.3) but who had been depressed in the past (scored in top 20 per cent of 'retrospective' Beck Depression Inventory). This is consistent with recent reports from Hammen et al. (1986) that previous occurrence of depression affects performance on cognitive tasks even when current mood is not disturbed. It raises the important possibility that trait mood memory biasing may exist independently of current state level of mood.

Although the experiments of McDowell (1984), Breslow et al. (1981) and Zuroff et al. (1983) confirm that depressed mood biases the learning of word-lists, because the subjects are depressed both while learning and while recalling the list, they do not help us to determine the relative importance of encoding or retrieval operations.

Mood induction has been used to examine this issue. Isen et al. (1987) used success or failure at a computer game to vary subjects' mood. They were then asked to recall words from a list of positive and negative personality trait adjectives they had memorised in neutral mood prior to playing the game. Success experience caused more positive adjectives to be recalled, but failure did not facilitate recall of negative adjectives. Teasdale and Russell (1983) used a similar design, but manipulated subjects' mood with Velten-type negative or positive self-statements (Velten, 1968). Subjects read positively or negatively-toned statements with which they were asked to identify. They had previously been presented (in neutral mood) with a list of 36 adjectives (12 positive, 12 negative, 12 neutral). Mood at recall was found to affect significantly which words from the list were recalled. In a later experiment, Clark and Teasdale (1985) replicated this recall mood congruency effect, but showed that the effect was more characteristic of females than males, possibly due to the fact that the female subjects were found (even in neutral mood) to rate the stimulus words as more personally useful in their daily lives. Thus they would have been more likely to have used these words when depressed in the past.

Note that this explanation uses the concept of state-dependent learning. But all the experiments cited so far have not examined state-dependent learning in the strict sense at all — i.e. that material learned in one state or context will be more likely to be recalled if the subject is returned to the same state or context in which the original learning took place. In fact, experiments which have specifically manipulated mood at encoding and retrieval to examine state-dependent retrieval have produced equivocal results. A much cited study by Bower, Monteiro and Gilligan (1978) failed to find that making mood the same at encoding and retrieval facilitated recall of a single list (16 positive or negative abstract nouns). The mood manipulation was hypnosis, which has been used in the same laboratory many times to produce many more robust mood-biasing effects. Only when the authors, in a third experiment, used an interference paradigm where two lists were learned (one in happy mood, the other in sad mood) did they find that reinstatement of encoding mood at the retrieval stage facilitated the recall of the list learned in that mood. The fact that such large effects were found with only four subjects in each of the six groups was surprising, given the failure of the earlier experiments in the series. Indeed, Bower and Mayer (1986) have now attempted to replicate the experiment and failed.

Schare et al. (1984) did find a state-dependent learning effect but, like Bower et al. (1978), only when two lists were learned in an interference paradigm. The lists consisted of neutral words, one of which was learned when happy the other while sad (mood having been induced using the Velten procedure). This result will have to await replication before it can be considered reliable. One procedural feature which distinguishes it from the Bower procedure is that during the recall phase, words from either list were recalled. (In the Bower paradigm, subjects attempt first to recall List 1, then List 2 in counterbalanced order.) This seemingly minor procedural point may be significant since it allows interference between competing items during retrieval. Early retrieval of items from the list learned in the same mood will tend to cue other words from the same list. This process alone will tend to inhibit the later recall of other actually stored items and may be why McDowell (1984) found biased recall in depressives only when a mixed list was used.

It can thus be seen that mood state-dependent learning is far from easy to demonstrate experimentally. This weakens the case for explaining the fact that mood at recall facilitates retrieval of congruent material encoded in neutral mood (Teasdale and Russell, 1983) by reference to state-dependent learning theory.

5.2.3 Stories with Mixed Affective Content

Bower, Gilligan and Monteiro (1981) examined the effect of mood-congruent encoding by having subjects read a story about two characters playing tennis (one sad, the other happy). The story contained an equal number of sad and happy statements. Subjects read the stories after they had been hypnotized and a happy or sad mood suggested. In neutral mood on the following day, subjects attempted to recall the events narrated by the story. Eighty per cent of the facts recalled by subjects who had been sad while encoding were sad facts from the story. For subjects whose encoding mood had been happy, only 45 per cent of their recall was of sad facts. A similar result was reported by Bower (1981) in which subjects in happy or sad (hypnotically-induced) moods read events from a 'psychiatric interview' with an individual in which both happy and sad events were mentioned. In this experiment retrieval mood was also manipulated for the recall phase which took place 20 minutes later. Results showed a clear interaction between mood at encoding and type of fact retrieved (more sad facts if learned in sad mood; more happy facts if learned in happy mood). However, mood at recall did not affect retrieval. As a further check on this failure to find an effect of retrieval mood, another experiment was performed using the story about sad and happy tennis players. This time the stories were encoded in neutral mood and, six hours later, recalled both in happy and then in sad mood (counterbalanced within subject design). No effect of recall mood could be demonstrated.

What could explain this inconsistency in mood-congruent retrieval effects? Isen et al. (1978) and Teasdale and Russell (1983) have found such effects, but Bower (1981) did not. Two possible explanations suggest themselves. The first is that Bower's use of story material means that the individual items are associated with each other (e.g. one tennis player enjoys the sunshine, the other is scorched by the sun). If one is recalled it is likely to cue another item even if opposite in hedonic tone. Mood at retrieval may not be sufficient to override these inter-item associations which are not as strong if a list of words is presented.

There is a second reason why retrieval mood may have operated more on the words than the story. Both Isen et al. (1978) and Teasdale and Russell (1983) used personality trait adjectives. It is possible that these items tend to be encoded with reference to the self, unlike the Bower stories which are explicitly about other people. Depth of processing studies of the self-schema (see Chapter 6) find that material encoded with reference to the self often shows mood- or personality-congruent bias in recall, whereas the same item encoded with reference to another person does not do so. Consistent with this, Hasher et al. (1985), who used integrated story material which was not self-referenced, failed to find a mood-congruent retrieval effect. Further experiments on mood-congruent encoding and retrieval should include both integrated and non-integrated material under conditions which do and those which do not favour self-referential encoding in order to check explicitly the relevance of these possible mediating variables.

5.3 ASSOCIATIVE NETWORK — MODEL OR FRAMEWORK?

The evidence so far reviewed seems to indicate that mood-congruent encoding and retrieval are reliable phenomena: that it can be demonstrated for autobiographical memory and for laboratory word-lists or stories with mixed affective content. Difficulties in demonstrating some mood-congruent effects seem plausibly explained by the interconnectedness of the to-be-recalled material, or by the extent to which a subject may encode the material self-referentially. But there have been few successful demonstrations of mood acting as context in a strict state-dependent learning experiment. The question now arises whether associative network theory is the most appropriate model to explain the data.

As we have seen, however, several semantic network models exist. Johnson-Laird *et al.* (1984) review six of them, and identify nine distinguishing features by which some are different from the others. Yet none of these distinguishing features of the models makes any differential predictions concerning the mood and memory experiments reviewed in this chapter. This is consistent with the notion that network theory is best seen as a general framework for speaking about mood-memory phenomena, rather than a model whose specific predictions can be confirmed or refuted. Frameworks can be more or less helpful, they cannot be right or wrong. Other frameworks may be equally helpful in understanding the phenomena under discussion (e.g. encoding specificity framework, Tulving and Thomson, 1973; schema theory, Alba and Hasher, 1983). If there are data that it cannot explain it may not be because it could not in principle be extended to do so, but it may be more helpful to use alternative frameworks to describe that aspect of the data. (See Power and Champion (1986) for further discussion of the disadvantages of network models.)

There are two types of reason for rejecting a model as unhelpful. The first is conceptual; the terms used may not readily map on to what people normally mean when they refer to emotions. The second is empirical; experimental results may demand so much elaboration of the framework that it becomes more parsimonious to seek an alternative. In evaluating the usefulness of network theory we shall consider several examples where such issues arise.

5.3.1 Emotion as a Node — Hot vs. Cold Cognition

It is a major premise of network theory that different emotions are represented as units or nodes in the same semantic network with which memories of events are recorded. But the same semantic network underlies our ability to use emotional words appropriately in any context, not just when the emotion denoted by the word is being experienced. Why is it that any use of an emotion word does not activate the whole emotional apparatus? In Abelson's terms, when is a cognition 'hot' and when 'cold'? In reading this chapter, for example, depression nodes will have been activated repeatedly in the reader, but not (we hope) in a way that has brought to mind all the readers' worst experiences of failure and rejection. What is it that determines when 'depression' will or will not make a person feel sad? Bower's account is to assert that there are different types of node for each emotion word: 'We should distinguish the node corresponding to the concept of fear vs. the node for experiencing fear itself' (Bower and Cohen, 1982, p. 309).

Watts (1984) objects to this development of the theory. First, it is *ad hoc*. Bower could go on proliferating nodes indefinitely to get himself out of tight corners. Second, there are doubts whether it is plausible to build hot and cold nodes into the same network as though they are activated in the same way and had the same kind of spreading activation effects. In fact, Bower and Cohen did take account of some of these problems in their 'Blackboard Control Structure' — a hypothetical structure for integrating knowledge from various sources involving both Cognitive Interpretation Rules and Emotional Interpretation Rules. Cognitive Interpretation enables the organism to recognise objects, people, events, etc. and is a multi-stage process moving from sensory feature extraction to conceptual meaning interpretation. Emotional Interpretation Rules specify an emotional appraisal for any given cognitive interpretation. The output of Emotional Interpretation Rules is not a specification of a complete emotional state but an adjustment of intensity to the current level of a specified emotion. It appears to imply that individuals are feeling all emotions at some (minimal) level all the time.

There are some aspects of this extension to network theory that are intuitively appealing. First, it provides a framework for talking about mixed emotions. On occasions when the outcome of Cognitive Interpretation Rules is ambiguous or unstable, switching rapidly from one result to a plausible alternative, the system may fail to find the appropriate Emotional Interpretation Rule to apply. The result is that instructions to increase several incompatible emotions may occur at the same time.

Second, it explicitly allows that Emotion Interpretation Rules can be applied at any stage in the cognitive interpretation process. A loud noise may elicit emotion without a great deal of processing of the meaning of the stimulus, whereas a smile from a stranger might make heavy demands on the Cognitive Interpretation Rules before Emotion Interpretation Rules are brought to bear.

Despite these attractions, the model does not seem to make any novel predictions over and above those made in the absence of network theory by Lazarus, Beck, Meichenbaum and other 'cognitive appraisal' theorists in the 1960s and 1970s. Furthermore, the disadvantage of the model is that it fails to escape from the assumption that affect is represented in the network in the same way as mood-neutral propositions. Finally, it does not address a number of specific findings which have posed problems for network theory, and which we now consider.

5.3.2. Recall vs. Recognition

Bower and Cohen (1982) review several attempts to demonstrate mood effects on memory using recognition rather than free recall as the dependent measure, without success. They suggest that state-dependent learning and mood-congruency effects will not be demonstrable in recognition paradigms since, if sufficient alternative cues are available, they will swamp the rather weak mood cue. Recognition paradigms actually give the 'old' word — a very strong cue which overrides the mood cue. Simon (1982) offers an alternative explanation for why recognition fails to show mood dependency. He differentiates between the 'index' and the 'encyclopaedia' in episodic memory. The 'index' informs the subject of the probable location of a specific item, after which a search through the 'encyclopaedia' at that location retrieves the items. Recognition paradigms involve no search through the encyclopaedia, merely judgement about the items. Mood may act to bias the search through the encyclopaedia but does not affect reference to the 'index'.

Simon's suggestion would not, however, explain the fact that, though rare, state-dependent effects have occasionally been found in recognition (Leight and Ellis, 1981; Schare et al., 1984). Perhaps there is a third possibility. Recognition experiments in the memory literature typically find much higher rates of remembering than do free recall paradigms. Perhaps mood shows little influence because of a ceiling effect. A distinctive feature of the experiments which did show effects of recognition is that by use of nonsense syllables (Leight and Ellis, 1985) and long delay between study and test (Schare et al., 1983) the task may have been sufficiently difficult for ceiling effects to have been avoided. Thus there may be no qualitative difference between the way mood influences recall and recognition but only one of degree. (Further discussion of the role of response bias in recognition memory can be found in Martin and Clark, 1986a, 1986b).

5.3.3 Lexical Decision Experiments

Network theory would predict that subjects in a particular mood should be primed by that mood so that word–non-word decision times should be faster for words that are congruent with prevailing mood. In a series of experiments, Martin and Clark (1985) have found this not to be the case. Similarly MacLeod et al. (1987) found no difference between depressed patients and matched controls in the pattern of lexical decision latencies for positive, negative and neutral words. Both Simon's index vs. encyclopaedia model and the task difficulty explanation applied above to recognition experiments might explain this failure for lexical decision to corroborate network theory. Lexical decision both uses the 'index' and is easy. On both counts it might not be expected to show a mood-congruent bias. An alternative account, based on the possibility of different types of processing being involved in tasks such as lexical decision from those involved in memory, will be considered in the final chapter.

5.3.4 Judgements

This literature is reviewed in detail in Chapter 8. It is relevant here to mention the criticism of the 'spreading activation' component of network theory made as a result of Johnson and Tversky's (1983) experiments. They induced negative mood with different negative themes (e.g. dying of cancer) and asked subjects to predict the probability of certain events happening to them in the future, similar to the experiment reported by Gilligan and Bower (see above). However, Johnson and Tversky reasoned that on a theory of activation which spreads according to degree of semantic association between items, mood induced by one item should cause a greater degree of pessimism for a similar event (e.g. dying of another sort of cancer) than for a dissimilar event (e.g. being struck by lightning). This was not found to be the case.

Note that the judgements examined in this experiment do not demand retrieval of specific instances from a subject's past, even though in principle a person may be able to retrieve relevant instances. Indeed, despite the fact that Bower and Cohen (1982) cite studies by Isen (reviewed by Isen, 1984) on judgements of past performance of one's car or TV set soon after having been given a free gift, it is possible that the link between judgement research and that on memory we have so far been considering may be quite tenuous. Making the statement 'My car has given me a lot of trouble' assumes that there exists in memory some records of specific instances of when the car gave trouble, but the judgement itself appears not to need to make explicit reference to the memory records of specific instances themselves. We shall return in the final chapter to a discussion of whether the processes involved in judging whether a memory exists (or estimating the size of the database) are different from those involved in retrieving specific items from the database.

5.3.5 Negative Happiness

This refers to the phenomenon of feeling bad about otherwise happy events: for example, a patient who reports having had good times when she lived in a particular place in the past — and becomes upset and cries when telling her therapist. Another patient reports how a friend from work came with a gift from co-workers and 'it got me really down'. Many patients say, 'I've got a good home and family' — and are depressed just to mention the good things. Similarly, patients often report finding formerly pleasurable activities aversive in inverse proportion to how pleasurable they once were. Finally, a common feature of bereavement is becoming most easily upset when a happy memory of the loved one is brought to mind. There are many traditional explanations of these phenomena: that happy memories remind people more acutely of their loss; that a positive thought (e.g. 'I've got a nice husband') is hiding a negative implication ('...but I wish he were more considerate'); that kind acts from others induce conflict, so that anger cannot be so readily expressed and is 'turned in' and depression is shown. Some of these explanations may account for some of these situations but not others. It is perhaps wrong to categorise them all under a 'negative memory' heading. Nevertheless, the phenomena exist, and a network theory which claims to deal with mood and memory must deal with them. Remembering an affectively-toned episode may sometimes reproduce the mood of that episode, or sometimes produce the opposite emotion as a sort of comparison effect.

An experiment by Strack *et al.* (1985) has examined this phenomenon more closely. In a series of studies they asked students to recall positive or negative events either from their present life or from their past. They were interested in what effect recalling these events would have on the subjects' current level of subjective well-being. In one of their experiments they found that if subjects were asked to recall a positive or negative past event in the context of asking *why* it had occurred, their recall was less detailed and vivid than if they recalled it in the context of asking *how* it had occurred. In the *why* (non-vivid) condition, past positive events caused decreases, and past negative events increases, in current subjective well-being. In the *how* (vivid) condition a mood-congruent effect of recalled event on current well-being was observed (negative past events lowering current subjective well-being and positive past events enhancing it). Strack *et al.* concluded that only if recall of a past hedonic event altered one's current mood would it have a congruous effect on well-being. If it did not, it would produce a comparison effect and make well-being shift in the opposite direction. It is clear that the factors determining whether a past negative event has a pleasant or unpleasant effect on current mood are likely to be complex and will demand further elaboration of network models than have been given hitherto.

5.3.6 Mood Memory Asymmetry

A further complexity is introduced by findings of asymmetry in the effects of positive and negative moods. (See Isen (1984) for a review.) For example, Isen *et al.* (1978) found that success on a computer game facilitated recall of a positive trait adjective, but failure on the game did not facilitate recall of negative adjectives. Isen (1984) also refers to Teasdale and Fogarty's (1979) study, which seemed to suggest that biased recall of personal memories was mostly due to happy mood facilitating recall of happy memories and inhibiting recall of sad memories rather than sad mood having the reverse effect. More recently, Williams and Broadbent (1986) found that mood bias in suicidal patients was wholly accounted for by slower recall of positive memories, rather than speeded recall of negative memories.

A problem in interpreting asymmetries of this kind is that very few mood-congruency studies have examined memory for neutral material. Chapter 3 reviewed a great deal of evidence to suggest that depressed subjects remember neutral material less well than non-depressed subjects. This general memory deficit shown by depressives on neutral material may have implications for the interpretation of mood congruency memory effects. A consistent pattern of findings emerges from two studies which have included neutral materials

(Teasdale and Russell, 1983; Dunbar and Lishman, 1984). Both found that in normal subjects (or subjects in positive mood) positive words were remembered particularly well, but there was no difference in memory for neutral or negative words. Conversely, depressed subjects (or subjects in negative mood) remembered negative words particularly well but showed no difference in memory for neutral or positive words. This suggests that mood biases memory towards recall of congruent material, but does not bias it *away* from recall of incongruent material. Unfortunately, both these experiments were vulnerable to floor effects and this conclusion about asymmetry in mood congruency should be regarded with some caution until it has been replicated in an experiment that does not suffer from this problem.

Another issue about the interpretation of mood congruency studies raised by a consideration of memory for neutral materials is the finding that normals show better recall of emotional than of neutral words (Dutta and Kanungo, 1975; Rubin and Friendly, 1986). Though the interpretation of this effect is controversial, the basic phenomenon is not in dispute. It is conceivable that the effect holds even more strongly in patients with emotional disorders than in normals, and that their observed performance with positive and negative materials represents a summation of this effect with hedonic bias, i.e. the apparent bias towards negative words could thus be the summation of two distinct processes with different underlying mechanisms. It is clear that further research on the memory bias in depression needs to include neutral materials if it is to examine these possibilities. Only then will it become clear to what extent asymmetries arise from differences between different *moods* in their effects on memory, or differences between different *materials* in how susceptible they are to respond to any mood shift.

5.3.7 General and Specific Memories: the Need to Examine Retrieval Processes

Williams and Broadbent's (1986) study on mood and memory in parasuicide patients has already been mentioned in connection with their finding of asymmetry (bias appearing to be due to retarded recall of positive memory rather than enhanced recall of negative memories). However, a further finding of that experiment was that this delayed recall of positive memories was in a large part due to the clinical group responding at first with inappropriately general memories. Whereas control subjects would respond to a cue word with a specific memory (some event that had occurred at a specific place and time), parasuicide patients tended to respond with a general category (e.g. to the cue 'happy' the response 'playing squash'). A familiar finding emerged from a study of autobiographical memories in depressed patients (Moore *et al.* 1988). Moore presented patients and matched controls with sixteen situations involving social support or lack of social support (e.g. 'a neighbour helped me with some practical problem'; 'my partner criticized me'). The percentage of first responses to these cues that were inappropriately general was 40 per cent for depressives and 19 per cent for controls $(F(1,32) = 11.07; p < 0.01)$.

These results make us focus on the processes of retrieval, something largely ignored by network theorists. Several investigators (e.g. Williams and Hollan, 1979; Norman and Bobrow, 1979; Reiser et al., 1985; Kolodner, 1985) have suggested that retrieval from autobiographical memory involves an intermediate stage in which a general context or description is framed to aid the search for a specific exemplar. The cue 'happy' will first pose the question: 'What sort of activities, people, places, objects make me happy?' These general descriptions are recursively refined until a specific example is retrieved, its appropriateness checked and a suitable response made.

This retrieval process may work in most instances extremely rapidly so that one is not aware of it. People who are not emotionally disturbed appear to be able to pass rapidly through intermediate stages on about 80 per cent of occasions when cued by common emotion words. By contrast, emotionally disturbed patients in Williams and Broadbent's (1986) and Moore et al.'s (1988) experiments appeared to stop at the point where they had retrieved a context but not retrieved a specific example. Our current investigations are studying the processes which affect whether an item is encoded or retrieved at a general or a specific level in autobiographical memory. At the moment, network models explain the pre-potency of memories with a certain affective content in terms of the activation spreading from emotion nodes and other associated nodes. It leads to the conclusion that effective therapies must either change the patterns of association in the network, or manipulate mood state to diminish the impact of spreading activation. But if mood disturbs qualitative aspects of encoding and retrieval (e.g. level of specificity), such therapies are likely to be incomplete. We shall need treatment strategies that directly address the deficit being shown, and this requires better descriptions of underlying encoding and retrieval processes than have been given hitherto.

5.3.8 The Specificity of Mood-congruent Effects in Memory

One of the benefits of examining in detail the processes underlying encoding and retrieval is that it may help account for specificity in the effects of mood on memory. Network theory does not make distinctions between different moods in the effects they are predicted to have on memory. All moods should enhance encoding and retrieval of material congruent with them. It appears, however, that such effects are more difficult to find in anxious groups than they are in depressed groups. Although mood-congruent recall has been found in agoraphobic patients (Nunn et al., 1984) in a series of experiments on patients with a diagnosis of general anxiety state, Karin Mogg has repeatedly failed to demonstrate mood-congruent recall of threat-related words (cited in

MacLeod *et al.*, 1986, p. 19). In some of her experiments, there appeared to be a reversal of mood-congruent enhancement, with retrieval of threat words gradually diminishing over three learning and recall trials (Mogg *et al.*, 1987). Similar results have been found by Watts (1986, p. 229), using words relating to spiders (e.g. web, hairy) in a group of spider phobic subjects. In one experiment, despite enhanced recognition for spider words relative to control words, there was diminished free recall for the spider words. Subsequent research, though not finding inhibition, has confirmed that mood-congruent facilitation does not occur for these subjects using these materials. Watts suggests that the materials for this group may involve 'distate' or 'disgust' which inhibits rather than facilitates search through the semantic network. A parallel explanation could be advanced for Mogg's findings with threat-related words. Specifying exactly what aspects of encoding or retrieval are involved in this 'inhibition' is an important problem for future research, to which we return in the final chapter.

5.4 CONCLUDING REMARKS

Frameworks in psychology are often useful in suggesting research which then reveals the framework to be inadequate in interesting ways. Semantic network theory has been such a framework. Whereas models lead to 'predictions', frameworks lead to 'expectations' — and it is when these are violated that a phenomenon comes to our attention. The recall effects with threat and spider words; the asymmetry of mood and materials; the distinction between general and specific memories; these are unexpected within the model and lead us to pay attention to the processes which determine the phenomena. They raise potentially important issues about mood and memory: that the content of the to-be-recalled material makes a difference (e.g. threat- or loss-related); that the mood of the subject (e.g. anxiety or depression) makes a difference; and that the retrieval processes operating upon the material makes a difference (mood may block progress from general to specific memories). These represent the start of new lines of research, each of which is likely to yield much useful data relevant both to theory and clinical practice.

Chapter 6

Schemata

The previous chapters have reviewed evidence to suggest that in the specific field of emotional disorders, as in the wider domain of cognitive psychology, attention and memory processes are not merely passive systems dealing only with the input and output of literal representations for environmental events. People's reports on their environment are frequently incomplete, or even highly distorted and inaccurately elaborated. Furthermore, it has been reported that memory for unusual or atypical event descriptions is disproportionately poor. Subjects appear to 'normalize' such information, and tend to recall rather more stereotyped descriptions than were originally presented. The previous two chapters have shown how this state of affairs may arise from biases at encoding, storage or retrieval. This chapter considers the most widely researched theoretical framework capable of incorporating all of these aspects.

Bartlett's (1932) early demonstration of this phenomenon involved a North American Indian folk-tale, entitled 'War of the Ghosts', which contains many elements alien to English subjects. Although the general gist of this story could be recalled, many of the more peculiar details were quickly forgotten. Additionally, recall protocols included many errors of *commission*; that is, elaborations consistent with the protocol but which had not occurred in the actual story. Ultimately, therefore, the rather curious Indian folk-tale was remembered as a more stereotyped narrative, in some cases taking on the character of a standard Wild West story. Similar results have been produced by a large series of subsequent studies (e.g. Postman, 1954; Paul, 1959; Bransford and MacCarrell, 1975; Bower, Black and Turner, 1979; Spiro, 1980; Nakamura and Graesser, 1985). To accommodate such results Bartlett argued that pre-existing memory representations are employed constructively during retrieval, and impose their own structure on new information. Those representations, which Bartlett termed 'schemata' guide recall selectively and can contribute default information to fill in gaps in the new memory trace.

Despite surprisingly little initial impact, such ideas have received growing attention over the past twenty years or so, and a vast literature now exists concerning the potential role of schemata in a variety of information processing tasks (e.g. Minsky, 1975; Adams and Collins, 1979; Walker and Yekovich, 1984; Alba and Hasher, 1983). Schema-based theories have been proposed to account for various aspects of perception (e.g. Neisser, 1976; Goldstein and Chance, 1985), comprehension (e.g. Mandler and Goodman, 1982; Galambos and Rips, 1982; White and Carlston, 1983) and memory (e.g. Chi, 1978; Morris *et al.*, 1981; Mathews and Bradley, 1983; Griggs and Green, 1983). The potential of such models for illuminating the bases of cognitive distortions have led to their recent popularity in many applied areas including clinical (e.g. Beck, 1976), forensic (e.g. Loftus, 1979) and educational (Ausubel, 1968) psychology.

However, as the popularity of schema theory has grown, and the range of its application extended, so the meaning of the term 'schema' has become increasingly vague. Indeed, it is now generally accepted that the term has no single definition (cf. Taylor and Crocker, 1981; Brewer and Treyens, 1981). In the next section we briefly consider several different conceptions of this theoretical construct.

6.1 THE NATURE OF SCHEMATA

Different researchers use the term schema with widely varying degrees of precision, and this has consequently led to considerable confusion and misunderstanding. We shall here consider several, increasingly specific, uses of the term.

(i) At the most basic level all theorists agree that a schema is a stored body of knowledge which interacts with the encoding, comprehension and/or retrieval of new information within its domain, by guiding attention, expectancies, interpretation and memory search (cf. Graesser and Nakamura, 1982; Alba and Hasher, 1983). While some may consider this definition sufficient, the majority of researchers would require that such memory structures fulfil certain additional criteria.

(ii) One of the more elementary criteria is that the schema should have a consistent internal structure, which is imposed upon the organisation of new information. Such stimuli therefore come to be structured in a stereotypical manner. Thus, when subjects are presented with stories in which the positions of various statements have been rearranged, they tend to produce recall protocols with a more conventional organization. For example, thematic statements migrate towards the beginning of such protocols (e.g. Mandler and DeForest, 1979; Mandel and Johnson, 1983), and incorrectly arranged behavioural sequences are recalled in a more appropriate temporal order (e.g. Bower, Black and Turner, 1979; Lichenstein and Brewer, 1980).

(iii) Another common criterion is that the knowledge contained within schematic structures should be *generic* in nature, constituting abstract prototypical representations of environmental regularities. Thus a schema is often conceptualized as an organized summary of the attributes and relationships which typify certain classes of exemplar stimuli, ranging from personal stereotypes (e.g. Hamilton, 1983), through spatial scenarios (e.g. Biederman, 1982) and stereotyped actions (e.g. K. Nelson, 1977) to complex narratives (e.g. Thorndyke, 1977). Specific instances of such stimuli are then processed using the appropriate schematic prototype as a blueprint to impose structure, resolve ambiguity and provide supplementary information. The final representation may therefore include both elements from the specific stimulus event and elements from its generic prototype.

(iv) It has sometimes also been suggested that before such representations can be considered schematic they must constitute a modular-bounded package of such generic information, in the sense that activation of any part will tend to produce activation of the whole (Mandler, 1984). Suppose we are told: 'John sat down and looked at the menu.' A menu is probably a bound feature in most people's restaurant schema and, since the activation of this element will produce activation of the whole modular prototypical representation, we may immediately assume the presence of food, waiters and chefs; and anticipate more specific information concerning stereotyped schema-bound actions such as ordering food, eating, paying the bill, etc. Reading-time studies do indeed indicate that activating a schema establishes the mental representation of unmentioned scenario-bound information just as effectively as does the explicit introduction of this information, (e.g. Garrod and Sanford, 1982; Sanford, 1985).

In summary we have seen that while certain properties are necessary before any internal representation can be considered schematic, various additional criteria are required by most definitions of this concept. A schema certainly consists of a stored domain of knowledge which interacts with the processing of new information. However, certain definitions also require that this representation have a consistent structure which exerts an organizational influence, must embody only generic prototypical information, and be modular in nature. Later in this chapter we review several different areas of psychology where schema based models have been proposed and consider which of these criteria are commonly met.

6.2 THE FUNCTIONING OF SCHEMATA

Most schema theorists assume that the comprehension of a stimulus input involves first identifying the relevant schema, and then applying it to direct the intake of information and organize its representation (cf. Norman and

Bobrow, 1976). The first of these two processes is a 'bottom-up' or data-driven operation in which the cognitive system attempts to recognize the schema that is best able to accommodate the elements of the particular input. The second process is 'top-down' or conceptually-driven, with the chosen schema being employed in the control of attention, inferencing and the selective storage of particular details (cf. Graesser and Nakamura, 1982).

Sanford and Garrod (1981) point out that stimulus input may often take the form of a fragmentary description of a situation about which we already have further knowledge. When this happens then these components of our existing internal representation will become activated and, if they are a part of a modular schema, the entire structure will be activated in consequence. Selection of schemata by such 'partial matching' is a common device employed by schema-based AI systems. Of course, the system is not foolproof, and errors will occur when such partial matching leads to the activation of an inappropriate schema. These errors will only be detected when some later information cannot be accommodated by the currently active schema which, in consequence, must be revised. Such errors are subjectively obvious in 'garden-path' texts including the following examples from Sanford and Garrod (1980):

(i)   John was on his way to school.
(ii)   He was terribly worried about the maths lesson.
(iii) He thought he might not be able to control the class again today.
(iv)   It was not a normal part of a janitor's duty.

The schema activated by the first two sentences usually casts John as a pupil; sentence (iii) cannot be accommodated by this representation and a new schema is selected in which he is considered the teacher; while the final sentence indicates this also to be inappropriate and a further revision is required. In such instances the failure to accommodate the new information within the existing schema leads to comprehension difficulties, which are easily indexed by reading-time latencies.

Once an appropriate schema is operative, it is assumed to guide processing in a conceptually-driven fashion, and influence which aspects of the input receive most processing. Most attention is usually allocated to those elements which deviate from the schematic representation (e.g. Krueger, 1981; Bellezza and Bower, 1981). However, when confronted with diverse information concerning unrelated topics, a schema can be employed to guide attention selectively towards schema-congruent elements (e.g. Neisser and Becklen, 1975; Neisser, 1976). The active schema will also influence comprehension by determining pragmatic implications (e.g. Schweller, Brewer and Dahl, 1976), elaborating vague information (e.g. R.C. Anderson et al., 1976), filling in absent details (e.g. Paris, Lindauer and Cox, 1977), and simplifying complex information (Frederiksen, 1975).

Ultimately an integrated representation will be stored which is heavily influenced by the active schema used during encoding, and this will lead to a range of memory biases. There is, however, dispute in the literature concerning the exact nature of such biases, which partly reflects underlying differences of opinion regarding the detailed operation of schemata. Graesser and Nakamura (1982) identify four alternative formulations based on different aspects of experimental phenomenon.

(1) *Filtering hypothesis*: According to this account information which is typical of the active schema becomes cohesively organized in the final representation, whereas atypical information is only loosely associated. This predicts a recall advantage for schematically typical over atypical elements of the input. There is indeed empirical support for this prediction (e.g. Goldin, 1978; Bransford, 1979; Rothbart, 1981). However such an effect may stem from a guessing bias, favouring schematically typical information, rather than representing a true memory effect. In fact, memory discrimination between stated and unstated information is *poorest* for schematically typical elements (e.g. Bower, Black and Turner, 1979; Smith and Graesser, 1981).

(2) *Attention elaboration hypothesis*: This suggests that, due to the dis-proportionate processing resources which schematically atypical elements attract during encoding (e.g. Friedman, 1979; den Uyl and van Oostendorp, 1980), there will be a memory advantage for such information. Considerable experimental evidence is consistent with this alternative prediction (e.g. Going and Read, 1979; Goodman, 1980; Graesser *et al.*, 1980; Srull, 1981). However, attempts to relate such superior recall for atypical elements directly to patterns of resource allocation suggest that this account is not entirely adequate (e.g. Light, Kayra-Stuart and Hollander, 1979; Graesser, 1981).

(3) *Partial copy model*: Bower, Black and Turner (1979) proposed that, in addition to an episodic memory trace which is rapidly lost over a short time-interval, a stereotyped event sequence is encoded by activating the corresponding elements in its generic schema. At short delays explicitly stated elements are more highy activated than non-stated elements, which are only partially activated. However such activation fades and, after a longer retention interval, it becomes impossible to distinguish stated from non-stated elements. Several predictions arising from this model were confirmed by Bower *et al.* (1979). For example, false-alarm rates were high for unstated, schematically typical actions, especially when several episodes requiring the same schema had been presented (permitting incremental activation of relevant but unstated actions). Also, as predicted, memory discrimination between stated and un-stated actions was poorer for schematically typical than for atypical actions. Nevertheless, Graesser and Nakamura (1982) argue that the partial copy model is inadequate since, although the absence of memory discrimination for typical actions after a 30-minute retention interval indicates the loss of explicit

propositions by this time, recognition memory for atypical actions persists even after three weeks (Graesser, 1981; Smith and Graesser, 1981). The generic schema should provide no basis for remembering such information.

(4) *Schema pointer + tag*: According to Graesser's favoured account (Graesser, 1981; Graesser and Nakamura, 1982) the memory trace consists of (i) a pointer to the relevant generic schema, and (ii) a set of 'tags' or additional information, for schema atypical or marginally atypical elements. The predictions arising from this account are similar to those produced by Bower *et al.*'s (1979) partial copy model, but permit the continued retention of atypical information despite the complete absence of any ability to discriminate stated from unstated typical actions.

To some extent these four formulations of schema functioning appear to stand in direct conflict. However, they are each specifically tailored to account for rather different aspects of the experimental literature. The first two models, for instance, are particularly concerned with accounting for differential recall of presented details, while the partial copy model was developed primarily to account for the erroneous 'recall' of missing information. Furthermore, some apparent contradictions appear to be terminological rather than conceptual in nature. For example, advocates of the filtering hypothesis predict and confirm that memory for typical information will be superior to that for atypical information, while the attention elaboration hypothesis leads to the supported predictions that memory for atypical information will be disproportionately good. However, each group of theorists conceptualize 'atypical' rather differently — to mean either information *irrelevant* to a particular schema (such as blowing one's nose in a restaurant), or *incompatible* with this schema (such as driving a tractor in a restaurant). While irrelevant information may be filtered out, and therefore be poorly recalled, incompatible information may indeed attract disproportionate attention and therefore be well recalled.

Thus schema theory is currently fairly imprecise and embodies a range of rather different formulations. Schema selection itself is likely to constitute a probabilistic and error-prone process. According to schema theorists, once selected, the influence of an active schema can be diverse, and not always easily predictable. It can facilitate the processing of either schema-congruent or schema-incongruent elements of an input, depending upon the precise task conditions. Furthermore, it can appear specifically to facilitate memory for typical or for atypical information depending upon the definition of typicality and precise nature of the memory tests which are employed. Despite such complications, many have found schema theory useful to accommodate a wide variety of phenomena. Perhaps the most fully developed formulations of schemata are expressed in the related theoretical constructs of 'frames' and 'scripts', which we shall now consider in more detail.

6.3 FRAMES AND SCRIPTS

Perhaps not surprisingly, the most precise theoretical formulations of schemata have emerged from the field of artificial intelligence, within which such representational systems have been employed to model the perception, comprehension and retrieval of complex information (e.g. Roberts and Goldstein, 1977; Rosenberg, 1977; Grosz, 1978). Two related influential approaches within this field have conceptualised schemata as 'frames' (Minsky, 1975) or 'scripts' (Schank and Abelson, 1975, 1977), and will be considered in more detail in this current section.

Both frames and scripts represent highly structured modules of generic information. They are typically assumed to constitute organizational structures which serve to link in a coordinated manner 'slots' or 'terminals', capable of receiving particular details from the input. Each slot is designed to accept only one particular type of information, and may initially contain default values which, if no further details are supplied by the input, will be assumed valid. While frames may embody a wide range of organizational relationships to arrange components slots, from simple spatial position to such complex rule-defined systems as scientific paradigms, scripts represent a sub-set of frames in which the internal architecture primarily reflects temporal and causal relationships. Both theoretical concepts however have important aspects in common. Processing an input essentially involves assigning elements to appropriate slots in the relevant frame or script. The imposition of structure, the provision of unstated detail and the comprehension of inferences are all emergent properties of this representational system.

There is certainly compelling evidence that identifying the appropriate generic script can impose a meaningful structure upon an input which may otherwise be extremely difficult to process. Consider for example the following passage condensed from Bransford and Johnson (1971):

> The procedure is actually quite simple. First you arrange things into different groups. Of course, one pile may be sufficient depending on how much there is to do. After the procedure is completed one arranges the materials into different groups again. Then they can be put into their appropriate places. Eventually they will be used once more and the whole cycle will then have to be repeated.

Most readers find this text difficult to comprehend and to recall. However, if they are initially provided with the appropriate generic script by being given the title 'Washing Clothes', comprehension ratings and recall scores improve dramatically. Similar results have been reported by Dooling and Lachman (1971).

Providing such a schema *after* presentation is relatively ineffective for heavily metaphorical text (e.g. Dooling and Mullet, 1973), but for less obscure materials can retrospectively improve comprehension and memory. Indeed, the subsequent provision of alternative schemata can differently influence the availability of certain details, suggesting again that the frame can be employed as a retrieval device. For example, Anderson and Pichert (1978) presented subjects with a passage concerning a house which mentioned general layout, decoration, position of doors, open and closed windows, and so on. Some subjects were subsequently told to imagine they were house-buyers, and others burglars, and asked to recall everything they could about the house. Each group recalled significantly more of those details which could easily be accommodated by plausible slots in their adopted schema, e.g. 'house-buyers' recalled details of decor, while 'burglars' recalled details of access. Switching perspectives after initial recall led to further retrieval of much previously omitted information which could now be assimilated by the new schema.

While clearly indicating that generic representations can affect comprehension and retrieval of new information, such studies do not directly address the hypothesis that those representations exert a *structural* influence. The best evidence that frames and scripts impose a particular structure upon new information is provided by those experiments which demonstrate that recall protocols tend to approximate a stereotypical organization, even if this organization is not explicitly represented in the initial stimulus. For example, it has been proposed that simple stories are processed by assigning constituent elements to appropriate slots in a generic narrative frame (e.g. Thorndyke, 1975, 1976, 1977; Rumelhart, 1975). The hypothetical structure of this frame is hierarchical, with slots at the highest levels accepting propositions establishing the setting, the theme, the plot and the resolution. Lower slots accept more specific subordinate propositions, concerning discrete events, goals, sub-goals, and so forth. There is good evidence that clustering of propositions in the recall of text corresponds closely to this abstract theoretical schematic structure, even when such clustering is absent in the presentation order (e.g. Black and Bower, 1979; Buschke and Schaier, 1979; Yekovich and Thorndyke, 1981).

Furthermore, predictions concerning the recallability of story elements are more accurately based on the position of such elements within the hypothetical narrative frame, rather than on their position in the surface text. Recall is typically superior for information corresponding to higher-level slots in the narrative frame (e.g. Gentner, 1976; M.K. Johnson and Scheidt, 1977; Meyer *et al.*, 1980). Several studies also suggest that such information is disproportionately easy to access in order to carry out integrative processing during subsequent comprehension (e.g. Walker and Meyer, 1980; Cirilo, 1981). When we consider stereotyped action sequences, it has been shown that minor rearrangements of temporal orders in the surface text, which violate the generic script structure, tend to be rectified during recall (Mandler, 1978; Stein and Glenn, 1979; Bower, Black and Turner, 1979; Galambos, 1981, 1982). Not all theorists accept that such empirical phenomena require the postulation of pre-existing stereotyped narrative frames. Some, for example, argue that many of the observed effects may arise because of readers' attempts to establish referential continuity (e.g. Johnson-Laird, 1980, 1983; Garnham, Oakhill and Johnson-Laird, 1982; Garnham, 1983). However schema theorists usually interpret these results as supportive evidence for the existence of generic representations which exert an organizational influence on relevant new information.

It is more difficult to test directly the hypothesis that frames and scripts are *modular* representational systems, in which all component elements become activated when the frame is selected and deactivated when the frame is deemed to be no longer appropriate. However, Sanford and Garrod (1981, 1982, 1983; Anderson, Garrod and Sanford, 1983; Sanford, 1985) report a series of comprehension time-studies which support this argument. In all their studies these researchers measured the accessibility of schema-bound entities by recording the time taken to comprehend sentences which made a direct anaphoric reference to such an antecedent. Two kinds of observations supported the modularity of generic schemata:

(1) Activating a generic schema activates its schema-bound entities to the same degree as if those entities had been explicitly introduced. For example, Garrod and Sanford (1982) presented a short passage about a man being questioned, either explicitly stating the presence of a lawyer or not. Not surprisingly, a subsequent sentence which made a definite reference to 'the lawyer' was comprehended more rapidly when this character had already been mentioned. However, when the passage title introduced a schema within which the lawyer would be a bound entity, as with the title 'in court', this effect disappeared entirely. Activating the 'court' schema thus apparently activated a module of relevant information.

(2) Indicating the inappropriateness of a currently active frame immediately reduces the accessibility of its schema-bound entities. For example, Anderson, Garrod and Sanford (1983) presented a text which first described a fairly stereotyped situation (such as visiting a hairdressers, cinema or a restaurant), then indicated a shift in either time or space, and finally made a definite reference to a schema-bound entity within the initial frame. The magnitude of the time or distance shifts were judged, on the basis of raters' decisions, to be either within or beyond the likely boundaries of the initial frame. Thus a 'beyond-shift', but not a 'within-shift', implicitly indicated that the initial frame was no longer appropriate. Anderson *et al.* observed that the accessibility of the schema-bound entity (as indexed by the comprehension latency for the final definite reference) was markedly reduced by the 'beyond-shift' alone. Indicating the inappropriateness of the initial frame therefore appeared to have decreased the availability of a module of associated information.

In summary, there is considerable converging evidence to support the potential value of frame theory. Such generic structures not only appear to influence the comprehension and general accessibility of new information, but produce a specific pattern of memory effects which suggest that they impose a stereotyped organization upon this input. In addition, recent evidence suggests that they do indeed operate in a modular fashion.

6.4 SCHEMATA IN CLINICAL THEORY

Many aspects of cognitive content in mood disorders suggest that emotional information is processed in an idiosyncratic or biased fashion. Clinical observations of depressed individuals reveal that they tend to notice their failures rather than successes, infer the worst from situations which could be interpreted positively, and selectively recall unhappy memories from the past. By comparison with non-depressed controls, depressed subjects are more negative in their recall of performance feedback, evaluate themselves more negatively, and blame themselves for failure (Coyne and Gotlib, 1983; Blaney, 1986). Similarly, anxious individuals are selectively attentive to environmental cues related to threat, such as words descriptive of phobic situations. While phobics do not appear to have a particularly extensive knowledge of the non-emotional attributes of phobic stimuli, there is evidence that their knowledge base emphasizes threatening or other negative features to a greater extent than does that of non-phobic subjects (Landau, 1980). We may thus conclude that emotional disorders are associated with selective attention, knowledge and recall for mood-congruent information. The important question for present purposes, however, is whether these characteristic differences in cognitive content and processes result from the operation of schemata; that is, of generic and modular cognitive structures.

The major contributor to the development of clinical theories involving the schema concept is Aaron Beck (see Beck, 1976; Beck et al., 1979; Beck and Emery, 1985). In his terminology, schemata are cognitive assemblies of structural elements, which are themselves further organised into larger constellations. When activated, a specific schema or constellation of schemata directly influences the content of a person's perceptions, interpretations and memories — for example, by helping to select relevant details from the environment, or to recall relevant data. Individuals who develop specific emotional disorders are supposed to be characterized by the nature of those constellations of schemata concerned with interpreting emotional information. Thus depression is said to be associated with schemata concerned with loss, and with negative aspects of the self, the world and the future. Content concerned with personal vulnerability and danger activates the behavioural pattern of flight and the feeling of anxiety, and so on.

It is clear from this account that Beck's use of the term schema corresponds to our first and most basic requirement of the concept; that of a stored body of knowledge which interacts with encoding, comprehension and retrieval of information. Presumably, it is supposed that individuals who are prone to develop depression or anxiety either have a more extensive database concerning loss or danger, etc. or have greater ease of access to such a database.

A major problem with this view is that the relevant observations have been made on those who are currently in a depressed or anxious state, and there is little evidence that such individuals could have been distinguished from others not vulnerable to emotional disorders prior to its onset. The usual explanation offered is that the relevant schemata cannot be detected until activated by appropriate events. Thus Kovacs and Beck (1978) state: 'We postulate that the schemata that are active in depression are previously latent cognitive structures. They are re-activated when the patient is confronted with certain internal or external stimuli' (p. 529). A related suggestion is that vulnerability to depression or anxiety disorders depends on the type of information which is activated by a given mood state. If depressed mood activates highly aversive and deprecatory information, then the negative emotional state may persist and deepen rather than recover, as would be the case if little such information existed. This hypothesis predicts that vulnerability to emotional disorders arises more from the persistence of otherwise normal variations in mood than from initially different reactions to events (Teasdale, 1983).

If it is indeed the case that emotional schemata can remain latent but then be activated intact, at least a degree of modularity is being assumed. This assumption is not obviously required by any experimental data, and it seems equally possible to suppose that emotional information is stored in a more fragmented way, not necessarily leading to activation in unitary form. It is much less clear whether or not Beck views emotional schemata as containing *generic* representations. If so, then the theory would need to be more explicit concerning the type of representations involved, in order to become testable. One might propose that depressed individuals have generic cognitive structures for situations such as social encounters that resemble those employed by non-depressed individuals, but that the frames or scripts involved have different default values. For example, when another person fails to provide definite signals of approval in a social encounter, the depressed person might retain a default value corresponding to 'dislikes me' in the relevant slot. Alternatively, depression might affect the choice of frame that is appropriate to any particular situation. If there are different frames for accepting and rejecting encounters, then depression might be associated with a bias towards selecting the rejection frame.

Since no systematic research has been carried out on these issues they can only be the subject of speculation. In fact, the only attribute of emotional schemata which has attracted a considerable body of research is that of their internal structure. Specifically, it has been proposed that depression is associated with a particularly negative self-schema, and that it is this structure which explains the increased probability of recall for negative information about oneself. To evaluate this proposal we must first consider the nature of self-knowledge, and the extent to which this knowledge should be considered as a schematic structure.

6.5 SELF-KNOWLEDGE AND THE 'SELF-SCHEMA'

The term 'self-schema' has commonly been used to refer collectively to the knowledge about oneself stored in long-term memory. It is often assumed that this knowledge is organized as a single coherent structure, although there is comparatively little (if any) evidence that would force such an assumption. We shall first examine what evidence there is, and then return to the question of whether self-knowledge may be considered to constitute a 'self-schema'.

According to Marcus (1977), cognitive structures concerning the self develop out of individuals' attempts to explain their own behaviour, and are used subsequently in encoding or reporting information about oneself. To demonstrate self-knowledge operates in this way, Marcus proposes that within any designated self-descriptive domain, one should (a) make judgements of applicability to oneself relatively rapidly; (b) be able to retrieve consistent behavioural evidence; (c) find it relatively easy to predict one's own behaviour; and (d) resist counter-schematic information.

To provide evidence relevant to these propositions, Marcus showed that individuals who consistently rated themselves as independent, individualistic and a leader (or as dependent, conforming and a follower) were more rapid in arriving at a decision as to whether words related to such traits were self-descriptive than were other subjects who had less decided views (described as 'aschematics'). The same subjects also recalled more behavioural evidence, and predicted more future behaviour, that was consistent with adjectives related to their own self-descriptions. Finally, when subjects were given feedback on their supposed 'suggestibility' that was incongruent with these self-descriptions, those who had described themselves as either independent or dependent rated the feedback as less accurate than did the so-called aschematic subjects. Thus, on each of the four counts proposed by Marcus as necessary evidence to support the idea that a consistent body of self-knowledge is used to describe one's own behaviour, confirmatory data were reported.

In the same year, Rogers, Kuiper and Kirker (1977) reported further experimental evidence suggesting that self-knowledge is a particularly extensive database, using a depth-of-processing paradigm. Judgements of whether adjectives described oneself, meant the same as another word (semantic), rhymed with another word (phonemic) or were presented in large or small letters, were compared for their capacity to facilitate incidental recall. The probability of recall following self-judgements was twice as great as following semantic judgements, which were in turn more effective than either phonemic or size judgements. In discussing these results, Rogers *et al.* state:

> In order for self-reference to be such a useful encoding process, the self must be a uniform, well-structured concept. During the recall phase of the study, subjects probably used the self as a retrieval cue. In order for this to be functional, the self must be a consistent and uniform schema.

The superiority for self-referenced material is now a well-established finding, which has been replicated by many other researchers (e.g. Bower and Gilligan, 1979; Lord, 1980; Klein and Kihlstrom, 1986). None the less, it does not seem essential to invoke such concepts as a consistent and uniform self-schema in order to understand the self-referent recall data. The more extensive the information base within which new input can be encoded, the more associations are possible and thus the easier it will be to retrieve. This expectation arises because connections between old and new information may help in the search process. For example, in a network model of memory, search is said to occur via spreading activation from starting-points such as the context within which the to-be-recalled word was presented. If activation spreads simultaneously from such contextual cues, and from activation of information about the self, then intersection and consequent word retrieval will occur more rapidly.

Recent work by Klein and Kihlstrom (1986), while replicating the self-reference effect, has also provided further problems both for the self-schema concept, and for explanations based on elaborative encoding as an aid to retrieval. Essentially, they have shown that self-reference is no more effective than other forms of semantic encoding, provided that the categorial organization of the material is strictly controlled. Hence, if encoding involves category questions such as 'Is this an external body part: skin?', then recall is just as good as following questions like 'Can you think of an accident involving your: skin?' Furthermore, self-referent encoding may result in significantly poorer recall if it does not encourage categorization as self-descriptive vs. non-self-descriptive, as in questions such as 'I prefer to keep my ... short: hair?' Thus it would appear that in earlier experiments, self-referent encoding has been confounded with the organization of material into categories, and that it is this organization which is responsible for recall superiority.

Consequently, the evidence on self-referent recall does not necessarily tell us much about the structure of self-knowledge as opposed to the use of particular encoding or retrieval strategies. In free recall paradigms, a search process involving the activation of self-descriptors may be an easy and effective one, while equivalent strategies could not be used to search for words which happen to have similar meanings, or which rhyme with each other, or were written in capital letters. On the other hand, if simple categories are made explicit by the encoding instructions, then the organization which results will aid retrieval to the same extent as does self-reference. Thus it would seem that the effects of self-encoding could reveal something about the extent or type of self-knowledge, without necessarily requiring use of the schema concept.

Subsequent work by Rogers *et al.* (1979) provided evidence for a false-alarm effect with self-descriptive words, which they cited as indicating that self-knowledge functions as a cognitive prototype. A prototype is a collection of those features that are seen to be most representative of a category, and its use may lead to false recognition of new but prototypical items which were not in fact presented. Degree of self-relevance made no difference to accuracy of recognition of items actually presented; but accuracy of rejection for items that were not previously presented was reduced as self-descriptiveness increased, suggesting the existence of a false-alarm effect. This finding seems more difficult to explain away by reference to categorization at encoding, or retrieval strategy, and thus tends to support the idea that knowledge of oneself is organized within a cognitive structure of some kind.

There is no particular reason for believing that self-knowledge in the form of trait adjectives is unrelated to episodic memory. Rather, it is probable that links exist between self-descriptive adjectives, and specific episodes in autobiographical memory. Hence Bower and Gilligan (1979) tested recall of phrases such as 'a cheerful mood' or 'a broken bone' after these phrases had been encoded, using judgements of whether they had occurred to oneself, or using other semantic and graphic judgements. Once again, the self-reference condition was markedly superior when incidental recall was tested, with pleasant phrases being recalled better than unpleasant ones. The uniqueness of the self-reference encoding task was tested in further experiments reported by Bower and Gilligan (1979), and also by Kuiper and Rogers (1979), in which judgements either referred to oneself or to another named person. Other-person referent encoding took longer, but was usually associated with poorer recall, although it is of interest that very familiar other people (such as one's mother) lead to levels of recall approaching those achieved with self-encoding. This suggests that there is nothing very special about the structure of self-knowledge: any person or topic that is well known to the subject can be used as an aid in encoding or retrieval. The more extensive the knowledge base about the person or topic, the easier it will be to find points of contact between this knowledge and the new information to be remembered.

The existing evidence can thus be interpreted as strong support for the idea that an extensive knowledge base about oneself exists in memory, and that this knowledge base can be used in encoding by categorisation, and as an aid to subsequent retrieval, but does not conclusively show that self-information is structured as a 'self-schema'. It is possible, but by no means certain, that self-knowledge has a consistent internal structure, and is typically activated as a modular unit. However, even if so, it remains difficult to see how it could be regarded as a generic representation which is used when processing instances of a more general category. In discussing the evidence for the related concept of a self-prototype, Rogers (1981) lists three predictions which he argues have been confirmed. Probability of saying that a previously unseen item was seen before (the false-alarm effect) should increase with similarity to the prototype; decision times should be faster for items that are very similar or very dissimilar to the prototype; and recall of highly self-descriptive (prototypic) words should be better than those that are less self-descriptive. Since all three propositions can be supported from the experimental evidence, Rogers claims that this argues very strongly for the concept of the self as a prototype. However, alternative explanations have already been discussed for the superiority of self-referent recall, and it is not clear that the data on decision speed require assumptions beyond that of an extensive existing database of self-knowledge. The false-alarm effect, demonstrated by Rogers *et al.* (1979) does provide support, since it implies that representations of never-presented items were in fact activated, presumably because of their central position within a cognitive structure. On the other hand, the generic domain to which a self-prototype refers remains quite unspecified, so that whether it is reasonable to refer to a 'self-schema' remains to be demonstrated.

6.6 DEPRESSION AND SELF-SCHEMA THEORY

Although the question of whether or how information about oneself is organised as a structure in memory has not been resolved by the experimental data discussed so far, such research has had the effect of stimulating related work on cognitive processes in depression. Early experiments by Davis (e.g. 1979), modelled on that of Rogers *et al.* (1977), failed to show superiority for self-referred recall in depressive subjects, and this result was taken to throw doubt on the existence of a well-differentiated self-knowledge structure in depression.

In subsequent work (e.g. Derry and Kuiper, 1981) it became clear that demonstration of a self-reference recall advantage in depressive subjects depends crucially on the use of negative mood-congruent words. Comparisons of positive and negative words showed that clinical depressives have a self-reference advantage for negative (but not positive) words, while with non-depressed subejcts the self-encoded positive words are recalled better. This distinction between the two groups persists when self-encoding is compared with judgements concerning other people (Bradley and Mathews, 1983). Clinically depressed individuals recalled more negative words that had been encoded in relation to themselves, but more positive words encoded in relation to unfamiliar others, while non-depressed controls recalled more positive words both for themselves and others. Furthermore, this and other studies of depressed subjects (Ingram and Reed, 1986) have shown that, consistent with the criteria advanced earlier by Marcus (1977), latency to arrive at negative self-judgements during the encoding task is shorter for depressed subjects, while non-depressed subjects are quicker to give positive self-judgements (see Kuiper and MacDonald, 1982).

Results such as these cannot be attributed to a general response bias in depression which favours the endorsement of all negative words, since both the recall and the latency data show differences between self- and other-person judgements. At the same time, it remains unclear whether or not such data constitute support (as they are often taken to be) for the self-schema concept. While they certainly could arise from the operation of an enduring and unitary cognitive structure, they might also be attributable to the variable use of encoding or retrieval strategies. Perhaps depressed individuals tend to use retrieval strategies in which negative information about onself or positive information about others is selectively generated for subsequent recognition. Alternatively, rather than arising from an enduring cognitive structure, the recall bias might depend on the selective activation of mood congruent information (Bower, 1981).

In a study of normal students, Mathews and Bradley (1983) found that the extent of self-related recall bias varied considerably across two occasions of testing that were separated by several months. In a similar but more extensive study, Hammen et al. (1986) found that the extent of reported past depression contributed to current recall bias in depressed students, but that when their mood improved, all evidence of enhanced recall for negative words disappeared. Parallel results were obtained for the generation of behavioural examples and decision latency, providing broad confirmation that both past experience of depression and current mood jointly determine the extent of positive or negative bias in the processing of self-knowledge. We have recently gathered similar data on current and recovered clinical samples (Bradley and Mathews, in press) and results were consistent with those of Hammen et al. in that the fully recovered depressives no longer showed any negative self-related bias in recall, and in fact recalled more negative words that had been encoded in relation to other people. Rather different results were obtained by Teasdale and Dent (1987), who compared previously depressed patients with never-depressed controls, and found that the recovered group still showed a more general negative bias in recall. While thus indicating that retrieval operations may not be fully normalised following recovery, it is clear that the negative recall bias for self-encoded material in depression is not stable over time, and that the earlier suggestion that it reflects the operation of a unitary and consistent self-schema, are no longer viable.

One way of accommodating these results is to suggest that some aspects of the self-schema remain latent until activated by events or mood states (e.g. Kovacs and Beck, 1978). However, it is equally plausible to argue that some emotional states serve to facilitate the recall of congruent self-related material

(Bower, 1981), and this mechanism maintains depressed mood by selectively activating unpleasant episodic and semantic information in memory (Teasdale, 1983). Perhaps the most satisfying way of integrating the present data is to suppose that individuals differ in the extent and type of information about themselves in memory (without necessarily postulating a unitary and consistent self-schema) and that different types of self-knowledge are activated and used under different circumstances or mood states. If so, then the recall of self-encoded material may be a useful index of clinical change, but not necessarily of vulnerability to future depression (Hammen *et al.*, 1985).

In contrast to the fairly consistent findings on the relationship between recall of self-encoded material and depression, similar experiments with anxious subjects have proved much less conclusive. Although test anxiety has been found to be associated with a variable recall deficit (cf. Mueller, 1980), self-encoded emotionally threatening material is not typically recalled better than is neutral information by clinically anxious subjects compared with controls (Mogg *et al.*, 1987). This last result was interpreted as evidence that, unlike depression, anxiety is not associated with a negative bias in recall, so that such measures would not be applicable to the assessment of change in anxiety states. It is also apparently inconsistent with predictions arising from Bower's network model of mood and memory, which makes no such distinction among different mood states. However, if we allow the possibility that different emotional states serve different cognitive and behavioural purposes, it is quite plausible that some emotions (e.g. depression) will be associated with biases in recall, while others (e.g. anxiety) will be associated with biases in perceptual scanning (cf. MacLeod *et al.*, 1986).

Having now reviewed the evidence concerned with self-knowledge, and having determined that we are not forced by this evidence to conclude that it is necessarily structured as a consistent, generic and modular schema, we can now consider various alternative ways in which such self-knowledge might be organized.

6.7 ORGANIZATION OF SELF-KNOWLEDGE

First, self-knowledge may be considered to be one particular instantiation of a more general 'person schema'. Here it is assumed that the schemata for people is similar to those schemata involved in representing other categories of objects or events. That is, the general person schema would include knowledge that people have specific physical attributes such as body parts, or psychological attributes such as intelligence, and so on. Some of these attributes will be common to all people, such as possessing a head, and thus will be permanently incorporated into the person schema. Other attributes will be variable, such as gender, although we know that this must be either male or female. Thus the person schema should contain a 'slot' for gender information which is filled in the case of any specific person by either male or female. Slots of this kind within schemata are also assumed to have 'default' values corresponding to the prototypical person. For example, it will generally be assumed that a person has two eyes, even though occasionally people have only one eye or none at all. Thus if we are talking to a stranger over the telephone, we naturally assume that the person has two eyes even though we have never actually seen him/her. Psychological attributes might also have default values in some cases, as for example when we assume that a new acquaintance is honest until evidence suggests otherwise.

How might knowledge about oneself fit into this view of things? Presumably, we observe our own behaviour and attributes in the same way as we observe those of others, and thus store the information similarly. If so, then the 'self-schema' is simply a particular instantiation of the generic person schema, with all available slots filled appropriately. This view would lead us to expect that we would be particularly likely to characterize ourselves using attributes on which we differ from the typical or average person. Thus in this sense the 'self-schema' is a set of 'tags' or additional information which is attached to the general schema for people (cf. Graesser and Nakamura, 1982).

Alternatively, it is possible to consider that the self-knowledge is uniquely structured, and totally differentiated from the schemata used to process information about others. That is, the self-knowledge may not be part of a more generic knowledge structure at all, but simply consists of all information that we have about ourselves, encoded and stored differently from the information that we have about others. For example, judgements of our own appearance or behaviour are clearly made in a quite different way from similar judgements made about others. To some extent this may be attributable to the obvious fact that we cannot directly perceive ourselves interacting with the physical and social environment as we can perceive others. In a study by Lord (1980), self-reference was once again found to be a better mnemonic than relating the same words to others, but the use of mental imagery was a more effective retrieval aid for information about other people than for oneself. This may be taken as evidence that information about others, but not oneself, is easily encoded iconically; presumably because we possess relatively little visual information about our own behaviour. If information about oneself is encoded quite differently from information about others, then it might appear inappropriate to use the term 'schema' for self-knowledge, since the use of the term is taken to imply a more generic structure.

A final perspective on self-knowledge is not to assume any unitary memory structure representing oneself exists in enduring form at all. Conceivably, there are many 'selves' depending on current role, circumstances or mood. Clearly, we encode information about ourselves quite differently in different situations, such as when we are at home or at work, and thus may be considered to be using quite different schemata or frames. If at work I am required to teach students, then presumably there will be slots in my work schema for lectures, students, and so forth; while at home there will be other slots for recreation and housework tasks. Similarly, it is not impossible that other aspects of self-knowledge, such as personal attributes, are also differentially available in different contexts. It does not seem inconceivable that one such 'self-schema' may be active at any one time, and then be replaced by another 'self-schema' at another time, depending on circumstances.

This use of the term self-schema as a means of selecting relevant information from a more extensive database is similar to the selective effect on recall that is observed when the same story is viewed from different perspectives (Anderson and Pichert (1978)). Thus, clusters of self-descriptive features that are recalled differ according to the particular role (e.g. wife, mother, etc.) being considered at the time (Linville, 1982). In this sense the self-schema could be used to refer to the particular frame that we are currently using to extract information from the general database. As a result of this selective extraction we construct a varying mental model of ourselves at different times, dependent on selective retrieval of information associated with the present circumstances (Power and Champion, 1986). A different self-model would thus be constructed according to current situation or state, by selectively drawing on information I have about my own behaviour and attributes. In our view this is more satisfactory than other conceptions, which have difficulty in accounting for apparent inconstancy in the structure and content of the 'self-schemata' over time. Changes in negative recall bias with recovery from depression do not have to be attributed to the 'latent' status of a negative self-schema, but rather to a change in the choice of frames used to encode or retrieve information about oneself. Future research could thus be directed towards investigating the factors that influence frame selection, rather than the content of any particular schema.

Chapter 7

Thoughts and Images

The biases in attention and memory found in anxiety and depression have often been explained in terms of the distinctive cognitive structures presumed to be associated with emotional disorders. These can be formulated in various ways, such as associative networks (Chapter 5) or schemata (Chapter 6). Mental models are another possibility (Johnson-Laird, 1983a), and one that Power and Champion (1987) have argued is well suited to cognitive theories of emotional disorders. However, it is moment-to-moment thoughts and images which are the main focus of therapist–patient interaction and the route by which all other cognitive phenomena are brought on to the therapeutic agenda. It is therefore important to consider their role in emotional disorders. Thinking and imaging probably do not exhaust the range of possible conscious cognitive phenomena, but they are the most ubiquitous.

One of the central issues that has been discussed in connection with imagery recently is how it relates to underlying cognitive structures. Though this debate has focused on visual imagery, there is scope for a closely parallel debate about the relationship between thoughts and knowledge structures. This theoretical question of the relationship of thoughts and images to knowledge structures has a close bearing on several of the important clinical questions concerned with images and thoughts.

The first two are concerned with the properties of emotional imagery. Thoughts and images are used in therapy to explore (or 'access') emotional reactions and preoccupations, and there is a need to give a theoretical account of how such accessing occurs. One of the questions that has been posed is whether images are better able than thoughts to access emotion. Secondly, there may be special characteristics of *emotional* thoughts and images. One possibility is that though they have considerable phenomenal impact, they tend to be lacking in detail.

The next two issues are concerned with the role of phenomenal experience in bringing about underlying cognitive change. Processes of natural recovery from traumatic events such as bereavement involve a process of 'working through' which appears to be carried on at the phenomenal level of thoughts and images. This raises the issue of how phenomenal aspects of 'working through' relate to more basic changes in knowledge structures. Finally, many therapies use the medium of images and thoughts to bring about fundamental and long-term changes in people's beliefs and reactions. Such changes also appear to depend on changing knowledge representations through the medium of work on images and thoughts.

We shall consider each of these issues in turn. However, as background for a discussion of these questions about thoughts and images in emotional disorders, it will be helpful to briefly set out the recent general debate about the nature of imagery, and to review Peter Lang's extensive body of theoretical and empirical work on imagery which has taken this debate as its starting point.

7.1 THEORIES OF IMAGERY

7.1.1 The general Debate

There are essentially two major schools of thought about the nature of imagery: the 'pictorialists', such as Kosslyn (1980), Shepard and Cooper (1982) and Paivio (1986); and the 'descriptionalists', such as Pylyshyn (1973, 1984) and Kieras (1978). A convenient collection of position statements in this controversy has been edited by Block (1981).

The pictorialists emphasize the similarity between images and the objects they represent. Thus, they claim that the relations between the components of an image are analogous to the components of the corresponding external stimulus, and that the experience of an image is substantially similar to the perception of the external stimulus. The pictorialists have demonstrated a variety of phenomena relating to the manipulation and use of images — for example, that people can rotate them (Shepard) and use them to facilitate memory performance (Paivio). Studies of mental image acuity and scanning (e.g. Kosslyn et al., 1978) are perhaps the most compelling evidence for the pictorialist position. The pictorialists assert that the functional properties of images depend on their pictorial qualities.

Are these claims denied by the 'descriptionalists'? The problem in answering this is that the focus of the argument seems to have shifted subtly over time, with each side finding a way of incorporating all the available facts into its own position. It may therefore be useful to go back to Pylyshyn's (1973) early trenchant statement of the descriptionalist position. His view was that 'the representation corresponding to an image is more like a description than picture.' In his theory, 'seeing the image has been replaced by a set of common and completely mechanical processes.' It 'eliminates all reference to perceptual process' (p.22).

The impetus to develop such a theory of imagery perhaps stems from a general problem in cognitive science about how to handle the relationship between process and representation (e.g. Dreyfus, 1979; Searle, 1980; Pylyshyn, 1984). Computational models of cognitive processes developed within the functional tradition of artificial intelligence have no need for representations of the analogue kind that correspond to the thoughts and images of introspection. It has therefore seemed attractive to some psychological theorists to develop a theory of human cognitive processes which does not give any unique functional properties to thoughts and images.

The pictorialists have wished to stress the perception-like character of imagery, and have had some success in establishing this. In his introduction to the controversy, Block (1981) suggests that it is now generally accepted that images and perceptions share many properties, and that the real issue is whether both are pictorial or both are descriptional. However, he was premature in thinking that the question of similarity had been settled. Chambers and Reisberg (1985) have recently attempted to show that the properties of images can remain unspecified in a way that is not possible in percepts, and that questions of interpretation do not arise for images in the same way as in the perception of external stimuli. Images represent what they are intended to in a way that percepts do not.

Another point at which the ground of the controversy has shifted concerns whether images have functional properties (e.g. play a causal role in information-processing) as the pictorialists would claim to have demonstrated, or whether they are merely epiphenomenal (i.e. do no useful work) as the descriptionalists appeared to claim at the outset of the controversy. Both Shepard and Kosslyn have taken this to be a key point of disagreement, though Block (1981) doubts whether this is so. Some descriptionalists are willing to admit that there is *something* associated with imagery (perhaps even uniquely associated with imagery) that has functional properties. However, they question whether it is the *experience* of the image that has these properties, as opposed, for example, to the neural substrate associated with imagery. What is uncomfortable about this latter suggestion is that, unless ways are found of controlling the neural and experiential aspects of imagery independently in experimental work, it will be impossible to decide whether it is the phenomenal image or the neural substrate that has the causal properties.

An alternative proposal that the descriptionalists can make is that images contain no information that is not contained in non-imaginal encodings of the same knowledge, but that they encode it in a form that facilitates processes of access and manipulation (Clark and Chase, 1972). This is a plausible view, but it probably concedes more than the descriptionalists would wish.

One of the descriptionalists' points that would probably be widely accepted relates to storage and construction. How are images stored? There is probably no one in the current debate who would claim that images are stored in pictorial form, or that when people 'form' an image they simply pluck a fully-formed visual image from their library of mental pictures. Presumably, previous images are 'retrieved' using the same kind of constructive processes as are involved when new hypothetical images are generated or existing images are manipulated or revised. Currently, most of the pictorialists (e.g. Kosslyn, 1980) would accept this. If this is conceded, then the classification of encodings has to include, in addition to imaginal and linguistic representations, a third form of encoding in which knowledge is stored when it is not in consciousness. Johnson-Laird (1983) among others has adopted such a three-fold classification of encodings into images, propositions and 'mental models', a particular form of non-conscious encoding. For him, images are 'the perceptual correlates of models from a particular point of view' (p.165).

This brief account of the current debate among experimental psychologists about the nature of images will have to suffice as a background to a discussion of issues relating more specifically to emotional disorders.

7.1.2 Lang's Approach to Emotional Imagery

Next, we shall consider the extensive programme of theory and research on emotional imagery carried out by Peter Lang, which takes descriptionalist theories of emotional imagery as its starting-point. Lang's theoretical views have been set out in a series of papers (Lang, 1977, 1979, 1984; Lang et al., 1980, 1983) and reviewed in more detail than is possible here by Watts and Blackstock (1987). Like Pylyshyn and others, Lang proposes that 'affective images are conceptualised as propositional structures, rather than as re-perceived, raw, sensory representations' (Lang, 1977, p.863). Following Kieras (1978), Lang proposed that the associative network (see Chapter 5) is the most satisfactory way of formulating the propositional structure of representations, though this is not a necessary aspect of the descriptionalist position. The other key feature of Lang's position is his emphasis on response aspects of imagery, and this is the one that has largely guided his experimental work on emotional imagery.

Originally, Lang (1977) claimed that imagery contained two elements (stimulus and response aspects), though subsequently (e.g. Lang, 1979) he proposed that imagery also contained semantic propositions (e.g. the proposition in a snake phobia that snakes are dangerous). The response aspects include perceptual, visceral, motor and verbal response systems. Central to his research is a procedure for training subjects to include response aspects in their imagery, which he has contrasted with training for stimulus detail in imagery. Response training (but not stimulus training) results in the amplification of physiological responses when phobics imagine their particular phobic stimulus (e.g. when snake phobics imagine a snake, but not when speech phobics do so). Another important consequence of response training is said to be that it promotes greater *concordance* between verbal and physiological response systems, though it now appears that this can be achieved by using response-laden imagery scripts without prior training in response imagery (e.g. Robinson and Reading, 1985). The clinical importance that Lang attaches to concordance follows from his early finding (Lang *et al.*, 1970) that it is correlated with a good response to desensitization. However, there is as yet no experimental demonstration that it improves the effectiveness of desensitization, and in fact response training seems to impede short-term emotional habituation (see Watts and Blackstock, 1987). Lang also proposes that response training makes imagery more vivid by making it more complete, vividness being defined as the 'completeness of the evoked propositional structure' (Lang, 1977, p.872).

Lang's view is that response training facilitates accessing and retrieval of the 'deep structure emotion prototype' (Lang, 1984, p.208), especially the efferent aspects. In fact, a variety of different accounts can be offered to explain why response training should increase the level of emotion associated with imagery. First, response training may increase the 'completeness' of imagery more effectively than stimulus training, perhaps due to a kind of ceiling effect for stimulus aspects. Second, if subjects imagine responses such as heart-rate being activated, this might lead directly to the activation of that response system. Third, response aspects of imagery could be more closely linked to affect in the cognitive structure than the stimulus aspects. Lang's research programme has not yet enabled us to rule out any of these alternative explanations of the effects of response training.

Lang sees a connection between his general descriptionalist position about the nature of imagery and his emphasis on its non-stimulus aspects. However, it is not clear that there is any necessary link between the two. There would be no dispute between descriptionalists and pictorialists about the fact that imagery *can* have response aspects. This fact does nothing to settle the theoretical debate about the nature and function of imagery. For example, motor responses to a phobic stimulus can be 'pictured' as readily as the phobic stimulus itself.

Among the issues that any propositionalist theory of imagery has to face is whether the activation of visual imagery has any functional value not shared by, say, verbal representations of what is presumed to be the same basic propositional structure. Though it is not entirely clear where Lang stands on this, his implicit assumption seems to be that the evocation of emotional imagery is functional. He is descriptionalist in his assumption that the value of imagery in desensitization depends on how well the corresponding cognitive structure (the 'emotion prototype' as he calls it) is accessed, but he seems to be unorthodox among descriptionalists in at least tacitly assuming that generating response-laden experiential imagery is a valuable way of accessing the prototpye.

7.2 PROPERTIES OF THOUGHTS AND IMAGES

7.2.1 The Role of Images and Thoughts in Emotional Disorders

One of the most interesting issues that has been raised about the emotion-inducing properties of images and thoughts is their relative effectivness in accessing emotion. Sheikh and Panagiotou (1975) among others have claimed that images have a greater capacity than language for attracting and focusing emotionally-loaded associations. Klinger (1980), Horowitz (1983) and Sheikh and Jordan (1983) have made similar claims. It has also been suggested that material that is associated with painful or complex associations can be retrieved more readily in pictorial than in linguistic form. However, these claims have been based largely on anecdotal reports of clinical observations. The methodological problem is that this clinical literature may be based on an unrepresentative minority of people for whom imagery is unusually powerful. There are probably marked individual differences in the functions served by different kinds of representations.

Further, the results of the few available experimental comparisons of the emotive properties of imaginal and linguistic representations are conflicting. Reyher and Smeltzer (1968) presented subjects with words and instructed them to generate in response either a word-associate or an image. The imagery condition produced significantly greater skin conductance reactions, and also higher scores on a measure of 'primary process' responses. One of the limitations of the study is a lack of information about the volunteer sample used; there is no assurance of its representativeness. Baker and Jessup (1980) report results which suggest that emotions differ in how they are best accessed. Subjects were required either to verbalize or to visualize a series of scenes. Physiological responses were higher for verbalizations. Rating scales tended to show interactions with the hedonic properties of the scenes: depressive scenes were rated as stronger and more vivid when verbalized, whereas neutral and pleasant scenes got higher ratings when visualized. Neither of these studies used self-report ratings of emotional reactions to the linguistic and pictorial representations, which makes them somewhat tangential to the hypothesis that pictorial representations are more emotive. However, it is clear that this hypothesis is one that could readily be investigated experimentally.

Despite this conflicting evidence, let us assume that it is correct that pictorial representations are more emotive than linguistic ones. How could this be explained? There are two main possibilities: either we must postulate that pictorial representations can *incorporate* information about emotional reactions more readily than linguistic ones; or that pictorial representations can *access* emotional reactions more readily than linguistic ones. The idea that imagery is well adapted for accessing emotion can be seen as parallel theoretically to the claims made by Kosslyn and Shepard that imagery gives access to spatial information and facilitates the manipulation of spatial information in a way that other representations do not. There would be no serious theoretical problems involved in conceding that imagery allows emotional information to be accessed more readily than do other representations. However, it would be more problematic to concede that imagery contained emotional information that was not, and could not be, contained in other forms of representation. For example, this would raise problems about how the information was stored when images were not in consciousness. It seems unnecessary to postulate that imagery contains unique emotional information in order to accommodate any special emotional properties it may have.

There is another claim that has been made in the clinical literature that would have more far-reaching theoretical implications if it were substantiated. This is that imagery is uniquely effective in recalling experiences from the pre-verbal stage of childhood (Kepecs, 1954). If correct, this would imply that it was easier to retrieve information in the same representational form as it was originally experienced. A descriptionalist theory of imagery that (1) regards imagery as an epiphenomenon of more basic cognitive processes, and (2) assumes that all non-experiential encodings are of the same general form, could not readily accommodate such a finding.

Though no theoretical problem is raised by the idea that imagery facilitates the accessing of emotional information, there is a sense in which this may not be the appropriate way of handling the supposed emotive properties of imagery. The problem is that emotional information is not the same as emotion (Russell, 1987). How representations access emotion itself is less easily explained than how they access emotional knowledge. A parallel problem has arisen in associative network theories of relationships between mood and memory. Bower and Cohen (1982) were led to make a distinction in their associative network model between nodes for emotional feeling, for emotion words, and for emotional concepts. Though Bower and Cohen include feeling nodes in their network, it is not yet clear that this is appropriate, i.e. that feelings are elicited by connections in the network in ways that are essentially similar to those by which knowledge is accessed (see Chapter 5, section 5.3).

Linguistic representations lend themselves to classification more readily than do images. The simplest level is the single word. A number of information-processing tasks involving emotive words (e.g. colour-naming) have been discussed in earlier chapters of this book. The success of these tasks is evidence that individual words can be potent emotional stimuli. As yet we know little about what kinds of word are best able to produce such effects, though Watts et al. (1986b) speculated that colour-naming effects may be strongest with concrete, highly imageable words. This would parallel word variables that are relevant to the strength of learning phonomena (e.g.

Christian *et al.*, 1978). The representational effectiveness of single words is also attested by the fact that therapeutic benefit can be derived from semantic desensitization using individual words (Sergeant, 1965). There is an analogy between this procedure and the laboratory phenomenon of semantic satiation (Di Caprio, 1970) but it remains to be explored in detail.

Though the effects that can be obtained with single words are striking, it is probably correct that the important linguistic determinants of specific behaviours (including emotional reactions) are sentences/facts rather than words/things (Rozeboom, 1972). Distinctions can be made between sentences that (a) describe particular stimuli or events, (b) contain general semantic knowledge, and (c) provide guidance for actions. This classification roughly parallels that between episodic, semantic and procedural memory (Tulving, 1983). It is probably in the semantic and procedural domains that language has the advantage, as it is better able to represent general statements than images. In the clinical domain, negative cognitions in depression, such as Beck's well known triad of negative views about the self, the world and the future, seem to represent general semantic propositions rather than specific episodes.

An interesting issue here is the relationship between semantic and episodic representations. Either type of representation can be biased in emotional disorders and clinical observations suggest that dissociation in either direction is possible. Thus a depressed patient might have a preponderance of negative specific memories of parenting, but have a general proposition in semantic memory that parenting was good. Equally, as we described in Chapter 5, there are patients who have negative general statements in semantic memory, but when pressed for detailed episodes have surprising difficulty in substantiating what they are based on. Perhaps the potentially opposing effects of mood-congruent retrieval (Teasdale, 1983) and repression (Erdelyi and Goldberg, 1979) are partly responsible for these apparently assorted clinical phenomena.

Though both imagery and language can be used to guide actions, the advantage of language seems to lie in the fact that it can more readily be used concurrently with action. The effects of imagery in rehearsal for action can be powerful, a fact that has been best demonstrated in sports psychology (Suinn, 1983). However, it is harder to use imagery than language concurrently with an activity; this gives imagery less flexibility than inner speech. As discussed in Chapter 3, anxiety and depression are associated with an excess of task-irrelevant worry and rumination. However, there have been fewer studies of whether they are also associated with a poverty of the kind of inner speech that might guide coping behaviour. It is relevant that Watts *et al.* (1986c) found that spider phobics' descriptions of how to remove a spider from a bath were significantly less elaborated than those of non-phobics. There may be a general impoverishment of coping inner speech in patients with emotional disorders.

There has also been surprisingly little comparative evaluation of the effects of treatments based on linguistic and pictorial representations. Imagery enthusiasts have made claims for the therapeutic value of imagery-based techniques (e.g. Sheikh and Jordan, 1983). On the opposite side, it has been suggested that linguistic treatments involving representations have more widely generalised effects. Meichenbaum (1977, p.114), in a seminal study, explored this issue by examining treatment effects in subjects who had two discrete phobias (snakes and rats). The imagery treatment was desensitization and the verbal treatment was a stress innoculation technique focusing on anxious 'self-talk'. It seems that stress innoculation affected both phobias, whereas desensitization affected only the phobia to which it was applied. Methodological questions can be raised about this study as the two treatments may have differed in their relative emphasis on stimulus and response processes, as well as in their use of verbal or visual representations, thus making interpretation difficult. A stress-management technique using rehearsal in visual imagery would have been a more appropriate comparison with verbally-based stress innoculation to answer the question being raised here of the relative generalizability of language- and imagery-based treatments. Nevertheless, it is plausible that language produces better generalization of treatment effects than imagery.

7.2.2 Properties of Emotional Imagery

Clinical researchers have shown considerable interest in the vividness of emotional imagery. This no doubt partly reflects the long history of general research on imagery vividness (Marks, 1972), but also follows from a more specific interest in the hypothesis that response to imagery-based treatments such as desensitization is dependent on the vividness of the subject's imagery. Several studies directed at this hypothesis have used standard questionnaire measures of imagery vividness, though these scales have generally been unsuccessful in predicting response to desensitization (e.g. McLemore, 1972; Dyckman and Cowan, 1978). Awareness of the limitations of these scales has led to interest in developing performance-based measures of imagery vividness that might relate better to desensitization outcome (Rimm and Bottrell, 1969; Danaher and Thoresen, 1972; Rehm, 1973; McLemore, 1976; Hiscock, 1978). These studies have generally obtained weak and inconsistent relationships between objective and subjective measures of vividness. Apparently, no one has yet looked at whether these objective measures actually predict response to desensitization, the purpose for which they were purportedly developed.

It is not clear why performance tests of visuo-spatial imagery would be any more closely related to desensitization than are general imagery measures. The basic mistake seems to lie in seeking to infer the vividness of emotional imagery from general imagery measures (whether questionnaire or performance) rather than looking specifically at the vividness of emotional imagery. Dyckman and Cowan (1978) obtained ratings of the vividness of desensitization scenes and found that this *was* related to desensitization outcome. This kind of direct examination of emotional imagery seems the appropriate strategy. Fuller reviews of this literature on vividness of imagery and desensitization can be found in Strosahl and Ascough (1981) and Anderson (1981).

Perhaps the most basic question about the vividness of emotional imagery is the nature of the relationship between such vividness and the degree of emotion associated with it. This may well be complex. Most image theorists have accepted uncritically that vividness is a unitary dimension, though Klinger (1978) has questioned this and suggested (on the basis of factor-analyses of imagery ratings) that there are two main components which he designated 'sensory saturation' (i.e. richness and impact) and 'clarity' (i.e. precision). Watts et al. (1986c), working with the related components of 'awareness' and 'detail' in phobic imagery, found that awareness was positively related to phobic anxiety, though detail was not. Indeed there may be a *negative* relationship between anxiety and some aspects of vividness. Consistent with this, Mathews (1971) suggested that relaxation serves to increase the vividness of imagery in desensitization and Borkovec and Sides (1979) found that vividness increased during desensitization. On the other hand, Marzillier et al. (1979) found no difference between phobics and non-phobics in the vividness of imagery. In a very different clinical field, Parkes (1972) observed a tendency in bereaved people for the clarity of imagery for the deceased person to improve as preoccupation decreased.

It has been suggested (Watts et al., 1986c) that the detail and precision of phobic imagery is particularly important in the effectiveness of imagery-based treatments. Watts (1974) attempted to manipulate the detail of imagery in desensitization by either describing each scene in full each time it was imagined, or simply instructing the subject on the second and subsequent presentations to 'imagine the same scene again'. Detailed presentations resulted in more long-term (between-session) anxiety decrement. This was interpreted in terms of a dual-process habituation theory of desensitization in which one of the component processes is relatively stimulus specific and depends on a clear cognitive representation of the stimulus (Watts, 1979).

There have been no specific investigations of whether the sensory awareness component is related to treatment effectiveness, though there is no clear theoretical reason for predicting that there should be a relationship. Even for clarity of imagery, the theoretical question remains of whether this has a direct causal effect on the desensitization process, or whether the causal properties are to be located in an underlying non-conscious cognitive encoding of which experiential detail is only an epiphenomenon. However, even if this latter is the case, increasing experiential detail may be an effective strategy for bringing about the desired changes in the nonconscious encodings.

If images are generated from underlying cognitive representations they may show parallel characteristics. The lack of precision in emotional imagery may result from relatively undifferentiated cognitive representations. Landau

(1980) found that dog phobics are able to list fewer instances of dogs than non-phobics, suggesting a less differentiated conceptual structure. However, this was also true of mammal instances, leaving it unclear how general were the cognitive differences between groups. As discussed in Chapter 3, section 3.1.6, obsessionals show a general tendency to use narrow categories in sorting tasks, but especially so with 'feared' material such as contamination or making serious mistakes (Persons and Foa, 1984). Similarly, studies of relationships between personal constructs have found that they are unusually highly correlated in patients with anorexia (Button, 1983a), depression (Sheehan, 1981), spider phobia (Watts and Sharrock, 1985b) and mixed neurotic problems (Ryle and Breen, 1972; Winter, 1983). Makhlouf-Norris *et al.* (1970) also found this for obsessionals, but Millar (1980) failed to replicate this finding. Some of these studies have used constructs related to the disorders, others have used neutral constructs. Relationships between constructs are especially strong when constructs related to the disorder are used (Winter, 1983). For a more detailed review of this literature see Button (1983b).

Though sufficient positive findings have emerged to indicate some kind of association between emotional disorders and conceptual organisation, several problems of interpretation remain. It is not clear how far the findings are specific to emotional materials. It is also not clear whether the different methodologies (listing, sorting and repertory grid) provide indices of exactly the same cognitive phenomena. Further, any assumptions about relationships between these structural phenomena and the properties of conscious representations such as images must be tentative, as they have not been studied directly.

7.3 IMAGES AND THOUGHTS IN EMOTIONAL PROCESSING AND TREATMENT

7.3.1 Intrusive Thoughts and Emotional Processing

We shall turn now to the role of thoughts and images in 'working through' the stressful impact of life-events such as bereavement. In this process, conscious thoughts and images occur frequently and involuntarily. The important theoretical question is how, if at all, this contributes to the process of 'working through' and to such changes in underlying knowledge structures as may accompany this.

Freud's observations regarding repetition compulsion following trauma have been influential and will serve as a starting-point. Horowitz (1983, p.131) summarizes Freud's position as follows:

> A harrowing or frightening experience exceeded a person's state of pre-
> paredness and/or capacity to master the resulting stimulations and affects. A

temporary protective mechanism shunted the experience out of awareness where it resided as a kind of undigested foreign body; the memory traces were still extremely vivid and the affects were still of potentially overwhelming intensity. At some later date, the 'repetition compulsion' asserted itself — the person relived the experience repeatedly until it was mastered — until associated feelings such as helplessness diminished. Until such mastery of affects, recall of the experience tended to evoke very vivid images. With mastery the memory traces were processed for storage in the usual way: they were stripped of sensory intensity and related to various schemata and concepts.

Such clinical observations have been supplemented by experimental studies. Horowitz has reported a series of studies comparing the effects of stressful and neutral films on subsequent intrusive representations and found that stressful films were followed both by more intrusive thoughts and more intrusive imagery (e.g. Horowitz, 1975). His interpretation of these findings hinges on the notion of 'completion' of information processing. Until this point is reached, material remains in what Horowitz calls 'active memory', and shows a tendency to surface repeatedly in conscious representations.

It is not clear how well this formulation can explain why *stressful* material is apparently more likely to surface in consciousness than other material in active memory. Another problem is whether the critical notion of completeness can be defined sufficiently independently for it to be of scientific value. If such an independent measure were available, it might be found that stressful and non-stressful materials that had both been processed only to similarly 'incomplete' extents would differ in their capacity to generate intrusive representations. Another problem is that it appears from Horowitz's experimental report (though his report is not wholly clear on this point) that stressful films led to increased intrusive representations of material that was unrelated to the film as well as of related material. It is not clear how Horowitz's theory can predict the intrusion of unrelated material.

Intrusive cognitions in emotional disorders to not seem to be confined to reactive conditions which follow trauma (or experimentally induced stress). Depressive mood states have similar effects. For example, Sutherland *et al.* (1982) tested and confirmed the hypothesis that depressed mood (experimentally induced in normal subjects) makes intrusive thoughts difficult to remove. There are also intrusive thoughts associated with anxiety that tend to be more emotionally intense than depressive ones (Clark and de Silva, 1985). Indeed, clinical observations suggest that intrusive visual images are a feature of many conditions. For example, patients with compulsions (e.g. to eat certain foods, to steal, etc.) quite commonly report intrusive imagery relating to the compulsion. A broader view is thus required that allows (a) that any current concerns can generate intrusive preoccupations, not just one relating to a previous stressful event; and (b) that a variety of emotional disturbances or disorders can result in increased intrusive thoughts and images.

Rachman (1980) has offered an integrative review of what he terms 'emotional processing', i.e. the processing of stressful events. His position is similar to that of Horowitz at many points. Like Horowitz, he has a concept of incomplete or unsatisfactory emotional processing. Among his comprehensive list of signs of unsatisfactory processing are unpleasant intrusive thoughts. Intrusive imagery is not included, but would be compatible with Rachman's general position. Rachman's analysis concentrates on the factors that promote or impede emotional processing. Of particular interest is his proposal that calm rehearsal promotes emotional processing, whereas agitated rehearsal impedes it. This is an advance in specificity on Horowitz's position, which includes no hypothesis about different types of cognitive repetition.

There is a need for caution about theories such as that of Horowitz that assume that a psychological function is served by the intrusion of a representation. Just because there is a function that *might* be served, it should not be concluded that the function concerned is actually being served. The intrusive representations might be an *index* of incomplete processing without contributing to the completion of that processing.

Even accepting that emotional processing needs to be completed, why can this not be carried on without any conscious representation? A specific possibility that might be considered (and could be tested experimentally) is that the repeated retrieval of conscious representations from long-term memory contributes importantly to their transformation. This may be more helpful to the completion of processing than either sustained conscious processing or sustained non-conscious processing. The role of intrusive thoughts and images in emotional stress and recovery is an intriguing phenomenon that deserves more research attention than it has received.

7.3.2 The Role of Representations in Psychological Treatments

All psychological treatments make use of thoughts or images. Probably the most widely used treatment employing visual imagery and certainly the most thoroughly investigated is the technique of imaginal desensitization developed by Wolpe (1958). A wide variety of other techniques making similar use of imagery have also been developed, including covert sensitization, covert reinforcement, covert negative reinforcement, covert extinction, covert modelling and covert response cost (Upper and Cautela, 1979). Imagery has also been the basis of a variety of psychotherapeutic techniques (Singer, 1974). There is an equivalent family of techniques based on linguistic representations. Verbalizations are also, of course, the foundation of most psychotherapeutic techniques, including psychoanalysis. One of the first behavioural techniques to make use of verbal material was Homme's (1965) coverant control method. More recently Meichenbaum (1977) has developed a treatment for anxiety based on modifying 'self-talk', and Beck a related treatment for depression

(Beck *et al.*, 1979) and anxiety (Beck and Emery, 1985) based on modifying negative thoughts and assumptions. Indeed, there is a burgeoning family of clinical techniques making use of verbalizations.

With all treatments that use symbolic representations, there is a question to be answered about how their effects transfer to situations in the real world. Clinical theories about how the effects of imaginal treatments such as desensitization 'transfer' to external stimuli have been almost embarrassingly naive. The simplest view would accept the extreme pictorialist assumption that phobic imagery is an analogue of an external stimulus. It is simply assumed that modified reactions transfer from the image to the stimulus, rather in the same way as conditioned reactions to one stimulus transfers to other related stimuli along a stimulus generalization gradient.

The poverty of theorising about how transfer from representations to external stimuli occurs is so serious that few people have explicitly stated the assumptions involved. However, Cautela and Baron (1977) set out what they regard as three key assumptions: (a) there is 'homogeneity' between overt and covert behaviours (i.e. that they share similar properties); (b) there is 'interaction' between overt and covert events such that one can influence the other; and (c) both are governed by the same laws of learning. Evidence can be adduced in partial support of these assumptions, but they remain problematic (see Strosahl and Ascough, 1981). For example, it is true that the physiological reactions to imagery are similar to those to external stimuli, and that conditioning procedures have been successfully adapted to imagery-based exercises with acceptable therapeutic effects. However, this does not explain how the effects of imagery treatments on external stimuli come about.

Another, somewhat more sophisticated suggestion that can be made is that imagery and perception involve common psychological processes, or rather that imagery represents the anticipatory phase of visual perception (e.g. Neisser, 1976). Modifying processes involving imagery would therefore require the modification of the section of the pathway through which external stimuli are processed. Imagery-based treatments might be able to modify the processing of external stimuli by operating on the common processes involved in both. A variant of this view would assume that, even though imagery processes themselves may not have a role in mediating reactions to external stimuli (Franks, 1974, pp. 237–40), they may influence the long-term structures that modulate reactions to external stimuli. However, it is not clear whether or how imagery can affect subsequent stimulus processing in this way. It may be that imagery is a form of conscious representation that is *derived from* long-term memory, but is not itself involved in determining how external stimuli are processed.

Another possibility is that the apparent transfer from imaginal exercises to real-life situations is mediated by expectations (e.g. Powell and Watts, 1973). A key question for such a theory to face is how imaginal exercises affect expectations about real-life situations. One possibility is that there is a simple failure of 'reality monitoring' (see Chapter 3, section 3.1.6). People often fail to distinguish in memory between what they have seen externally and what they have generated internally (Johnson, 1985). However, failures of *memory* for whether events actually occurred are altogether different from a failure to distinguish between imagination and reality at the time of occurrence. A repeated failure to do the latter would represent a psychotic state.

There are other, perhaps more plausible ways in which imaginal expectations might change expectations regarding real events. For example, for phobics to imagine a feared situation with only minimal anxiety may lead them to *believe* that they could cope with the real situation. Beliefs may thus play an important part in mediating the effects of imaginal exercises. However, clinical observations suggest that beliefs alone may not be sufficient. Sometimes a phobic may believe he can do something but find that in practice his level of anxiety prohibits it.

A fundamental issue for all theories of therapeutic transfer is the distinction between representations of the *real* world and representations of *possible* or *imaginary* worlds (e.g. Johnson-Laird, 1983a, p.423). Such a distinction is crucial in psychological theory for a variety of purposes. Perceptual input seems to contact the models of the real world in a way that is different from whatever subsidiary contact it has with models of hypothetical worlds. Also, models of the real world have behavioural consequences in a way that models of hypothetical worlds do not. Consequently, the therapeutic benefits of treatments based on images or linguistic representations would be very limited if all they achieved was to give people a model of a hypothetical but unreal world (for example, a hypothetical world in which phobic objects could be approached without fear, or in which a depressed person was loved and esteemed by others). There are two possible alternative consequences of a phobic person entertaining representations of a world in which the phobic object can be approached without fear. One would be the creation of an additional model of a hypothetical world in which this was the case; the other would be the revision of the existing (phobic) model of the real world. The clinical results would be very different.

The question of whether a representation relates to real or imaginal worlds cannot be settled on the basis of whether or not it is *true* of the real world. Many depressed people have a distorted perception of the world which, though inaccurate, is clearly intended to be a representation of reality; they are not likely to confuse this and a model of a bleak but imaginary world. Though there are a number of ways in which models of real and imaginal worlds *tend* to differ, it is not clear that any provide a wholly reliable way of making the distinction. For example, it has been suggested in the literature on reality monitoring (Johnson, 1985) that external events are associated with greater contextual information, though this is probably not invariably correct. It might not be true for an author who spent nearly all his time creating fictional characters. Johnson-Laird (1983, p.423) suggests that people know the status of a model 'because they can remember what led to the construction of the model in the first place'. However, the fact that reality monitoring is very imperfect shows that this criterion is also likely to fail.

Perhaps the essential property of a model of the real world is simply that it is *intended* to refer to the real world. There is a great deal of difference between a phobic patient imagining an explicitly hypothetical world in which he had no phobic anxiety, and imagining himself functioning in the real world without phobic anxiety. Imaginary exercises divide according to whether they are intended to refer to hypothetical worlds or to the real world. It can be proposed that only exercises involving models intended to refer to the real world will affect subsequent functioning in it.

Whether or not people take a model as being intended to refer to reality is not necessarily an all-or-nothing matter. People are capable of giving varying degrees of credence to alternatives to their current model of reality. For example, someone might entertain conflicting judgements about the risks associated with a particular activity and be genuinely uncertain which was correct. The amount of credence given to the alternatives might vary over time depending on circumstances. This prompts a question about the impact of new information. If new information suggests that an existing model of reality is incorrect, one possible consequence would be to create a new alternative model and discard the old one. Another would be to retain both the old and the new models, but to assign to the new one a higher level of credence than the old one. Some clinicians have the impression that the latter is the more common situation. In therapy, old models seem to be retained alongside new models, but with less credence attached to them, rather than being discarded.

As with most of the issues raised in this chapter, a great deal of additional empirical research is required before clear conclusions can be reached. However, there is one category of verbal representation, judgements of frequency and probability, which has been extensively researched, and it is to this literature that we now turn.

Chapter 8

Judgement

When the patient [a flying phobic] was not planning a flight in the predictable future, he would feel that the chances of the plane's crashing were one in a hundred thousand or one in a million. As soon as he decided to make a trip by air, his estimated probabilities of a crash would jump. As the time for the flight approached, the likelihood increased progressively. By the time the airplane took off, he would figure the chances as 50–50. If the trip was bumpy, the odds would switch over to 100 to 1 in favour of a crash. (Beck, 1976, p. 164)

Why should the anticipation of a flight increase the subjective probability of a crash? Are emotional states associated with systematic distortions in judgemental processes? The above quotation strongly suggests that they are. However, an issue arises here that parallels that considered in the previous chapter about whether the thoughts and images involved in emotional processing differ from those involved in processing neutral material. Similarly, it is by no means clear that biases in judgement are confined to people with emotional disorders, or even to highly emotional states. Systematic biases in judgement can be demonstrated in quite normal individuals whenever they make judgements concerning uncertain events. To establish the extent that emotional states or disorders are associated with unusual degrees of judgemental bias requires us to examine our state of knowledge concerning errors or bias in the normal population.

Before turning to a discussion of normal errors and biases, a brief comment is necessary to indicate what will and what will not be covered in this chapter. Much has been written about attributional style (e.g. Seligman *et al.*, 1979) and judgements of self-efficacy (Bandura, 1977) in relation to depression and anxiety. None the less, we have taken the decision not to cover these topics here, on the grounds that the relevant research is based almost exclusively on self-reports of cognitive content with the implicit assumption that these closely reflect underlying and causal cognitive processes. While such an assumption may be valid under some circumstances, it is likely that these reports are often misleading, since subjects may attempt to explain their own behaviour and feelings, even in the absence of conscious access to the relevant cognitive processes (see Chapter 9). Lacking any objective criterion for the validity of reported content, we prefer to treat such reports as data to be explained, rather than explanations in themselves.

Consequently, this chapter will focus on studies of judgemental heuristics and biases, and the extent to which these may vary in different emotional states. The nature of normal judgemental biases are first described to demonstrate that non-emotionally disturbed individuals are prone to errors associated with the use of simplifying heuristics, such as availability or representativeness. Next we discuss evidence that emotional states affect judgements of past performance and of future risk. Other evidence will be cited to show that similar effects occur when ambiguous events are interpreted such that the perceived meaning is congruent with emotional state. Finally, the implication of this research for clinical practice is discussed, both in relation to errors of clinical judgement and the psychological treatment of emotional disorder. At the most general level, errors in judgement are associated with the overuse of intuitive heuristic devices, and a corresponding failure to use logical or statistical decision methods. In their seminal (1974) paper, Tversky and Kahneman list three commonly used heuristic devices: availability, representativeness and anchoring.

8.1 HEURISTICS

8.1.1 The Availability Heuristic

In using the availability heuristic people are influenced by the relative availability, or accessibility from memory, of events related to the judgement they are making. When judging the probability of an uncertain future event, for example, it may often be useful to base one's estimation on the ease with which similar events can be accessed from memory. Generally speaking, the ease of such access will be correlated with past event frequency, so that the use of this heuristic often leads to quite accurate judgements. However, there are many factors associated with accessibility other than objective frequency, including vividness or salience, which may render the use of the availability heuristic misleading.

If one is required to estimate the relative frequency of English words that begin with the letter R, and compare this estimate with a similar one made for words in which R is the third letter, most subjects estimate the former as more frequent. In fact, words in which the letter R appears in the third place are far more common. The explanation offered by Tversky and Kahneman (1973) is that it is much easier to generate words that begin with R than words that have R as their third letter, thus producing the inaccurate impression that the former are more common. In another experiment, subjects were presented with a list of male and female names, in which either the males or the females were famous personalities, while the other sex names were those of an equal number of relatively unknown people. When subjects were later asked to estimate the number of men and women in the list, those who had seen the names of famous women but unknown men, tended to overestimate the number of women, while those whose list contained famous men and unknown women overestimated the number of men. Apparently, the more salient and memorable the exemplars within a category, the greater the estimate of their frequency.

It also seems possible that the availability heuristic is involved when people overestimate the likelihood of unpleasant and frightening events occurring to them. For example, if we have just read an extremely lurid account in the newspaper about a victim of violent crime, the increased availability that results may lead us to overestimate the true probability of being involved in such a crime ourselves. In systematic studies of this effect (Lichtenstein *et al.*, 1978; Johnson and Tversky, 1983) the subjective probability of death from a number of causes was shown to be related to disproportionate exposure to lethal events via media descriptions, or to their memorability and imaginability.

Tversky and Kahneman are not entirely explicit about the mechanisms thought to underlie availability; for example, whether availability refers to differential ease of generation in retrieval, and whether subjects actually engage in such retrieval at the time of making a judgement. Some evidence indicates the number of items which can be recalled when required does correlate with frequency estimates (Williams and Durso, 1986) consistent with the possibility that subjects actually generate examples in at least some tasks. However, since subjects can sometimes give judgements very rapidly, it would seem more likely that frequency information, sometimes in biased form, is encoded at the time of initial presentation.

8.1.2 Representativeness Heuristic

Imagine tossing a coin six times. Of the following possible head (H) and tail (T) sequences, which is the more likely to occur: HTTHTH or HHHTTT? In fact, both sequences are equally probable, since each occurrence of a head or tail has the independent probability of 50 per cent, so that the probability of any one unique sequence of six events is 0.5 to the power of 6 (or 0.0078). However, most people have the idea that runs of three heads or tails in a row are extremely unrepresentative of random sequences, and for this reason tend to select the first sequence as being the more probable. In doing so, according to Kahneman and Tversky (1972) they are using the representativeness heuristic. This representativeness heuristic is said to be used whenever people base their judgements on the extent to which a specific event is seen as prototypical of a larger group of events.

The heuristic can be particularly misleading when we ignore base-rate information as a consequence of its use. Suppose one has the information that an individual is relatively shy and withdrawn, is very fond of reading, and is good at keeping things neat and orderly. In deciding whether this individual is more likely to be (say) a librarian or a farmer, many people would estimate the former as more likely, on the dubious basis that the personality sketch given resembles our prototype of a representative librarian. However, use of representativeness in making this judgement has led us to overlook completely the fact that the frequency of librarians in the population (base rate) is very many times lower than that of farmers, and the latter group must also contain at least a proportion of individuals who also fit the description.

It is clearly a desirable intention that clinicians and therapists should be aware of the biases and heuristics which their emotionally disturbed clients may use when judging situations as threatening or depressing. It is also worth remembering, as was indicated at the beginning of this chapter, that judgemental bias is not the prerogative of emotionally disturbed populations. Since we all use heuristics in making judgements, clinicians are by no means immune from similar errors.

To illustrate this, suppose a specific form of cancer has a prevalence rate of 1 in a 1000. A screening test for cancer is 95 per cent accurate, that is, the false positive rate is 5 per cent. If you obtained a positive result in the absence of any other symptoms or indications, what is the probability that you actually have the cancer? To answer this question, recall that in a sample of 1000 people, only one will actually have the cancer, while the 999 that do not will produce a 5 per cent false positive rate. Since 5 per cent of 999 is approximately 50, the chances are therefore only one in 50 that an isolated positive result means that you actually have the cancer. This fairly elementary application of base rates was sufficient to confuse the majority of students and staff at Harvard Medical School, many of whom gave the erroneous answer of 95 per cent (Casscells *et al.*, 1978).

8.1.3 The Anchoring Heuristic

Initial positions taken may continue to influence subsequent judgements even under circumstances when their irrelevance should be obvious. In their description of anchoring effects, Tversky and Kahneman (1974) note that when subjects were asked to adjust an arbitrary initial estimate that is given to them as a starting-point, their expressed judgement remains closer to the offered anchor-point than it would have been otherwise, despite it being made clear that the anchor is irrelevant to the task. In other experiments subjects have been noted to cling to initial hypotheses, even when the evidence on which they were originally based has been totally discredited (Ross *et al.*, 1975). Subjects given the task of judging the validity of real and faked suicide notes persisted in the beliefs they had formed about their accuracy in making these judgements, even after they had been informed that the feedback given by the experimenter had been totally fabricated. It would appear that once formed, a hypothesis leads people to focus on reasons why it might be true, and to disregard evidence of its falsity.

8.2   CONFIRMATION BIAS AND OVER-CONFIDENCE

8.2.1   Problem-solving Tasks

Research on problem-solving has clearly demonstrated that normal individuals show a persistent bias that favours gathering information which confirms their beliefs, rather than challenging them. In experiments in which subjects are invited to test the validity of a rule, they typically proceed to do so by generating positive instances of that rule, and neglect to test negative instances (see Wason, 1971). For example, suppose that you are given the numbers 2, 4 and 6 and told that this sequence is an example of a specific rule. Your task is to establish the nature of this rule by generating more number series, and be told if each sample conforms to the rule or not. Only when you are confident that you know the rule should you announce your decision. In fact, the rule used by Wason was that of any series of ascending numbers; but subjects typically generated a few other ascending series of three consecutive even numbers (which do conform to the rule) and then announced this as their answer.

8.2.2   Judgements about People

Confirmation biases are by no means restricted to abstract problems, but extend to judgements about other people. Consider the case of an individual who is told that a new colleague is much more friendly than appearances suggest. To test out this idea, the individual might strike up a conversation and probe for examples of friendliness, or for examples of unfriendliness, or both. In a direct test of the preferred strategy under such circumstances, subjects who were told to determine if another person was introverted (or extraverted) typically chose confirmatory rather than disconfirmatory questions from a prepared list (Snyder and Swann, 1978). Interestingly, blind judges who listened to the target person's answers to these questions and then judged their personality tended to be swayed in the same direction, suggesting that confirmatory testing elicits social behaviour consistent with the hypothesis being tested. Such results strongly suggest that, once established, judgemental biases about people are very hard to change.

8.2.3 Probability Judgements

A related effect is the frequently cited degree of over-confidence expressed when making probabilistic judgements, under conditions of known uncertainty. Individuals typically express complete certainty in judgements that have true accuracy rates of only 80–90 per cent (Fischhoff *et al.*, 1977). This effect has often been attributed to a kind of confirmation bias; having arrived at a decision subjects appear selectively to rehearse reasons why that decision was a good one and often completely neglect any consideration of alternatives, or possible reasons why they might be wrong.

8.2.4 Hindsight: 'I Knew it Would Happen'

The confirmation bias tends to favour beliefs that we currently hold, and as a result may make us view the world as a less surprising place than it really is. If subjects are asked to reconstruct their pre-outcome estimate of the probability that an event will happen after it has in fact occurred, they typically adjust their remembered or reconstructed probability judgements so as to match their present knowledge. Prior to President Nixon's trips to Peking and Moscow, Fischhoff and Beyth (1975) asked subjects to rate the probability of various possible outcomes of the visits. Shortly after, subjects were asked to reconstruct their prior predictions, and these were compared with the estimates actually made. Reconstructed probabilities for events that had actually occurred showed a significant increase, while those for events that had not occurred showed a corresponding decrease.

It is not even necessary for real events to have occurred for this kind of reconstructive bias to manifest itself. When presented with clinical case histories, and required to explain a hypothetical outcome (such as suicide), likelihood estimates for this outcome occurring in fact are systematically increased (Ross *et al.*, 1977). The inflated probability estimates occur to the same extent regardless of whether subjects were first led to believe that the event had actually occurred, and later told that this was a fabrication; or whether they were simply asked to explain an outcome that was presented as clearly hypothetical in the first place. Again, it appears that selective focus on possible reasons why a hypothetical outcome might occur leads to a failure to consider reasons for alternative outcomes, and thus results in increased subjective likelihood. It seems likely (see Kahneman, Slovic and Tversky, 1982) that the prior existence of a causal schema consistent with one outcome renders subjects particularly vulnerable to the effects of *post hoc* explanation. This is, if the subject can find a highly plausible causal explanation for why an event, real or hypothetical, may have occurred, the judgmental bias resulting will be a relatively strong one.

8.3 EMOTION AND REPORTED SATISFACTION OR SUCCESS

It seems fairly clear from the foregoing review of intuitive judgements, that the predominant bias in normal individuals is a positive and sometimes self-serving one. The tendency to focus on evidence that is consistent with one's beliefs may be seen as serving a protective function, similar to that served by the positive recall bias and attentional avoidance bias discussed elsewhere (Chapters 3 and 7). Indeed, explanations of confirmatory and hindsight bias effects often draw on the idea of differentially available material from memory, so that mood effects on retrieval might lead us to expect equivalent mood effects on judgement. Hence if a negative mood state were to increase the relative accessibility of unpleasant material in memory, then use of the availability heuristic in judging subjective probability would produce a consistent negative bias in judgement.

A large number of experimental studies involving mood manipulations have demonstrated effects which are entirely consistent with this expectation. In an influential paper, Isen and her colleagues (1978) suggested the existence of a cognitive loop connecting mood state, accessibility of positive or negative material in memory, and behavioural consequences. Positive-feeling states were induced by giving passers-by a free gift, and in a second (apparently unrelated) interview the same subjects were required to rate their satisfaction with their own car and television set. Compared with controls, the subjects who had received free gifts rated themselves as significantly more satisfied with their own possessions.

Current-mood state also influences normal subjects' ratings of their performance on a mental task. After induction of a sad mood prior to performance of the mental task, subjects were significantly less satisfied with their own performance, even though this had been standardized by providing predetermined feedback of success or failure (Wright and Mischel, 1982). In similar vein, Schwarz and Clore (1983) found that mild happy or sad moods induced either by describing mood-congruent events or by simply interviewing subjects on sunny or rainy days, resulted in concordant changes in ratings of satisfaction with their life as whole.

In such studies it is sometimes assumed that the results support an explanation which draws both on ideas related to Bower's (1981) network model of mood and memory, and Tversky and Kahneman's (1974) account of the availability heuristic. That is, it is assumed that information relating to negative events is stored in memory in such a way that it can be activated by re-establishment of the mood which was present at the time of its encoding. Thus a depressed mood will make negative material more accessible, and this will in turn bias one's judgements of present circumstances or past events. However, as was discussed in the earlier description of the availability heuristic, it remains unclear which mechanism might underlie this effect. In judging satisfaction with one's television set for example, the possibilities include: the retrieval of specific episodes (e.g. when it has gone wrong); more general episode categories (e.g. periods of trouble-free viewing); the recall of previous feelings of satisfaction; or a mood-congruent shift in response criterion for what constitutes satisfactory performance.

In discussing their results, Schwarz and Clore (1983) offer yet another explanation, involving the attributions made by subjects about their emotional state. One of the manipulations involved in their experiments was to alert some of the subjects to the probable cause for their happy or sad mood (e.g. a small uncomfortable room, bad weather, etc.). Such subjects showed a much reduced mood-congruent effect on their judgements of life satisfcation, and these were not significantly different from those of controls. Schwarz and Clore argue that this shows that people use their current mood as a source of information in making judgements, *unless* a ready alternative explanation springs to mind. That is, a negative-mood state leads to judgements of low satisfaction with one's life, possessions and so on, to the extent that the existence of the negative mood is taken as evidence for an unsatisfactory life, as opposed to some more transient environmental event. Although it seems unlikely that such an explanation could apply to all mood-congruent cognitive biases, it is of theoretical importance in showing that, at least in the case of some judgemental tasks, mood effects are not completely automatic.

Very similar results have been reported in a series of studies concerned with naturally occurring depression and the assessment of one's own performance in a variety of tasks (Blaney, 1986). Both depressed students (Nelson and Craighead, 1977) and depressed psychiatric outpatients (DeMonbreun and Craighead, 1977) underestimated the amount of positive feedback that they had received during an earlier laboratory task. In other studies (Gotlib, 1983; Cane and Gotlib; 1985) similar effects were found when depressed patients rated standard evaluative feedback that they thought described their social performance, and when students directly rated their behaviour in simulated social situations. Even when confronted with identical neutral descriptions of their personality, depressed individuals rate such descriptions of their behaviour and themselves in a less positive way (Vestre and Caulfield, 1986).

This congruence of results arising from temporary mood manipulations, and more permanent states of depression, has been interpreted as implying that they arise from effects of depressed mood state on accessibility, possibly interacting with more enduring aspects of depressives cognitive organization (Teasdale and Spencer, 1984). However, very few studies have systematically investigated possible interactions between mood state and these more enduring individual differences; while equally, very few have considered whether the negative judgemental biases observed arise from depression or anxiety, or both. This last question certainly remains an open one, since at least one study in which both anxiety and depression were measured found that negative subjective evaluation of performance related more to trait anxiety than to depression (Zarantonello *et al.*, 1984).

8.4 JUDGEMENT OF CONTINGENCY AND CONTROL

It has sometimes been noted that reports on frequency of past successes or failures in experimental tasks are provided more accurately by depressed than by non-depressed subjects (for example, Nelson and Craighead, 1977). More consistently, depressed individuals appear to be relatively pessimistic (but more accurate) than non-depressed individuals in their judgements of contingency and control. In a study by Alloy and Abramson (1979), depressed subjects proved very accurate at detecting a lack of contingency between their own button-pressing responses and a desired outcome. Non-depressed controls were both less accurate and less consistent in their judgements across situations in which outcomes were either desirable or otherwise. If the outcome were desirable, normals tended to overestimate their control, but then underestimated their control if outcomes were undesirable.

In another related experiment, normals consistently succumbed to a positive illusion of control over success regardless of exposure to induced helplessness manipulations; whereas depressed subjects were consistently more accurate in correctly judging non-contingency (Alloy and Abramson, 1982). This accuracy is apparently confined to observation of oneself however, in that judgements of contingency made for others by depressed subjects tended to err in the direction of overestimating control (Martin, Abramson and Alloy, 1984). It would thus be misleading to characterise depressed people as invariably 'sadder but wiser' with the implication that their judgements are in some sense less biased than those of normals. Rather, it would appear that both depressed and non-depressed people can make biased judgements of contingency and control, but under circumstances where non-contingent success is being judged for oneself, the cognitive distortions shown by non-depressed people may be absent in depression. None the less, these findings may have implications for psychological treatments, since they suggest that therapists could try to induce the illusion of control over positive outcomes. Even if normals are less accurate in this respect than are depressives, such a positive bias may be a valuable defence against becoming depressed under circumstances when one cannot always have control over events.

8.5 SUBJECTIVE RISK

8.5.1 The Effect of Imagining on Outcome

In an extension of the research work concerned with judgements of past or present events, manipulations designed to alter the availability of specific future scenarios have also produced evidence of subjective probability changes. Suppose that you were asked to estimate the probability of a Government or Opposition victory in the next election. Having made your prediction, you are then asked to imagine as vividly as possible a detailed scenario involving plausible events that culminate in a victory for your less favoured party. Would this procedure lead you to revise your expectation, despite knowing that the exercise was a purely imaginery one? Based on research studies such as those by Carroll (1978), the answer is apparently yes. Subjects required to imagine either Jimmy Carter or Gerald Ford winning the 1976 Presidential election shifted their predictions so that these more closely matched the outcome that they had just imagined.

In a related experiment, Gregory et al. (1982) asked subjects to imagine themselves involved in positive event (e.g. winning a contest) or negative event (e.g. being arrested for a crime they had not committed). Once again, systematic shifts of probability judgements occurred in which subjects moved towards increased likelihood of the event they had imagined. While both these studies were once again interpreted as being due to the imagined scenarios making related material more accessible in memory, an obvious alternative explanation which might occur to the reader is that of demand characteristics. It would seem fairly apparent that experimenters expected a shift of ratings in line with the imagined scenario, so that perhaps subjects simply changed their predictions to meet this expectation.

Such an explanation seems unlikely in view of checks carried out in some of Gregory et al.'s (1982) experiments, in which a confederate telephoned the subject some time after the experiment under the pretext of carrying out a survey on judicial reform. Subjects who had imagined being falsely accused of a crime provided clear evidence in their responses that they had become more accepting of the idea that they themselves could possibly be accused in this way. Furthermore, in a probe prior to debriefing, none of the subjects indicated any suspicion that the telephone survey was anything other than it was represented as being. Finally, in a further experiment in which subjects were required to imagine subscribing to a cable TV service, experimental subjects were more likely actually to subscribe to cable TV when offered it by company sales people (47 per cent in the imagination condition versus 20 per cent of the control group). This effect of imagined scenarios on later behaviour was subsequently replicated independently by Anderson (1983) who found that changes persisted over at least a three-day period. Under the pretext of asking subjects to plan a series of creative cartoons, they were asked to imagine themselves as the main character in scenarios which involved giving blood or joining a political action group. Three days later, subjects who had imagined donating blood were more likely to volunteer to do so than were subjects who had imagined the political scenario. Anderson (1983) suggests that these experimental results imply that the effectiveness of imaginary rehearsal is due to the formation of behavioural scripts, although it seems unclear whether this is via the priming of previously existing schemata, or is attributable to new information that is acquired during the presentation of imaginary scenarios.

Either way, since the phenomenon appears to be fairly robust, it may be worth considering how it relates to psychological treatment methods that involve imagining new behaviours. Systematic desensitization, covert modelling and role-play rehearsal in imagination are all examples of treatments in which clients imagine themselves performing otherwise avoided behaviours. It would be useful to investigate whether explanations of such treatment effects might also include enhanced availability of new behavioural scripts.

8.5.2 Mood and Subjective Risk

Where mood has been experimentally manipulated, it appears to have surprisingly pervasive effects on estimates of risk across a wide range of future events, both positive and negative. In the previously cited study by Johnson and Tversky (1983), reading newspaper accounts describing the death of an individual in detail apparently resulted in quite global increases of estimated risk across all causes of death, rather than local increases related to the similarity between the newspaper account and the causes of death to be rated. A similar global increase in subjective probability across a range of disasters was found by Bower (1983) in ratings completed after the induction of an unhappy mood by hypnotic suggestion. While both authors cite Bower's (1981) network model of emotional state-dependent effects to explain their results, it seems on the face of it a little puzzling that there was no trace of differential effects attributable to event similarities. As Kavanagh and Bower (1985) argue, this appears to imply that activation spreads equally to all events linked to a particular emotional state, rather than only to those that would be primed by their semantic association with the activating events. Alternatively, one could suppose that subjects simply take their own mood state into account when making judgements of this sort (cf. Schwarz and Clore, 1983).

Rather similar global effects have been obtained with depressed and anxious populations (Butler and Mathews, 1983). In this study, normal, anxious and depressed subjects rated the risk of a range of positive and negative events, both in relation to themselves and to others. No significant differences were found between the groups in the analysis of the ratings for positive events. On the other hand, ratings of negative events showed highly significant differences, with both anxious and depressed subjects rating negative events as more likely to happen than did normal controls. Furthermore, although normal individuals did not differentiate between probability ratings for themselves or for others, ratings of negative events made by both anxious and depressed subjects for themselves were significantly higher than ratings for the same items when made for another person.

Once again, the most obvious explanation of these findings appears to be that negative-mood states (whether anxiety or depression) increase the accessibility of all emotionally congruent negative material in memory, or at least that which is related to oneself, and thus bias predictions concerning future events. At least two aspects of this explanation would seem to require additional investigation prior to its general acceptance. One that has already been mentioned is the assumption that mood effects alone are a sufficient explanation, without need of supposing an interaction between mood state and more enduring cognitive characteristic. The second is that no clear correlation has been demonstrated between increased availability of the relevant material in memory and shift in judgement, despite the success in modifying judgements with manipulations that are aimed at changing availability.

One way of testing whether the inflation of subjective risk for negative events in emotionally disturbed populations is entirely attributable to current-mood state is to investigate populations varying in trait anxiety (or vulnerability to depression) when they are also in different moods. Although ideally this should be carried out in a population known to be vulnerable to clinical disorders, the only available data concern high and low trait anxious normals tested prior to an important examination (Butler and Mathews, 1987). Subjective probability questionnaires concerned both with examination outcome and a range of other hypothetical negative events were given to students one month, and one day, before their examination, and the results compared with data from students who had no such examination in the immediate future. In examination candidates, state anxiety rose as the examination approached, and there was a related tendency to rate all negative events as more likely.

Unlike the completely global effects reported by Johnson and Tversky (1983) and Bower (1983), results obtained immediately prior to the examintion showed some evidence of specificity. All items were rated in two ways — for oneself and for another person — in the anticipation that self–other differences might be found paralleling the earlier results with emotionally disturbed individuals. On the second occasion of testing, students about to take an examination rated negative examination-related events as significantly more likely than other miscellaneous negative events, and tended also to rate them as more likely to occur to themselves than to others. Perhaps more interesting was an interaction between type of event and trait anxiety level, which applied to both examination and control groups. Individuals high in trait anxiety scores tended to predict that all positive events were less likely to happen to themselves (rather than others) and all negative events were rated as more likely. Thus, in the case of emotionally vulnerable individuals there was a relatively global elevation in judgements of personal risk which was not restricted to those currently feeling anxious about an examination. Since there were also more specific effects attributable to examination stress (that is, relative elevations in probability of examination failure), it would appear that there are both general effects associated with enduring individual characteristics and more local situational or mood-dependent effects.

One theoretical framework within which these results can be understood supposes that trait anxiety levels reflect the extent, elaboration or accessibility of cognitive structures concerned with the evaluation of threat. In this view, high trait anxiety is associated with extensive, well-elaborated schemata which encompass a wide range of threatening information. Due to the increased accessibility of threatening information, judgements of future risk across a wide range of negative events are elevated. Low trait anxiety, in contrast, would be associated with less extensive and elaborated threat-related information in memory. Under appropriate circumstances, such as immediately before an important examination, specific information pertaining to the current threat will be accessed. However, spread to representations concerned with other negative events would be limited by their restricted extent, or lack of interconnections among threat schemata.

8.5.3 Availability and Subjective Risk

The view outlined above allows us to extend the link between availability and subjective risk in such a way as to accommodate subjective risk differences between high and low trait anxious individuals, or between emotionally disturbed and normal populations. However, there is a fundamental methodo-logical difference between studies that involve subjective risk ratings of events that have been previously encountered (either in reality or in imagination) in comparison with new information about events that can be manipulated at the time of an experiment. For example, subjects in the study by Butler and Mathews (1983) were asked to rate the probability of events such as being attacked by an intruder in their own house. Although such an event will not have actually happened to the majority of people, most will have considered the likelihood of such an event at some time in the past. For this reason, subjective probability estimates may not be based on the retrieval of specific related events in memory, but on the recall of probability judgements that had been made earlier.

To illustrate this distinction further, consider the study by Sherman *et al.* (1983) in which subjects were given the task of estimating the probability of a victory by one particular football team in a forthcoming match. All subjects were required to read a passage about the two teams giving detailed factual information possibly relevant to each team's chances of winning. Subjects read these passages under two quite different instructional sets — either they believed they would be required to recall as many facts as possible from the passage, or that they were required to form an impression of the match outcome as they were reading. After having read the passage, some subjects were also required to produce possible explanations for a hypothetical victory by one specified team. Previous research, which has been discussed earlier in this chapter, would lead one to expect that the task of having to account for why one particular team might win the match should systematically shift probability judgements of the expected result in the direction favouring that team. As expected, subjects given the recall set came to believe it more probable that the outcome explained would also occur in fact. However, virtually no such differences were found in those groups that had been required to form an impression of the likely outcome of the game *prior* to having to explain a particular outcome. That is, in the presence of a structured and organized schema consistent with one particular outcome, explaining an alternative outcome does little to change subjective probabilities.

The implication of these findings is that manipulations of availability via imagined scenarios or explanations of particular outcomes is only likely to be effective under conditions where the individual has no pre-formed opinion on the issue to be rated. Where no such previous impression exists, presumably subjects access information from the imagined scenario or explained outcome when making their judgement. When a previous impression does exist, however, all that a subject needs to do is to retrieve that pre-formed opinion, and this alone will suffice to form the basis of a judgement. If such is the case, one would expect that in the case of subjects forming an opinion for the first time, there will be correlation between judgemental bias and the selective recall of facts that have been provided and/or generated. In a second experiment reported by Sherman et al. (1983) exactly these results were found. Shift in judgement was correlated with a measure of recall bias in those subjects who had been given a recall set (.61) but not in those subjects previously given impression set instructions (.24).

Given these findings, it is not clear that we should expect a correlation between the extent of judgemental bias in an abnormal mood state and the ease with which specific negative events can be recalled. To examine this issue, we required anxious subjects and normal controls to rate the subjective risk of a number of negative and positive future events, and also to recall or imagine specific examples of such events (Mathews and MacLeod, unpublished). If probability judgements depend on availability of relevant information, one would expect to find a correlation between the extent of judgemental bias and the latency with which subjects could either recall or imagine specific instances of positive or negative events. In fact, although anxious subjects judged negative events as significantly more likely than did non-anxious controls, and tended to be more rapid in imagining negative events than were non-anxious subjects, there was no correlation between probability and speed of producing an image. There were no significant differences in latency to recall events between groups, and no correlation between these latencies and probability ratings. While it could be argued that latency is only one out of many possible indices of availability, latency measures were found to be very highly associated with other indices such as the total number of events of that type which could be recalled.

Although not conclusive, it would certainly appear possible that the inflated subjective risk judgements which occur in mood disorders arise from pre-formed impressions rather than being formulated at the time on the basis of the recall of specific examples or one's current mood state. The question remains of the manner in which such pre-formed impressions could arise. One plausible explanation arises from consideration of results cited in Chapter 3, concerning perceptual bias favouring threat-related information. If we suppose that when under stress high trait anxious individuals show a consistent tendency to attend to mildly or ambiguously threatening stimuli in their environment, it seems likely that they will form the impression of an environment in which dangerous events are relatively common. Equally, if depressed individuals frequently rehearse thoughts of inevitable disaster (see Chapter 7) a similar inflation of negative probabilities will result. Thus no relationship will be expected between subjective risk and later retrieval of specific episodes, since all that is required is the recall of an earlier impression about the frequency of unpleasant events. Similarly, during the process of recovery a cognitive shift away from possible threat or disaster will lead to the gradual development of an alternative impression, and subjective risk estimates will decline.

8.6 INTERPRETATION OF AMBIGUOUS EVENTS

On the basis of the foregoing discussion, it seems reasonable to expect that emotional disorders might be associated with an increased tendency to interpret ambiguous events in a threatening manner. In the same way that anxiety states are associated with selective allocation of attentional resources to the location of threat cues (McLeod et al., 1986) a similar attentional bias might be expected whenever there are two competing interpretations for the same event.

Suppose you wake with a start in the middle of the night thinking you heard a noise, but all is quiet. What do you suppose woke you up? Faced with imaginary scenarios of this kind, anxious and depressed subjects appear to be more likely than controls to offer a threatening interpretation. In the study by Butler and Mathews (1983), after first providing an open-ended response, subjects were required to place possible explanatory alternatives in the order in which they would be most likely to come to mind in a similar situation. Threatening explanations (e.g. it could be a burglar) were ranked as more likely to come to mind by anxious and depressed subjects than they were by normal controls.

Clearly there are a number of possible interpretive schemata that one could use in understanding such ambiguous scenarios or equivalent real life events. We have discussed the extent to which emotional disorders may be associated with systematic bias in the use of such different schemata in Chapter 6, and there is considerable overlap between the concept of judgement and selection of schemata in order to arrive at an inference. In this chapter we have been concerned for the most part with reported subjective judgements of uncertain situations, rather than with comprehension and inference. However, this is necessarily an arbitrary division, and in some of the experimental paradigms that have been used it is not clear whether reports should be classed as subjective judgements, or as inferences which have been arrived at through nonconscious processing.

Eysenck, MacLeod and Mathews (1987) required subjects differing in level of trait anxiety to write down homophones as they were read out in list form. Homophones consist of words that have more than one meaning associated with the same pronounced sound, and in this case they consisted of words where one of the meanings was neutral, while the other was mildly threatening (e.g. dye, die; pane, pain). In such homophones one or other of the meanings tends to be dominant, and this was balanced so that in half of the words the dominant meaning was threatening and in the other half it was non-threatening. Similarly, half of the threatening meanings were physical and half were social. Anxiety level of subjects did not affect results associated with these last two factors, but overall there was a highly significant correlation between trait anxiety score and the total number of threatening spellings chosen for the homophones. As expected, the higher the trait anxiety level the more threatening interpretations were selected.

In an extension of this work Eysenck, Mathews and Richards (unpublished) used a paradigm in which anxious and non-anxious subjects read sentences that have either a threatening or non-threatening interpretation (e.g. 'The men watched as the chest was opened'). If anxious subjects are biased in the interpretation that they make of such sentences, we can expect that they would be more likely to select disambiguated threatening as opposed to non-threatening versions as having the same meaning (e.g. 'The men watched as the chest was cut open' vs. 'The men watched as the lid of the chest was opened'). Preliminary results using such a paradigm have shown significant differences in the expected direction, with currently anxious patients selecting more threatening versions than did either non-anxious controls or patients who had fully recovered.

As in most of the judgement tasks considered previously, the mechanism underlying the effects observed in these last two paradigms is not entirely clear. It may be that a relatively automated and nonconscious process is involved, in which emotionally disturbed subjects perceive ambiguous events as unambiguously unpleasant or dangerous. Alternatively, such subjects may be well aware of the ambiguity present in situations, but then select the more unpleasant version for further processing. In the last paradigm, for example, anxious subjects may have been aware of both the surgical and container meanings of chest, but then subsequently chose the more threatening meaning when required to make a choice. Even if this response bias explanation is partially correct, however, other paradigms involving text comprehension (discussed in Chapter 6) lead us to believe that anxious and depressed subjects also make inferences at the time of encoding which are biased in a mood-congruent direction. Thus whatever the exact mechanism, the experience of a mood-disordered individual will be that of a relatively threatening and upsetting environment.

8.7 CLINICAL JUDGEMENTS AND DE-BIASING

The discussion earlier in this chapter of heuristics and biases common in normal individuals suggests that clinicians will not be immune from making similar errors. Of particular relevance to clinical judgements is the early work of the Chapmans (Chapman, 1967: Chapman and Chapman, 1967, 1969) and the later studies that have extended their conclusions. These researchers were originally interested in why clinicians persist in believing that certain features of projective test responses are diagnostic of emotional disorders, despite evidence that they were actually invalid. The Chapmans hypothesised that clinicians' prior beliefs about the aetiology of certain conditions led them to perceive an illusory association between specific reactions and diagnostic category. That this was indeed the case could be demonstrated by providing clinical judges with totally random pairings between test reactions and individual clients, and showing that an illusory correlation persisted despite the lack of any real association. It would seem that the occasional random pairings which apparently confirm a clinician's prior theory are particularly salient, and for this reason are noticed and retained, while disconfirming instances are ignored or forgotten. More recent reviews of this and subsequent work are provided by Ross (1977) and Turk and Salovey (1986).

If the use of heuristics and consequent biases are so common, what corrective measures can be taken? Although the obvious answer is to warn people of their existence, abstract educational methods alone appear to have limited success in removing bias from intuitive judgements. Most discussions of methods which could be used to reduce bias suggest that, beyond educating judges about common sources or error, it is most helpful to provide corrective feedback which allows individuals to observe the nature of judgemental bias in their own responses. Specific errors, such as the confirmation bias, can be countered to some extent by practising corrective heuristics, such as listing reasons why one's initial solution might be wrong (Turk and Salovey, 1986).

De-biasing research may eventually lead to helpful suggestions that can be used in cognitive or behavioural therapies, although relatively little work has been specifically directed at modifying the powerful judgemental biases encountered in emotional disorders. Consider, for example, the problem of an anxious and hypochondriacal patient who is convinced that palpitations are a warning of imminent heart disease. Such a conviction is likely to be maintained by a series of heuristics and biases. Vivid and emotionally arousing scenarios of heart attacks, derived from the media, family or friends, may be a particularly compelling and available form of evidence. Palpitations are a representative symptom of heart disease, although in using this heuristic the client is overlooking the high base rate of palpitations which occur in the absence of physical health problems. Once convinced that a threat of heart disease is present, the confirmation bias will ensure that attention is selectively drawn to corroborating evidence while disconfirming instances will be ignored.

De-biasing attempts in such a client might be attempted in the context of cognitive therapy in the following ways. The high emotional salience of thoughts and images may be pointed out, while encouraging the client to see that they constitute ideas rather than real evidence. Attention may be drawn to the high rate of palpitations found in normals, and the client might be encouraged to gather information about the frequency of palpitations among healthy friends. Perhaps most important, given the documented power of pre-formed causal hypotheses, may be to provide an alternative causal model which the client can use in actively countering judgemental bias. By offering the client a model in which frightening scenarios of heart disease may cause autonomic symptoms which in turn serve to maintain anxiety, therapists may be able to help their clients to use judgemental heuristics in a positive rather than a negative way.

In the clinical example cited at the beginning of this chapter we posed the question of whether emotional disorders are systematically associated with distortions in judgement, such as subjective probability. A great deal of evidence has been summarized to show that, although judgemental distortions are also common among non-emotionally disturbed populations, depressed and anxious individuals are indeed characterized by particular types of bias which distinguish them from normals. Hence emotionally disturbed people judge their performance more negatively, consider they have less control over success, rate the risk of unpleasant future events as more likely, and interpret ambiguous events in a more threatening manner. Many of these effects can be attributed to the use of current-mood state as evidence, or to the effects of mood in making congruent events more available. Certainly, the characteristic distortions observed become more pronounced as mood becomes more negative, and tend to reverse on recovery. On the other hand, some research suggests that judgemental biases cannot be wholly attributed to short-term mood changes, and perhaps depend on previously acquired impressions and strategies. To the extent that this is true, the results of de-biasing research are likely to find useful applications in the psychological treatment of emotional disorders.

Chapter 9

Nonconscious Processing

This book has raised many issues about the relation between conscious and nonconscious processing. It is now time to address these directly. As discussed in Chapter 7, much theorising about the function of nonconscious processes assumes a simple isomorphic mapping with processes which are consciously accessible. However if the relationship is more complex, it is difficult to assess whether, in changing conscious cognitive appraisals during therapy, one is modifying the underlying bias in information-processing. A further reason for examining the way in which conscious and nonconscious mental processes interact is to prepare the ground for building a framework into which the results of the experiments on emotional disorders can be integrated. We shall leave such attempts at integration until the final chapter, where we shall also discuss the role of underlying processing biases in the maintenance and remediation of emotional disturbance. First, however, we shall review some relevant issues concerning the relationship between conscious and non-conscious processing.

9.1 HISTORICAL OVERVIEW

The conceptual distinction between conscious and nonconscious mental processes enjoyed a long and relatively uncontroversial history before the advent of experimental psychology in the nineteenth century. Pascal anticipated the psychoanalytical concept of the unconscious by three centuries when he wrote: 'the heart has its reasons, which reason knows not.' Similarly, the seventeenth-century English Platonist John Norris provided a prophetic description of a more cognitive account when he made the claim: 'there are infinitely more ideas impressed on our minds than we can possibly attend to or perceive.' Indeed, Whyte (1978) reviews excerpts from the writings of over fifty philosophers, between AD 130 and 1800, all of which demonstrate an awareness of both conscious and nonconscious mental operations.

The nineteenth-century experimental psychologists, such as James and Ebbinghaus, were severely restricted by their exclusion of nonconscious processes from scientific investigation. Although Freud attempted to reintroduce a more detailed account of the unconscious, defining it both in terms of a hypothetical unique content (instincts, motivation, repressed memories, etc.) and distinctive processes (pleasure principle and defence mechanisms), the psychoanalytical approach was ultimately too unreliable to qualify amongst experimental psychologists as a formal scientific method. The thorny issue of consciousness was subsequently simply avoided by the advent of behaviourism in the mid-1920s (Watson, 1925), and for the next 35 years scientific progress within psychology was restricted to the rigorous study of how environmental factors influence and control behaviour. Ultimately, however, theoretical psycholgists found the constraints of behaviourism too restrictive and in the late 1950s, by borrowing concepts from the newly established science of information technology, it became possible to reintroduce mentalism to psychology without reducing scientific rigour. In this way the information-processing paradigm was established. As this approach developed so the distinction between conscious and nonconscious processes gradually re-emerged. Early resistance to reinstate the concept of the unconscious has left a legacy of terminological confusion, with labels such as 'pre-conscious', 'pre-attentive', pre-cognitive', etc. being used in preference to the term 'unconscious', with its controversial Freudian implications.

The past fifteen years or so have seen a great revival of interest in this issue within experimental psychology. Experimental psychologists have asked the questions concerning the extent of nonconscious processing. How fully is information processed in the absence of consciousness? Do we comprehend the meaning of stimuli which never reach our awareness? Are the rules of nonconscious processing different from those of conscious processing? How does information enter consciousness, and why? Chapter 1 indicated how the traditional commitment to behaviourism shown by clinical psychologists has been weakened recently by an increased appreciation of how cognitive concepts may illuminate various psychological disorders. In attempting to determine how patients construe their world, clinical psychologists have addressed similar issues concerning consciousness to those which have interested the experimentalists. Can nonconscious processes, such as biased assumptions and inferencing, affect our conscious appraisal of various situations? Can such nonconscious operations be made available to consciousness and, if so, how can this best be achieved? Do certain psychiatric or neurological disorders reflect disruptions in the transfer of information from nonconscious levels into awareness?

Evidence concerning the nature of nonconscious processing is now available from several areas of research. In evaluating this evidence, it is helpful to relate it to two alternative forms of postulate regarding the 'psychological unconscious', introduced by Shevrin and Dickman (1980). The weak form of this postulate states simply that nonconscious processes exist and actively affect conscious processes. The strong form adds that these nonconscious processes follow different laws of organization. Having established the reality of the weak form, and argued that the balance of evidence supports the strong form of this postulate, we shall consider the nature of the relationship between conscious and nonconscious aspects of the processing system. One important issue concerns how information comes to be represented in awareness. It will be seen that different models conceptualise this 'transfer' in rather different ways.

9.2 EVIDENCE FOR NONCONSCIOUS PROCESSING

9.2.1 Verbal Report of Higher-order Cognitive Operations

Few would argue that low-level processes, such as feature extraction, need be available to consciousness. However, it is often assumed that the higher-order cognitive operations underlying choice, evaluation and judgemental behaviour are represented in awareness and can thus be addressed through introspection. Frequently, clinical psychologists will ask patients to report verbally on such higher-order processes. What is the main thing which upsets you about your marriage? Why does this aspect of the situation exacerbate your anxiety? And so on. However, many theorists (e.g. Miller, 1962; Neisser, 1967; J. Mandler, 1975; Nisbett and Wilson, 1977) have argued that such operations in fact proceed nonconsciously. Nisbett and Wilson (1977) provide an extensive review of evidence, which supports the existence of nonconscious higher-order processing by demonstrating that subjects are often entirely inaccurate when asked to report verbally on their cognitive processes. A few examples from the many illustrate the point.

The central idea behind dissonance theory is that behaviour, which is intrinsically undesirable, will, when performed for inadequte extrinsic reasons, be seen as more attractive than when it is performed for adequate extrinsic reasons. Thus, for example, subjects receiving shock in an experiment experience the shock as more aversive when they are given adequate justification for the necessity of the shock procedure by the experimenter (Zimbardo et al. 1969). Closely related to this line of research is attribution theory, which claims that subjects' attitudinal, emotional and behavioural responses to any particular event or experience will be influenced by the particular attributions which that subject makes concerning the event or experience. For example, Storms and Nisbett (1970) treated two groups of insomniacs with a placebo pill. One group of subjects were told that this pill would produce increased heart rate, alertness and other symptoms of insomnia. The other group of subjects were told that the pill would reduce arousal, lower heart rate, and so on. As anticipated the former group's insomnia improved 28 per cent whereas the latter group took 42 per cent longer to get to sleep than they had previously. The most common explanation for such effects is that when the arousal symptoms can easily be attributed to the pill they are interpreted as less threatening, and therefore easier to ignore.

Nisbett and Wilson's central claim, when reviewing such areas of research, is that subjects typically do not mention the influence of dissonance or attributions when asked to report verbally on the factors which influence them. Instead, they produce plausible explanations, which reveal no awareness of their critical influence. For example, the insomniac subjects explained their improvement by reporting that previously worrying problems had been resolved and they had therefore felt more relaxed. All denied having thought about the pills at all. A similar inability to report verbally on awareness of influential factors on a wide range of problem-solving, appraisal and choice behaviours has been demonstrated. When asked to assess the relative quality of four identical pairs of nylon stockings, Nisbett and Wilson's subjects tended strongly to select the stockings on the right-most side of the display. Yet all subjects explained their choice by reference to the quality of material and denied that the article's position had affected their decision in any way.

Nisbett and Wilson argue from this and similar kinds of data that conscious awareness is limited to the products of mental processes, and that the processes themselves are beyond the reach of introspection. Verbal reports are based not on true introspection, but on culturally supplied, implicit, *a priori* causal theories about the likely cognitive operations involved. Such verbal reports will be accurate only to the extent that the actual processes coincidentally correspond to such *a priori* theories. According to this view, the anxious patient may willingly report, for example, that he becomes tense in social situations because he anticipates people are likely to criticize him. However, this may reveal only his *a priori* theory, rather than the actual cognitive basis of his emotion.

While Nisbett and Wilson's review certainly casts doubt upon the validity of subsequent verbal reports concerning higher-order cognitive processes, it has been argued that it provides an inadequate basis for the claim that such processes are necessarily nonconscious (Smith and Miller, 1978; White, 1980). One feature of all the studies reviewed is that there is a separation in time between the report and actual occurrence of the process. This clearly permits the possibility that inaccurate verbal reports may reflect memory failure. In fact, Nisbett and Wilson's discussion acknowledges this possibility when they tell us:

> at this (immediate) point ... subjects have some chance of accurately reporting that a particular stimulus was influential ... at some later point, the existence of the stimulus may be forgotten, or become less available, and thus there would be little chance that it could be correctly identified as influential.

A second problem is that subjects' limited ability to provide accurate verbal reports may not reflect the absence of a conscious representation of the process but rather may stem from a difficulty in translating this conscious representation into a verbal code. This argument also applies to more recent work by Donald Broadbent and his colleagues (Berry and Broadbent, 1984; Broadbent, Fitzgerald and Broadbent, 1986) which has examined subjects' ability to control complex dynamic systems, such as computer-simulated transportation systems or economic systems. Subjects are allowed to interact with the system by changing various parameters and observing the effects, and attempt to achieve certain targets. One central finding in such tasks is that subjects' actual performance improves to levels quite unpredicted by their limited ability to report verbally an understanding of the dynamics of such systems. While one tempting conclusion may be that subjects indeed learn such dynamics nonconsciously, it remains plausible that they are simply unable accurately to translate their conscious experience of the systems' dynamics into a verbal code. This possibility may be more simply illustrated by a common example. We would all admit to consciously experiencing, say, the taste of an apple. However, it is unlikely that we could fully convey the conscious experience of this taste verbally to another individual who had never eaten an apple. This failure does not imply that the taste was only experienced nonconsciously but, rather, that the conscious experience cannot be fully reported verbally. Thus failure to report verbally the nature of a process can never be sufficient to demonstrate a lack of conscious awareness of that process.

The assertion that only the products of processing are available to consciousness, while the processing itself remains nonconscious (e.g. Miller, 1962; Neisser, 1967; Mandler, 1975) can also be criticized on logical grounds (Smith and Miller, 1978; White, 1980). As no satisfactory definitions of mental product and mental process currently exist, there are no criteria whereby a mental event can be defined as one or the other. We run the risk of circularity if we decide to use consciousness as the criterion for making the distinction —calling everything that gets into consciousness product and everything else process — as no experimental predictions can be derived from such a viewpoint.

In summary, then, the results of studies which have investigated the relationship between verbal report and other more objective processing measures are consistent with the weak form of Shevrin and Dickman's (1980) postulate, according to which nonconscious processes do exist which actively affect conscious processing. Such studies, however, have provided little evidence for the stronger claim that such nonconscious processes follow different laws of organization. Furthermore, there are interpretive problems with these data. An inability to report may often reflect memory failure or difficulty in conveying the nature of certain conscious mental events through the use of a verabal code.

Stronger evidence for nonconscious processing is required, and is readily available from other paradigms.

9.2.2 Attentional Studies

In the above section, subjects were seen to be unable to report verbally the way in which certain information influenced their responses. Nevertheless, much of the relevant information which they must have utilised was typically represented in consciousness. Thus they were aware of the reasons supplied by the experimenter for giving shock, they were aware of the stockings' positions, and so on. If subjects' responses could be influenced by information, which itself is *never* represented in consciousness, then this would constitute more concrete evidence for the existence of nonconscious processing. A variety of attentional paradigms provide evidence of this sort. Such studies commonly involve subjects attending to one information source while ignoring another. Although, typically, subjects are never conscious of the semantic content of the unattended message, there is considerable evidence that this information has indeed been nonconsciously processed to a semantic level. The most heavily researched paradigm in this field has been based on the dichotic listening procedure introduced by Cherry (1953). Subjects attend to, and usually 'shadow' or repeat aloud, the message played to one ear, and ignore the message which is simultaneously presented to the other ear. In Chapter 4 we saw how this paradigm has been used to investigate the extent to which threatening material in the ignored message can disrupt anxiety patients' performance on a reaction-time task, despite the subjects being unable to report the content of this unattended message.

Early models of how such selectivity was achieved and maintained (Broadbent, 1958) proposed that signals enter the perceptual system through multiple parallel channels and, prior to awareness, all this information is structurally analysed. On the basis of structural factors alone certain signals are permitted access to a single limited-capacity channel which leads to semantic analysis and, ultimately, to awareness. Even this early filter model, therefore, is consistent with Shevrin and Dickman's weak postulate endorsing the reality of nonconscious operations. There is also a hint of support for Shevrin and Dickman's strong postulate, since such nonconscious operations, by proceeding in parallel and being unconstrained by capacity limitations, can be said to follow different laws of organization from those which govern conscious processes.

Subsequent studies have demonstrated that the processing of unattended input is likely to be more extensive than Broadbent first suggested. Since the meaning of the unattended message has been shown to exert considerable influence, it has been argued that nonconscious processing extends beyond structural analysis to the level of semantic access. Moray (1959) found that subjects often consciously perceive their own name in the unattended message. Treisman's (1960) more powerful demonstration involved instructing subjects to shadow one ear, but unexpectedly switching the messages at the two ears half-way through the task. When this occurred subjects typically switched to shadowing the previously unattended channel. If the information in the ignored ear was not being semantically analaysed, then how could subjects know that it provided a meaningful continuation for the message they had been attending to? Such evidence led Deutsch and Deutsch (1963) to formulate a late selection model of attentional control according to which all stimuli, whether attended or unattended, are fully processed, and selection for conscious awareness occurs subsequently.

A considerable body of research supports this hypothesis. Many studies, employing a range of paradigms (Lewis, 1970; Treisman, Squire and Green, 1974; Underwood, 1976; Philpott and Wilding, 1979) have demonstrated that the processing of an attended message can be biased by semantic attributes of the ignored information. For example, in Mackay's (1973) study, subjects were likely to interpret the sentence 'she sat by the bank' in quite different ways when the words 'river' or 'money' occurred simultaneously in the other ear. Furthermore, there is evidence that subjects not only semantically process unattended information, but also categorise that information, relate it to past learning experiences, and respond with the appropriate emotions, all in the absence of awareness (Corteen and Wood, 1972; Corteen and Dunn, 1974; Von Wright, Anderson and Stenman, 1975; Forster and Govier, 1978; Govier and Pitts, 1982). In these studies an initial phase conditioned a GSR response to a certain class of stimulus word, such as city names, by pairing such words with shock. In the second phase these words, together with others, were presented to the unattended ear in a dichotic listening task. Despite their absence of awareness for this material, subjects showed a GSR response not only to the originally shocked words, but also to synonyms and members of the same category.

There is therefore good evidence from attentional studies that extensive semantic processing can proceed nonconsciously. In reviewing this area of research Posner et al. (1973) proposed that consciousness is bound up with a limited-capacity mechanism which 'serves to impose a serial order on what are essentially widespread parallel processes initiated by a stimulus'. Such a formulation is clearly consistent with Shevrin and Dickman's strong postulate regarding nonconscious processing operations. According to Posner et al. such operations not only occur but also follow distinctively different laws of organization.

Many of the attentional studies, however, could be criticised for failing adequately to ensure that subjects were *never* consciously aware of the unattended information (cf. Holender, 1986). Most commonly, subjects were simply asked at the end of the experiment whether they could report anything they had heard in the unattended channel. Sometimes they also attempted to recognize words from this channel, among distractors, in a subsequent test. While the results of such questioning suggest that subjects were indeed unaware of the unattended information, it could be argued that occasional momentary awareness may mediate semantic processing, even though this momentary awareness may be of insufficient duration to permit subsequent recall or recognition. Attempts to check for momentary awareness, by unexpectedly stopping the tape and immediately asking subjects to report the unattended information, have often failed to support this argument (e.g. Bargh, 1982). However, Glucksberg and Cohen (1970) found good evidence for memory of unattended material at delays of five seconds, and Klapp and Lee (1974) argue that this memory can persist for up to 10 seconds. Furthermore, when the probability of momentary awareness is reduced, then some of the evidence for the semantic processing of unattended information is weakened. For example, Newstead and Dennis (1979) modified Mackay's (1972) procedure to make attentional switching less likely. The gaps between sentences were shortened, and filler material was added to the unattended channel to ensure that critical words did not emerge out of silence as in Mackay's study, which Poulton (1956) has argued may provoke a shift of attention. Under such conditions Newstead and Dennis found it impossible to replicate Mackay's original results which, they therefore argued, may have been mediated by momentary awareness arising through attention switch.

Thus attentional studies cannot be taken as conclusive evidence supporting the occurrences of extensive nonconscious processing. One problem is that, in such studies, all subjects are aware of hearing 'something' in the unattended ear. They are thus conscious of the existence of the unattended message, they could voluntarily bring that message into awareness, and they must retrospectively assess the depth of awareness which actually occurred — a fairly complex task which may lead to erroneous reports. However, it is possible to present stimuli in ways that preclude the possibility of awareness, even under instruction to apprehend consciously the stimulus information. Though subjects typically cannot detect the existence of such stimuli whatsoever, there is nevertheless evidence that the information is nonconsciously semantically processed, and exerts an influence on conscious operations. The next section reviews this evidence in more detail.

9.2.3 Effects of Subliminal Stimuli

The hypothesis that subliminal stimulation can influence conscious processing, while giving rise to *no* intervening perceptual experience whatsoever, has been frequently investigated throughout the history of experimental psychology (Sidis, 1898; Stroh, Shaw and Washbourne, 1908; Coover, 1917; Baker, 1937; A. Williams, 1938; J.G. Miller, 1939, 1940; Spence and Holland, 1962; Gordon, 1967; Dixon, 1968, 1971, 1981; Marcel and Patterson, 1978; Marcel, 1983a, 1983b). Most experiments have ensured that the stimulus evokes no conscious perceptual experience by reducing its energy content below that which would permit awareness. This has been achieved by reducing either stimulus intensity or duration. A wide range of studies has demonstrated that, even when stimuli are made undetectable in this way, they are nevertheless processed. The earliest experiments to reveal structural processing of undetectable stimuli were conducted by Dunlap (1900). Dunlap found that the Muller–Lyer illusion, in which two lines of equal length are judged to be unequal, still occurs even when the 'arrows' which produce the illusion are too faint to be consciously perceived. Although later researchers have made methodological criticisms and reported some replication failures (e.g. Titchener and Pyle, 1907; Trimble and Eriksen, 1966), there are now numerous studies which, under more rigorous conditions, have demonstrated that the structural properties of undetectably brief tachistoscopic displays can indeed affect conscious perception (Bressler, 1931; Smith and Henriksson, 1955; Farné, 1963; Worthington, 1964; Walker and Myer, 1978; Gellatly, 1980).

There is also compelling evidence that undetectable stimuli are not only processed structurally, but reach the level of semantic representation. For example, the semantic content of a subliminally presented message has been shown to affect the conscious perception of expressionless faces (Smith, Spence and Klein, 1959; Allison, 1963; Somekh and Wilding, 1973; Henley, 1975; Sackeim, Packer and Gur, 1977). Descriptions of such faces are significantly more pleasant when accompanied by the subliminal word 'happy', rather than 'angry'. It has also been reported that measures such as imagery (Henley and Dixon, 1974; Mykel and Daves, 1979), projective test responses (Goldstein and Barthol, 1960) and dream content (Fisher, 1960) may be influenced by the semantics of stimuli made entirely undetectable by their brevity or low intensity.

Stimuli can be made undetectable by techniques other than brevity or low intensity though, as yet, relatively little effort has been made to compare systematically the processing consequences of such variations. Backward visual masking is a rather different technique which has been employed to render stimuli undetectable (cf. Neisser, 1963, 1967). This technique involves brief presentation of stimuli under conditions which would normally permit conscious perception. However, the immediate subsequent presentation of a different stimulus can 'mask' or obscure the earlier one, which therefore is never experienced consciously. Two different kinds of masking field have been employed, each producing a characteristic function. In its simplest form the mask is a high energy (i.e. bright), usually homogeneous, field. This procedure has been termed energy masking and such masking effects are most pronounced when the two stimuli are simultaneous, dropping off gradually as they are separated in time (Kolers, 1962; Eriksen and Collins, 1964, 1965). Alternatively, the masking field can be a patterned figure, the energy content of which need not exceed the stimulus field. Pattern masking produces a rather different function from energy masking, with the effectiveness of the mask initially increasing as it is separated in time from the stimulus. Beyond a delay of 20 to 100 ms the effectiveness of the mask drops off again (Kolers, 1962; Fehrer and Smith, 1962).

Those studies which have investigated the ultimate fate of the masked stimulus have yielded contradictory results. Some have failed to find any evidence that such stimuli achieve the level of semantic representation (e.g. Severance and Dyer, 1973), whereas others provide evidence that meaning is indeed nonconsciously processed (e.g. Marcel, Katz and Smith, 1974; Marcel, 1976, 1980, 1983a; Allport, 1977). One possibility is that the precise nature of the masking procedure is critically important. The basis of the masking effect is incompletely understood, and it has been argued that energy and pattern masking are most probably mediated by different mechanisms (Turvey, 1973; Marcel, 1983a). Energy masking is thought to operate peripherally, obscuring the stimulus before any central processing has occurred. In contrast, pattern masking may operate centrally, thus permitting nonconscious processing to take place. In support of this claim, Turvey (1973) reports that pattern masking, but not energy masking, will occur dichoptically, i.e. when the initial stimulus and the mask are presented to separate eyes.

Although pattern masking can make a stimulus entirely undetectable it would appear that semantic processing nevertheless proceeds in the absence of awareness. Marcel (1983a) presented subjects with a stimulus field which either contained a single word or was blank. The effectiveness of the subsequent pattern mask was gradually enhanced by decreasing the asynchrony between the onset of the two stimuli. Subjects were required to make three judgements: (a) Presence: did any word appear? (b) Graphic: which of two subsequently presented words had the more similar structural appearance to the masked word? (c) Meaning: which of two subsequently presented words had the more similar meaning to the masked word? The subjects were instructed to guess an answer for (b) and (c), even if they did not believe a word had actually appeared. As the asynchrony between stimulus and masking fields were decreased, subjects first lost their ability to report accurately the presence or absence of a word. While simple detection was at chance level, however, they could still accurately judge the graphic structure and the meaning of the word, although such judgements were typically experienced as guesses. A further decrease in the word–mask onset asynchrony reduced graphic judgements to chance level without eliminating accuracy on the semantic judgement task. Clearly, this is powerful evidence that semantic processing need not be mediated by conscious awareness. Marcel (1976, 1985a) has employed a range of paradigms which further supplement this evidence. For example, in a variant of the Stroop paradigm, undetectable pattern-masked colour words (such as red or blue) were found to reduce colour naming latency for congruent colour patches and to increase such latency for incongruent colour patches. Indeed, the masked words had an identical effect in this study to unmasked, consciously perceived, colour words.

Similarly, Marcel reported a variant on the traditional lexical priming paradigm (Meyer, Schvaneveldt and Ruddy, 1972; Schvaneveldt and Meyer, 1973). Meyer and his colleagues showed that, when subjects have to categorize letter-strings as words or non-words, they classify words faster when they are preceded by a semantic associate. Thus BUTTER is classified as a word faster if it follows BREAD than if it follows NURSE. Marcel demonstrated that this priming effect occurs with equivalent magnitude, even when the first word is rendered undetectable through pattern masking.

Such pattern masking studies appear, at the very least, to confirm Shevrin and Dickman's weak postulate regarding the reality of nonconscious processing. Marcel (1980) provides additional evidence, also using pattern masking, which suggests that conscious and nonconscious processes may follow different rules. In this study, subjects again were required to decide whether letter-strings were words. Two words preceded the critical string. Immediately prior to this string was a polysemous word, with one of its two meanings possibly sharing a semantic relationship with the target word. The first word was related semantically to one meaning of the polysemous word. Thus subjects may be sequentially presented with HAND–PALM–WRIST or with HAND–PALM–TREE. Without pattern masking the word PALM facilitated classification of WRIST but not TREE when preceded by HAND. Therefore when consciousness was permitted, only one meaning of PALM was represented, and this was constrained by prior context. However, when PALM was pattern masked then it facilitated classification of both WRIST and TREE, even when preceded by HAND. Thus both interpretations of PALM appear to be represented simultaneously when the word is processed nonconsciously.

Marcel (1983b) argues from such data that nonconscious perceptual processes 'automatically redescribe sensory data into every representational form and to the highest level of description available to the organism'. Such multiple representations exist simultaneously, unconstrained by capacity limitations, and it is only when representations enter our limited-capacity, serially organized consciousness that inhibitory processes operate to suppress ambiguity. Thus Marcel's view is firmly in keeping with Shevrin and Dickman's (1980) strong postulate that fundamentally different rules govern conscious and nonconscious mental operations.

It is important to note that Holender (1986) has criticized certain pattern masking studies on methodological grounds. In particular, he has shown concern over the manner in which the appropriate stimulus mask onset asynchrony is often calibrated in an initial block of trials, to establish an interval at which subjects are unable to report accurately the presence or absence of a stimulus. Holender points out that, if the eyes are not fully dark-adapted during these early calibrating trials, then as dark adaptation progresses the stimuli encountered later in the study may be consciously perceived. However, not all pattern masking studies are vulnerable to such criticisms. For example, when Marcel (1983a) mixed priming and detection conditions throughout his experimental trials, he still found reliable priming in the absence of any ability accurately to detect the presence of primes.

This review of evidence for nonconscious information-processing, obtained from verbal reports of cognitive operations, attentional studies, and experiments on weak, brief or masked stimuli, makes no pretention to be exhaustive. The range of paradigms providing further evidence is wide indeed. Undetectable olfactory stimuli have been shown to influence cognitive and affective judgements (Cowley, Johnson and Brooksbanck 1977; Kirk-Smith et al., 1978). Tones with frequencies higher than the audible spectrum have been conditioned to produce GSRs (Martin, Hawryluk and Guse, 1974). Stabilized retinal images which have faded from awareness nevertheless evoke the same visual cortical response as when they were consciously perceived (Riggs and Whittle, 1967). Ruddock and Waterfield (1978) report that monocularly presented red patterns, entirely imperceptible to their colour-blind subjects, could lead to a stereoscopic image when an appropriate, perceptible stimulus was presented to the other eye. Weiskrantz's (1977) patient, blind in his left visual field through neurological damage to his right calcarine fissure, could accurately 'guess' the locality, orientation and form of stimuli presented to this field, while insisting that he could perceive nothing whatsoever.

The current wealth of such evidence is beyond the scope of this text, and the reader is referred to Dixon (1981) for a more extensive review. However, the selected examples considered in this chapter suffice to demonstrate that extensive higher-order information-processing, including the analysis of both structure and meaning, the retrieval of associates, conditioning, access to past learning experiences involving similar information, and the evocation of both cognitive and affective responses, may not be mediated by conscious awareness. Furthermore, the weight of evidence suggests that conscious awareness may actually restrict information-processing in certain ways, particularly by imposing the constraints of capacity limitation and seriality on those operations which are conducted with awareness.

Six decades ago our psychoanalytically-oriented predecessors wrestled with the problem of formulating a credible account of the unconscious. Paradoxically, perhaps, having gathered such convincing evidence for the existence of extensive and elaborate nonconscious information-processing in more recent years, contemporary psychologists are now faced with the opposite problem of adequately accounting for the nature and purpose of consciousness itself. How do certain aspects of processing result in a conscious experience, and why? The next section examines some alternative models developed in response to this issue.

9.3 ACCOUNTING FOR CONSCIOUSNESS

While the evidence reviewed so far strongly suggests that a considerable amount of processing may proceed nonconsciously, it is clearly also the case that we all do experience conscious thoughts. Clinical psychologists are often faced with evaluating the significance of such conscious experiences, and may perhaps attempt to modify certain clinical disorders through techniques aimed at directly changing such patterns of thinking. It is therefore important to consider what aspects of information-processing correspond to conscious experience, and how such representations may be achieved. Shallice (1972) has suggested that consciousness may simply correspond to increased levels of activation within specific cognitive subsystems, which will increase their processing efficiency. Efficiency is of greatest importance for relatively complex processes, or those which have been poorly learned, and in consequence such processes may only take place consciously. With extensive practice, however, even complex operations may become over-learned, and can thus proceed in the absence of awareness. There is, indeed, ample evidence that many processing skills can be automatized in this way (e.g. Simpson, 1972; Schneider and Shiffrin, 1977; Shiffrin and Schneider, 1977). However, there are certain classes of mental operation which, it has been argued, can never occur without awareness (Mandler, 1975). Included among such operations are comparisons, serial ordering, conceptual grouping, and so forth. Such relational operations require the simultaneous juxtaposition of two or more 'mental contents' and, according to Mandler, this can only take place in consciousness. Through this mechanism consciousness permits the choice and selection of action systems on the basis of a current consideration of their likely relative merits; long-range plans can be interrogated and modified, and novel processing strategies can be formulated. Following the same line, Yates (1985) construes the content of awareness as an integrated model of the world — either real or imagined. This model is capable of simulating future events, anticipating outcomes, and thereby formulating appropriate actions, Ultimately, therefore, the content of consciousness forms the basis of our intentional behaviour.

Researchers have attempted to account for consciousness in rather different ways. Perhaps the simplest approach, within an information-processing framework, involves labelling one particular, usually late, stage of processing as 'conscious identification' or 'phenomenal awareness'. Erdelyi (1974) locates such a stage 'in or near the short-term storage system, beyond the encoding system but prior to long-term memory'. Indeed, there was considerable consensus for such a view among theorists at this time (e.g. Sperling, 1967; Haber and Hershenson 1973). Such an account postulates that information flows through a linear series of processing stages, often including feedback mechanisms reflecting the effects of attention or motivation which may modify signal strength. If information reaches the stage of conscious identification, then it becomes represented in awareness. Whether or not information reaches this stage depends upon its level of activation as it passes through the processing system. However, simple linear stage models have been rather discredited by evidence, some of which has already been reviewed, that information can be fully processed and enter LTM without ever passing through a stage where it has been represented in awareness (e.g. Fisher, 1960).

Mandler (1975) argues instead that consciousness is not a separate stage of processing but, rather, corresponds to a particular state of a cognitive structure. Cognitive structures may under certain circumstances become conscious but, when they do not, they continue to function nonconsciously. Certain operations already discussed, such as choice, reappraisal, comparision, etc., can only be performed by structures in the conscious state. The limited capacity of consciousness reflects the fact that only a restricted number of structures may be maintained in this state at any point in time. Mandler gives little indication, however, of the factors determining which processing structures become conscious. He argues that this will depend upon 'specific organism–environment interactions', though the precise mechanism remains unclear.

One line of argument is that processing structures vary on a continuum of activation, and it is their energy level which determines whether consciousness is achieved. Shallice (1972, 1978) has embodied a similar notion in his approach. He argues that the structures capable of becoming conscious are a set of action systems, and distinguishes these from perceptual, motivational and effector systems. The brain contains a vast number of action systems, each of which operates to attain a pre-set goal by means of output either to another action system or to effector units. The speed and accuracy with which an action system operates depends on its level of activation which can vary continuously, though simple or highly-learned action systems require only a minimum level for normal functioning. Level of activation will be influenced by the inputs, which every action system receives, from perceptual and motivational systems. However, one important feature of Shallice's cybernetic model is that each action system is inhibited by every other action system, the amount of inhibition increasing monotonically with the others' activation. In consequence, only one action system can become strongly active, or dominant, at any given time. It is this dominant action system (or, more precisely, inputs to this system) which corresponds to the content of consciousness. Though only one system can become dominant, others will continue to function at a much lower level of activity. Nonconscious processing will therefore proceed in those action systems capable of operating at such levels, i.e. those which are not complex or which have been highly learned.

Like Mandler, therefore, Shallice associates consciousness with the state of a processing structure. The operating rules of any action system remain unchanged whether it becomes dominant or not; only its speed and accuracy is affected.

A radically different account of consciousness has been offered by Marcel (1983b) and Yates (1985). Marcel's model was developed primarily to accommodate phenomenological aspects of perception, and his approach was subsequently developed and elaborated by Yates to encompass all aspects of awareness. Marcel's original model will be considered in some detail.

Marcel begins by rejecting those accounts which have treated the transfer from nonconscious to conscious processing primarily as a matter of activation strength. This is partly a reaction to his own experimental results. For example, Marcel (1983a) conducted a lexical priming study, where the prime was a masked word. This prime could be rapidly repeated, with its mask, from 1 to 20 times, before the target word was presented for lexical decision. Repetition of the prime was found to increase the energy of its semantic representation, as indexed by a steady growth in the magnitude of the priming effect. The probability of correct detection, however, remained unchanged as repetitions increased. On the basis of this finding, Marcel argues that 'all positions which rely only on energy for awareness seem to be discredited.' In addition, he dismisses such accounts due to their inadequate treatment of qualitative difference between conscious and nonconscious mental operations.

According to Marcel, phenomenal experience is neither identical to, nor directly reflects, the representations yielded by those processing structures capable of operating without awareness. Conscious experience requires a constructive act, whereby distinctive processes operate to retrieve and synthesise the output of nonconscious systems, thereby transforming this information into a qualitatively different representational code.

Marcel conceptualizes nonconscious processing as extensive and elaborate. Information is analysed, transformed and redescribed quite independently of consciousness, to the highest level of every possible representational form available to the organism. Such processing is not bound by capacity, and whenever there is ambiguity of any type all possible parsings and interpretations will be carried out and represented. Nonconscious analysis therefore leads to multiple representations at every level and in every available code, and such representations are not segmented in any way — for example, into events, objects or episodes. Phenomenal experience consists in the imposition of a particular segmentation, structure and interpretation on the records of nonconscious processing.

To clarify how this occurs, Marcel invokes the concept of 'perceptual hypotheses' which reside in LTM and mediate access to consciousness. Like Minsky's (1975) concept of 'frames', or Rumelhart's (1978) notion of 'schemata', perceptual hypotheses are stereotypical representations corresponding to complex structural descriptions of world knowledge. Together they form an exhaustive set of canonical representations for all things we are capable of consciously perceiving. A perceptual hypothesis is conceived of as a structural description which specifies its criterial features, non-criterial features, and their relationship. The values of those features, however, are left open to particular instantiations which vary from occasion to occasion. A fuller discussion of similar hypothetical structures will be found in Chapter 6 of this text.

The important point for our present consideration is that perceptual hypotheses are activated automatically if any of their criterial features can be detected among the immediate records of nonconscious processing. In practice, multiple hypotheses will be simultaneously activated and tested in parallel against the records of nonconscious processing. Which hypothesis will be selected depends partly on factors such as expectancy and frequency. However the chosen hypothesis will usually be that which accounts for most data in the records, and does so at the highest possible level of description. At any moment, what we are aware of is that hypothesis instantiated by the fit of data in the relevant records.

Thus in Marcel's model, data are recovered from the record of nonconscious processing, and a subset of these data is synthesized into a unitary model by being fitted into the highest-level perceptual hypothesis which can accommodate the greatest proportion of the record. We then become conscious of this instantiated hypothesis. By this account, consciousness depends upon two independent factors. First, nonconscious operations must leave adequate records for a sufficient period to enable hypothesis-matching to take place. Reducing stimulus intensity or duration (e.g. Henley, 1975; Sackeim et al., 1977) may result in inadequate records, whereas backward masking (e.g. Allport 1977; Marcel 1976, 1980, 1983a) may over-write such records, and therefore curtail their duration below that necessary for hypothesis-matching. Second, the range of perceptual hypotheses actually stored in LTM will impose limits on the potential scope of awareness. Conscious representations of events or episodes can only be accurate to the extent that appropriate hypotheses exist in LTM. It is interesting to note that the studies in Nisbett and Wilson's (1977) review involved specifically those situations where no schemata or hypotheses are likely to exist in LTM which can accurately account for the records of the nonconscious processing which actually took place. Introspection may have been inaccurate in these tasks, not because the records of the nonconscious operations involved could not be recovered, but rather because they could not be synthesized into an accurate pre-existing schema. Nisbett and Wilson argue that subjects supply introspective reports 'not by consulting a memory of the mediating process, but by applying *a priori* causal theories'. However, Marcel's model permits the existence of both *a priori* hypotheses *and* access to records of nonconscious processing. The *a priori* causal theories apparent in the introspective reports of Nisbett and Wilson's subjects may in fact correspond to the highest-level, existing perceptual hypothesis which could accommodate the greatest amount of data from the recovered records.

Can patients therefore be trained consciously to access cognitive processes previously beyond the reach of introspection? Could idiosyncracies in nonconscious processing underlie certain clinical conditions? In the final section we briefly examine consciousness from a clinical perspective, and illustrate how the reviewed research can aid our ability to understand, and further investigate, some of the central issues involved.

9.4 CLINICAL IMPLICATIONS

A central goal of cognitive therapy involves enabling patients to access their 'automatic thinking' in order to recognize its erroneous nature and substitute more rational, strategically controlled lines of processing where appropriate. Beck and Emery (1985) describe automatic thoughts as interpretations, inferences or predictions which occur so rapidly that the patient is often aware only of the emotion they generate. The implication, therefore, is that the interpretations or predictions themselves are often not spontaneously reportable. However, Beck does not clearly address the important issue of *why* such automatic thoughts may be difficult to report. One possibility is that they may occur with only momentary awareness, perhaps because they are not fully attended to, and therefore produce a relatively weak memory trace. Since such thoughts could otherwise be qualitatively similar to phenomenal mental events, they would be amenable to conscious representation. Straightforward introspection could therefore be a useful technique to access automatic thoughts and, indeed, most therapists do rely largely upon this approach. Patients are encouraged to search for answers to questions like: 'What did you think your wife was *really* saying when she told you to wash up — how did you interpret it deep down, automatically?' Or, 'You felt panicky before the speech; were you perhaps having the automatic thought that you would mess it up?' If the difficulty in reporting automatic thoughts does in fact stem from memory failure then another obvious implication is that introspective access will be most successful if attempted immediately, while it is taking place, as indexed by the occurrence of an emotional response.

Another possibility, however, is that a thought may be automatic, not because it has only briefly been consciously represented and is hence poorly remembered, but because it has actually occurred completely outside of awareness. If so, then theorists would disagree over the issue of whether or not such a thought could ever be introspectively accessed. Nisbett and Wilson would possibly argue that the *product* of automatic thinking may be accessed but not the underlying *processes* generating this product. While, as we have already argued, the distinction between product and process may be difficult to maintain, the implication is that conscious access may be limited to certain aspects of automatic thinking. For those theorists who conceptualize consciousness as a state imposed on processing structures, which nevertheless function in a qualitatively similar manner whether conscious or not, then processes which normally occur automatically may possibly be rendered conscious. For example, Shallice may argue that certain automatic thoughts occur outside awareness in particular situations because other cognitive action systems are more dominant at this time. An automatic thought could, therefore, become conscious if the relevant action system underlying this thought were to become dominant. This rationale may suggest certain techniques to enhance access to such automatic thinking. For example, during an episode of emotional distress, a patient may access automatic thoughts more easily by suppressing competing action systems through cessation of irrelevant activity and temporary abandonment of concurrent goals. In this way the possibility of the appropriate action system, underlying the automatic thought, becoming dominant and therefore consciously represented would be increased.

We have seen, however, that many theorists consider nonconscious processes to differ qualitatively from those which can be represented consciously (e.g. Marcel, 1983b). The former, for example, operate in parallel and are unconstrained by capacity while the latter are capacity-limited and usually serial in nature. For such theorists, if automatic thoughts represent nonconscious processes, then they can never be truly represented consciously. At best a therapist could hope to encourage some conscious experience which may give an indication of what may be occurring nonconsciously. Marcel, for example, conceptualizes conscious experience as an instantiated perceptual hypothesis which draws upon and synthesizes specific records left by nonconscious processing. The nonconscious processes cannot themselves be directly experienced, but can produce a conscious experience to the extent that the records of such processes instantiate available perceptual hypotheses. Thus, to identify consciously an automatic inference, prediction, inter-pretation, or whatever, one must have an appropriate 'blueprint' for such a mental event stored in LTM. This suggests one productive use of therapy time. The patient should be supplied with, and encouraged to speculate about, the hypothetical automatic thoughts which could feasibly have triggered certain negative emotional responses in the past. The evidence suggests that this will not permit accurate retrospective access to these thoughts. However, this procedure may generate the blueprints which would be necessary to recognize consciously such mental events, if indeed they do occur subsequently.

Cognitive research, therefore, suggests the procedures most likely to enable conscious access. Additionally, it is possible to adapt the paradigms used experimentally to study nonconscious operations, enabling objective measurement of erroneous or biased processing in such patients. Thus, even if conscious access to the processes themselves cannot be achieved, the patient may find it easier to question and reappraise his subjective experience if he has concrete evidence that his immediate automatic processing was distorted.

A number of assessment techniques, employing the use of subliminal threatening stimuli, have already been developed (e.g. Kragh and Smith, 1970; Smith and Danielsson 1979; Smith and Westerlundh, 1980). However, the potential therapeutic value of providing patients with the results of such assessments, thus demonstrating the biased nature of their automatic processing, has not yet been formally assessed.

An alternative approach is not to make patients consciously aware of biases, but rather to attempt to manipulate nonconscious processing directly. For example, a number of studies have begun to exploit the treatment potential of nonconscious perceptual processing. The rationale is that therapeutic information, implanted without permitting awareness, will evade intentional rejection, and may produce beneficial effects without causing the anxiety which may result from conscious appraisal.

Lee and his colleagues (Tyrer, Horn and Lee, 1978; Lee and Tyrer, 1980) have reported successfully desensitizing agoraphobic patients by presenting films of the phobic situation at levels of illumination which do not permit conscious perception. Using this procedure, fear and avoidance behaviour were reduced in the subliminal exposure group at least to the same degree as in a supraliminal exposure group, and both those groups improved to a greater degree than control subjects who experienced the same procedure with no film in the projector. The subliminal procedure, however, was experienced as significantly less stressful than either the supraliminal or even the control conditions, producing lower subjective ratings of muscle tension, sweating, shaking, difficulty breathing, and so on.

More recently, this general pattern of results has again been replicated (Lee, Tyrer and Horn, 1983). In this study a hybrid exposure condition, involving the 'fading' of initial subliminal presentations to a supraliminal level of illumination as treatment progressed, was found even more effective than either purely subliminal or purely supraliminal conditions. While such results are certainly encouraging, they are based on relatively small sample sizes with only five or six subjects in some groups, and await further independent replication with larger numbers of patients. Nevertheless they clearly indicate the clinical potential of exploiting procedures which may directly influence nonconscious processing without permitting rejection or producing the discomfort which can accompany the conscious representation of aversive stimuli.

A more extensive series of studies has been reported by Silverman which, though based on a rather more controversial theoretical framework, supports the potential clinical utility of subliminally presented information. One problem with evaluating this research is that it is is based on psychoanalytical hypotheses which are not always fully clarified. Nevertheless, Silverman and his associates do report that short statements presented at very brief exposure durations can serve a useful diagnostic and therapeutic purpose.

The potential diagnostic role of such presentations is based on the rationale that certain psychiatric disorders arise through underlying conflicts involving aggressive and libidinal wishes. Silverman argues that relevant statements capable of activating such conflicts, such as 'destroy mother', will, when presented subliminally, increase any psychopathology which is itself a consequence of those conflicts. Using 4ms exposure durations, Silverman reports that different types of stimulus material produce quite specific effects upon particular classes of psychopathology (Silverman, Bronstein and Mendelsohn, 1976). The effects of such subliminally presented statements have been offered as support for various psychoanalytical hypotheses, such as the role of oral aggression in schizophrenia (Silverman and Spiro, 1968), repressed aggression in depression (Miller, 1973), anal conflict in stuttering (Silverman et al., 1972), and incestuous wishes in homosexuality (Silverman et al., 1973). Control stimulus statements did not increase psychopathology, and the relevant conflict statement produced no effect when presented at longer supraliminal durations. Silverman has also extended this approach to the treatment of psychopathology, by presenting subliminal messages aimed at gratifying a common early symbiotic wish which, according to the psychoanalytical literature, should serve to counter adult emotional distress. The most common such phrase employed in this research has been 'Mommy and I are one', which has been reported to be surprisingly effective in reducing a remarkable range of psychopathology (cf. Kaye, 1975; Silverman, 1976, 1980, 1983, 1984). Four ms exposures to this message have been found to facilitate normal desensitization procedures, while similar exposures to neutral phrases such as 'people walking' has no such effect (Silverman, Frank and Dachinger, 1974). Such exposures have also been found effective in reducing thought disorder in schizophrenics (Silverman and Candell, 1970), and treating anxiety in male homosexuals (Silverman et al., 1973). Objective measures of improvement, such as weight loss in obese subjects (Silverman et al., 1978) or improved high-school grades in students (Arian, 1979) have also been reported using this procedure.

Related research suggests that mild manifestations of psychopathology in the normal population may be manipulated by the subliminal presentation of messages capable of influencing unconscious motives. Again, the actual nature of such hypothetical unconscious motives, and hence the subliminal statements which are employed, have been derived from a psychoanalytical framework. Hence it has been suggested that ability to perform well in competitive situations will be impaired by unconscious conflict over Oedipal wishes, and thus the influence of subliminal messages related to such conflict on competitive performance has been examined. For example, Silverman *et al.* (1978) report four studies in which dart-throwing ability was greatly impaired by 4ms exposures to the phrase 'Beating dad is wrong' and improved by similar exposures to 'Beating dad is OK'. Such effects were not, however, found when the exposures were made supraliminally. Similar effects of such subliminal messages on dart-throwing performance have been replicated by Lonski and Palumbo (1978).

The validity of the psychodynamic activation paradigm remains a controversial issue. Replication attempts have not always been successful (e.g. Condon and Allen, 1980; Heilbrun, 1980; Oliver and Burkham, 1982; Haspel and Harris, 1982; Porterfield and Golding, 1985), though Silverman (1985) attributes many such failures to procedural differences. In their own research Silverman and his colleagues report significant effects in approximately 80 per cent of their 60 or so studies, and a sufficient number of independent replications have been reported to demand that such results are taken seriously (e.g. Antell, 1969; Cherry, 1976; Parker, 1977; Sackeim, 1977). Many such replications have been reviewed by Mendlesohn and Silverman (1982).

It is easy to understand some resistance among many theoreticians to embrace a paradigm which rests upon so many controversial assumptions. The entire psychoanalytic framework, from which the specific experimental stimuli are derived, is itself largely unvalidated. The paradigm appears to require not only that subliminal words produce semantic activation, but that phrases can be syntactically parsed and encoded as relatively complex messages without awareness. There is little direct experimental evidence currently available to support this assumption. Nevertheless, the experimental procedures often resist trivial criticisms, employing double-blind methodology and including appropriate checks for subliminality. This area of research therefore adds further weight to the possibility that directly manipulating nonconscious processes may potentially play a therapeutic role, even if the precise mechanisms underlying subliminal dynamic activation effects remains unclear.

In this chapter we have seen that experimental psychologists have taken long strides towards understanding the nature of, and distinctions between, conscious and nonconscious processes. Novel paradigms have been developed, and progressively more powerful models generated. What the field lacks at the moment is a model within which the different types of processing bias found in emotional disorders can be understood. It certainly seems highly likely that, by drawing upon such research, clinical psychologists may now improve their ability to assess, treat and understand a wider variety of psychopathology,

Chapter 10

Theoretical Overview: Towards an Integrative Model

At the start of our book, we set as our aim to review how the information-processing paradigm has been applied to emotional disorders, and to consider theoretical and clinical implications of this body of work. The first chapter included a description of the relevant clinical phenomenology, how emotionally disturbed people are preoccupied with upsetting events. Was it that they experience more negative events, or do they notice them more than other events in their environment? Was it that, for them, the effect of even a mild stressor was exaggerated? Or could it be that the impact was initially the same, but by ruminating about and elaborating the event or its interpretations, emotional disturbance is increased. We pointed to the fact that until relatively recently there had been a dearth of methods for investigating these phenomena, and a lack of precision in clinical theorizing about cognitive aspects of emotional disorders. This final chapter examines how far the application of the techniques of experimental cognitive psychology has shed light on these issues.

10.1 SPECIFICITY IN PROCESSING BIAS

A number of experimental paradigms have now been used to examine differences between emotionally disturbed and control subjects in the processing of emotional materials: dichotic listening, lexical decision, the Stroop test, incidental recall of self-referent adjectives, intentional recall of personality trait adjectives, recall of stories with mixed affective context, cued autobiographical memory and probability judgements. If one were to summarize the cumulative conclusions of these experiments using these paradigms it might seem to be that, in emotional disorders, attention is biased, memory is biased and judgements are biased. One appears to be able to find bias in pre-attentive mechanisms as well as in the contents of consciousness. This would be consistent with the predictions of the two main frameworks within which these paradigms have been used: network theory and schema theory. Both these frameworks are relatively general in their predictions. They suggest that cognitive processing is biased in emotional disorders, but not that different emotions may have different effects or that any one emotion may have distinct effects on different aspects of processing.

However, our review of the experimental evidence has shown that bias favouring mood-congruent stimuli is not shown by all mood-disordered individuals on every paradigm. A considerable number of studies have found attentional biases in highly anxious subjects (Ray, 1979; Burgess et al., 1981; Parkinson and Rachman, 1981; Mathews and MacLeod, 1985, 1986; MacLeod et al., 1986, Watts et al., 1986a; see Chapter 4 for details of these experiments). Although further research will be needed to determine the extent to which failure to find effects is due to differences in tasks or materials, such attentional biases appear to be less associated with depressed mood. Gerrig and Bower (1982) failed to find that experimentally induced depressed mood affected perceptual threshold. One study which did appear to find an effect of depression on an attentional task (the Stroop task; Gotlib and McCann, 1984) did not assess anxiety levels, so could not determine which mood was responsible for the bias. Mathews and MacLeod's (1985) anxious patients who showed disruption on an emotional Stroop were also more depressed than control subjects, but partial correlational analysis showed that it was anxiety not depression which was associated with longer colour naming of negative words. To our knowledge, only one study has examined both anxious and depressed subjects on the same perceptual task (the visual dot-probe experiment of MacLeod et al., (1986). There was no evidence of biased processing by depressives.

By contrast, a considerable number of studies have found a memory bias in depressed subjects (Teasdale and Fogarty, 1979; Teasdale and Taylor, 1980; Teasdale, Taylor and Fogarty, 1981; Derry and Kuiper, 1981; Bower and Cohen, 1981; Clark and Teasdale, 1982; Bradley and Mathews, 1983, Fogarty and Hemsley, 1983; Frith et al., 1983; Mathews and Bradley, 1983; Teasdale and Russell, 1983; Dunbar and Lishman, 1984; McDowell, 1984; Teasdale and Dent, 1987). Similar memory biases have been reported in agoraphobics (Nunn et al., 1984), but findings with other highly anxious subjects have been negative. Indeed, some investigators have reported that repeated attempts to demonstrate a relation between anxiety and recall have failed (Chapter 5, section 5.5) despite the use of self-referent threat adjectives in a paradigm which exactly parallels that used with depressives (Mogg et al., 1987).

Finally, although memory bias appears a robust phenomenon in depressives (consistent with semantic network theory), another prediction of that model is that lexical decision would show mood-congruent bias. Clark et al. (1983) failed to find an effect of induced depressed mood on lexical decision; and MacLeod et al. (1987) similarly found no differences between depressed patients and controls in lexical decision on negative words relative to positive or neutral words.

It appears that different emotions may be more specific in their effects on cognitive processing than was originally thought. One possible interpretation of the data is that anxious subjects, but not depressed subjects, orient their attention towards threat. Depressed subjects (but not generally anxious subjects) may selectively remember negative material. One problem in interpreting this apparent dissociation between the effects of anxiety and depression is that studies vary in many more ways that simply 'attention' vs. 'memory', or 'anxiety' vs. 'depression'. Some assess state variables, others trait variables. Some use personality trait adjectives (especially memory research and especially with depressives). Others use words which denote the feared object (especially attention research and especially with anxious patients). Experiments vary in the time invervals over which biased responses are expected to be observed. No study has yet looked for a double dissociation between different emotions (e.g. anxiety vs. depression) on tasks which assess different aspects of processing (e.g. visual dot-probe and incidental recall of self-referent adjectives using the same type of stimulus material). Until such research is carried out, attributing patterns of results to differences between anxiety and depression or to differences between different aspects of processing, must remain speculative. Nevertheless it would be helpful to derive a model into which these preliminary results from the research literature might be incorporated for the heuristic purpose of directing further investigation.

10.2 AN INTEGRATIVE MODEL

We saw in the previous chapter how information-processing studies have yielded support for Freud's claim that unconscious processes moderate our conscious experience. Furthermore, the processes which operate non-consciously appear to follow different rules from those which are available to introspection. This conclusion corresponds to the distinction drawn by Schneider and Shiffrin (1977) between automatic and strategic processes (see Chapter 2). Automatic processes operate without awareness, are rapid, unconstrained by capacity and occur in parallel. Strategic processes on the other hand are capacity-limited, relatively slow and usually serial in nature. Such a distinction can be found in many areas of clinical and experimental cognitive psychology, often arising out of studies which examine very different aspects of cognitive function. It is similar to the distinction made by Hasher and Zacks (1979) between automatic and controlled processing. More recently, Baddeley (1983) has distinguished between an initial passive aspect of memory and a strategic awareness-based recollection procedure, the latter being a problem-solving process which requires strategic deployment of mnemonic cues. Similarly, in their theory of emotion, Leventhal and Scherer (1987) distinguish between an automatic sensorimotor level, a schematic level and a controlled conceptual level (see Chapter 1). The notion that there may be more than one form of process which acts on more than one form of representation is, as we have seen, assumed by many cognitive psychologists, but it is only relatively recently that this notion has been elaborated on the basis of detailed experimental results. We shall argue that both encoding and retrieval involve a passive, automatic aspect and an active, strategic aspect. Second, we shall suggest that a bias in one aspect need not entail a bias in the other. Third, we shall examine the suggestion that the results to date are explicable if different moods have their effects on different aspects of processing.

10.2.1 Priming vs. Elaboration

In chapter 4 we considered the possibility that the attentional biases shown by anxious patients may map on to the phenomena described in the perceptual memory experiments of Jacoby and Witherspoon (1982) and Graf and Mandler (1984). As described in Chapter 4, a central purpose of their experiments was to understand how a person could show evidence of having been exposed to a stimulus without necessarily being able to remember having been so exposed.

In perceptual memory paradigms, a study phase (in which, for example, a list of words is shown to subjects) is followed by a test phase involving such tasks as identification of briefly presented words (e.g. 35 msec) or completion of word stems (*for...*; forest, forbid, forget, etc.). These test tasks show evidence that a subject's responses have been biased by the material to which they were exposed in the study phase. However, the extent of this bias is independent of the subject's ability to recognize which items they saw in the study phase. Indeed, since amnesic patients show equivalent bias in such perceptual memory tasks without being able to recall anything about the study phase, such effects are clearly independent of 'aware' forms of remembering (Jacoby and Witherspoon, 1982).

The extent of perceptual memory bias also appears to be independent of the depth to which an item is processed. Graf and Mandler (1984) compared structural and semantic encoding in the study phase. They found that this manipulation had no effect on the extent to which word-stem completion was biased by the items which had been studied. Despite this there was the predicted large enhancement of recognition and recall for the items encoded semantically.

Graf and Mandler (1984) account for these results by proposing a distinction between two processes which operate upon mental representations: *integration* (priming) and *elaboration*. Priming is automatic, occurring because the processing of a stimulus (e.g. a word) involves automatic activation of the multiple components involved in the representation of that stimulus. The result is a strengthening of the internal organization of the representation, making the word more '*accessible*'. That is, the word will come to mind more readily when only some of its features or components (e.g. initial letters) are presented. Elaboration, a more strategic process, consists of the activation of a representation in relation to other associated representations to form new relationships between them and to activate old relationships. The result of the spread of activation to associates produced by this process of elaboration is to make the word more *'retrievable'* because such elaboration generates new and reinstates old paths for retrieving the word. In summary, processing a word results in activation which unifies or primes the representation of the word. (We use the concept of 'priming' rather than that of 'integration' because of the latter's ambiguity.) Such priming 'raises the probability that the word will be produced (or seen, or heard) when only some of its components are presented.' By contrast, 'elaborative processing is required to perceive relations among a set of previously unrelated words and to relate the occurrence of a word to its context' (Graf and Mandler, 1984, p. 554). These suggestions encourage us to look again at the information requirements of the tasks which have been used to assess emotional disturbance.

The level to which the representation of a word or concept has been primed is assessed by tasks such as perceptual threshold. These are similar to the type of attentional tasks used to study anxiety. This suggests the possibility that biases such as those shown by anxious patients on the visual dot-probe experiment (see Chapter 4, section 4.4) may reflect processes similar to those which underlie automatic priming. The extent of elaboration of a word or concept in relation to associated words or concepts is assessed by tasks such as depth of processing. These are similar to the types of task used to study memory in depression. This suggests the possibility that biases such as those shown on recall (in neutral mood) of negative material encoded in depressed mood (see Chapter 5, section 5.2) may reflect the extent to which that material has been elaborated at encoding. The important implication to note about the dissociation between pre-attentive priming and strategic elaboration is that one may observe bias in priming without observing bias in elaboration. This dissociation is not readily predicted by either schema or network theories.

In order to account for the attentional and memory phenomena seen in emotional disturbance we need to make additional assumptions about these two basic stages of processing. We need to assume that the processing which takes place at each stage is sensitive to emotionally valent information. Specifically, we assume that there exist decision mechanisms capable of judging the affective salience of an item. Such a decision process must take place both at the pre-attentive and elaboration phases.

10.2.2 Pre-attentive affective decision and resource allocation

The previous chapter reviewed evidence to suggest that a number of operations proceed pre-attentively. These include sensory registration, semantic labelling, associative spread and disambiguation of a stimulus. At this pre-attentive stage, all meanings of an item are activated. Disambiguation starts to occur when the activation of the range of meanings of the item up to any given point interact with activation from the context. A dominant meaning is selected and alternative interpretations rejected. How are these pre-attentive operations sensitive to the emotional valence of stimuli? We assume that at the pre-attentive stage of processing there exists a decision mechanism capable of assessing the affective valence (e.g. threat value) of an item.* On the basis of this decision, priorities for subsequent processing are determined; resources are oriented towards or away from the source of the stimulus. This account is similar to Neisser's (1976) characterization of perception as a cyclical process. The first stage involves the passive intake of partial information from the environment which is then mapped onto internal representations or schemata. These schemata both accommodate the information and direct processing resources during the next intake cycle toward particular elements of the stimulus array. It is at the point of this cycle, where processing resources are allocated for subsequent cycles, that decisions may be made on the basis of affective salience.

Non-disturbed subjects tend to orient processing resources *away from* the location of a stimulus which has been judged to be threatening. This may be protective, limiting increases in anxiety by excluding such minor threatening stimuli from the cognitive system at an early stage. By contrast, it appears that anxious patients shift processing resources *towards* the location of a threatening item.

We suggest that it is this switching of processing resources which MacLeod *et al.* (1986) were assessing in their visual probe task. It also explains the poorer performance found on a secondary reaction-time task when threatening material was played to anxious subjects in a non-shadowed message in a dichotic listening paradigm (Mathews and MacLeod, 1986). In this experiment the fact that subjects were not consciously aware of the threatening material in the non-shadowed message did not prevent it from depleting the resources available for the reaction-time task.

It is possible that once a negative item has received priority in the allocation of resources, it will increase the extent to which an item is primed ('integrated' in Graf and Mandler's sense). That is, increased allocation of pre-attentive resources towards an item may be functionally equivalent to multiple exposure to that item. If this is so, then irrespective of the degree of further processing of the item at the elaboration stage, the representation of that item will be more likely to be produced (or heard, or seen) when only some of its

---

*It is reasonable to assume that the system evaluates the valence of an item on several affective dimensions (e.g. threat, loss, irritation) but the data only allow us to speculate for the preattentive stage on the evaluation of threat.

components are presented. Furthermore, negative items may appear to come into consciousness of their own accord due to the operation of previously primed items acting to disambiguate otherwise neutral stimuli in a negative way. The person need not be aware that the original items have been encoded; the phenomenon is independent of a person's ability to recognise those items to which they have been exposed. In summary, the visual probe and dichotic listening experiments of MacLeod *et al.* (1986) and Mathews and MacLeod (1986) are explained in terms of these pre-attentive activation processes. We assume that high trait anxious individuals have a tendency at this preattentive stage to orient resources towards the location of threat. The greater the evidence that a stimulus has been disambiguated as threatening, the greater the tendency to orient towards it for these subjects.

10.2.3 Affective decision and resource allocation at elaboration

What mechanisms underlie differential elaboration of negative material? At the strategic* stage, relations between associates of the disambiguated item are activated (Graf and Mandler, 1984). We assume that, as such elaboration of an item begins, a further decision mechanism assesses the affective valence of the item. As at the pre-attentive stage, resource allocation is contingent upon the results of this decision. If additional resources are allocated, the stimulus will be more elaboratively encoded. These elaborations are encoded with the item, and are able to act as mnemonic cues to aid later recognition and recall, even if such recall is performed in neutral mood. We assume that enhanced incidental recall following self-referent encoding of negative material in depressives (Derry and Kuiper, 1981; Bradley and Mathews, 1983; Mathews and Bradley, 1983; see also Chapter 6) arises because of the extra resources deployed in the recruitment of mnemonic encoding cues.

In some types of emotional disturbance (e.g. spider phobia) there may be strong tendencies to direct processing resources *away* from valent (phobic) material at the elaboration stage. In this case, fewer mnemonic cues would be stored with an item rendering it less retrievable.

Different mood states may therefore have different effects on such tasks independently of the effect they have had on preattentive priming, by varying the type and extent of elaborative encoding that takes place. That is, they may differentially affect the degree to which mood-congruent mnemonic cues are recruited and encoded with an item.

---

*Although in principle these processes may be amenable to strategic control (as in depth-of-processing studies), we assume that people do not, in general, know how such processes could be brought under voluntary control.

10.2.4 Retrieval Effects

Retrieval from long-term memory also has a passive automatic aspect and a strategic 'recollection' aspect (Baddeley, 1982). It is possible that here too some emotional states affect the passive aspect and others the strategic aspect. The passive aspects of retrieval may determine which memories 'come to mind' apparently unprompted. The strategic aspect of retrieval determines how successfully one can make an active search of memory. The priming/elaboration distinction is again relevant. More highly primed material will come to mind more readily when only partial cues are available. This may, for example, explain the finding that highly anxious people are more likely to give a negatively-biased spelling of a homophone (e.g. weak, week; ail, ale; pale, pail). Although alternative explanations are available, e.g. that such highly anxious subjects consciously retrieve both spellings and then consciously select the more threatening interpretation, the notion that these biases arise independently of awareness is more consistent with the evidence of Jacoby and Witherspoon (1982). They used a similar paradigm and found that amnesics' spelling of a homophone could be biased by prior exposure to the non-dominant meaning, despite the fact that the patients could not recall having undergone the study phase. It would suggest that the anxious person may, either by virtue of mood or by virtue of frequent rumination on threatening themes, have relatively frequently activated representations which bias towards threat on these interpretive tasks. Such biases may exist without the anxious patient being able to recall the episodes which have primed the threat interpretations.

Depression may affect the active strategic element of memory retrieval. In particular, depression may enhance the deployment of mood-congruent cues at retrieval, enhancing the recall of negative material even if that material has been encoded in neutral mood (Teasdale and Russell, 1983). By contrast, if the material to be recalled involves an element of distaste or threat (as it may do in phobic or anxious patients) then mood-congruent recall may be inhibited. That is, there may be, for these patients on these materials, a reduction in the extent to which mood-congruent mnemonic cues are generated at retrieval whether or not such cues have been generated at encoding.

10.3 HOW MUCH EXPLANATORY POWER DOES THE MODEL HAVE?

The aim of the model was to provide a framework within which it would be possible to see how dissociations between different emotions arise. It accounts for the current pattern of findings regarding differences between general anxiety and depressive states by suggesting that anxiety preferentially affects the passive, automatic aspect of encoding and retrieval, whereas depression preferentially affects the more active, effortful aspects of encoding and retrieval. In the terms used by Graf and Mandler (1984), anxiety makes certain items more *accessible*, whereas depression makes certain items more *retrievable*.

The model has the potential to be elaborated so that it makes quite specific experimental predictions. For example, it might predict that the effect of exposing anxious and depressed people to the same list of emotional and neutral material would have different effects depending on whether one assessed their perceptual memory performance or their recognition/recall performance in the test phase of such a study. However, it is not our purpose here to search out specific predictions, but rather to examine the way in which the model may help elucidate some more general clinical and experimental issues. It is to the first of these, the issue of trait versus state, that we now turn.

10.3.1 Trait and State Effects

Most of the research described in this book has been aimed at finding differences in information-processing between emotionally disturbed patients and non-disturbed controls or between different types of emotional disturbance. From these findings it is difficult to determine whether the cognitive biases represent responses to particular events in a person's life, represent a particular cognitive style or trait disposition, or arise from transient affective disturbance. For example, Lloyd and Lishman (1975) demonstrated that the greater the level of depression in depressed patients the more biased the latency of recall of hedonically toned autobiographical memories. From this study it was not clear to what extent this phenomenon was due to the fact that the more depressed people may have suffered more negative events in the past. However, Teasdale and Fogarty (1979) showed that transient manipulation of mood in normal volunteers was sufficient to bring about a similar bias in recall latencies.

Similarly, it is difficult to determine whether the fact that anxious patients tend to overestimate the probability of unpleasant things happening to them is dependent on trait or state mood. Butler and Mathews' (in press) research on exam anxiety found that as the exam approaches, all subjects become anxious, but that high trait anxious subjects become pessimistic about a wider range of concerns. This suggested to them an interaction between transient state mood and trait predisposition. Let us consider how each of these in turn may be represented in terms of the model.

Transient mood shifts may affect the processes we have described by modifying the outcome of the decision on the affective salience of an item at both the preattentive and elaboration phases. We suggest that transient mood may adjust the decision mechanism in certain direction, similar to the effect of presenting the subject with a more negative item. The greater the affective

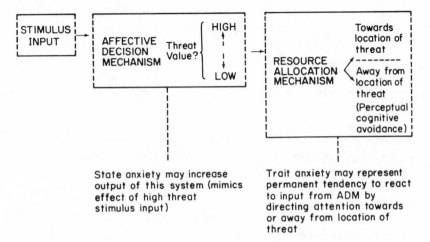

Figure 10.1 (a) Representation of how state and trait mood (e.g. anxiety) may affect resource allocation at pre-attentive stage.

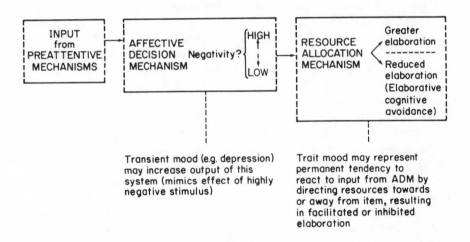

Figure 10.1 (b) Representation of how state and trait mood (e.g. depression) may affect resource allocation at elaboration stage.

disturbance, the greater the output of the decision mechanisms to those other processes which are contingent upon them; orientation towards or away from the source of threat at the pre-attentive phase (see Figure 10.1a); facilitated or inhibited search for associative mnemonics at the elaboration phase (see Figure 10.1b).

Trait predisposition may be represented as a permanent tendency to react to the output of affective decision mechanisms in a certain direction. Some individuals are prone to direct more processing resources towards an item if it is judged to be negative at the pre-attentive stage. For these individuals, threatening items will tend to be in a more activated state. Other individuals are prone to direct processing resources away from an item which is judged to be negative at this stage. The item will be less well primed. In particular, it is possible that high-trait anxiety reflects a permanent tendency to react to the affective decision at the pre-attentive stage by orienting resources towards the source of threat.

Independently of these predispositions, individuals may also differ in their tendencies to direct processing resources towards or away from an item if it is judged to be negative at the elaboration stage. The result will be differences in the extent to which a negative item is elaborated. In particular it is possible that depression-prone individuals have a permanent tendency to react to the affective decision at the elaboration stage by directing more resources to a negative item. For these individuals, negative concepts will always tend to be more elaboratively encoded.

Note that these assumptions allow us to specify why trait effects are not pervasive throughout the entire processing system; the tendency to allocate resources directionally at pre-attentive priming stage or elaboration stage may be independent of each other. Most importantly, however, it allows us to describe how transient state interacts with more permanent trait predispositions. If increases in transient anxiety or depression adjust the affective decision mechanism so that it behaves as if it were processing a more negative item, the resource allocation mechanisms would necessarily receive a greater input. The increased intensity will cause an increased directional effect. The result will be more orientation towards or away from the source of threat at the pre-attentive stage (the direction depending on trait tendency) (see Figure 10.1a); and greater facilitation or inhibition in the search for associative mnemonics at the elaboration phase (depending again on the directional tendency) (see Figure 10.1b). But is there any evidence that trait and state interact in this way?

It is a major assumption of the cognitive models of emotional disorder proposed by Beck (1976), Beck et al. (1979); Beck, Emery and Greenberg (1986) and Abramson et al.'s (1978) reformulated helplessness theory that some patients, even when not currently depressed, remain vulnerable because of relatively enduring cognitive characteristics. When the literature on this topic was reviewed by Williams (1984, Chapter 8) the evidence available suggested that such between-episode vulnerability did not exist. However two cautions were expressed at that time about accepting this negative conclusion. First, that the failure to find depressive cognitive style between episodes had relied on self-report questionnaire measures. It was possible that more sensitive cognitive assessments might produce different results. Since then Hammen et al. (1986) have used an incidental recall paradigm following self-referential encoding of character trait words to assess biased schemata in previously depressed college students. Although some aspects of their data supported the notion that prior depression had residual effects on schematic responding, other aspects suggested that self-schemata were mood-dependent rather than stable. Dobson and Shaw (1987) and Bradley and Mathews (submitted) have similarly found that recovered depressed patients show normal self-referential memory.

But there was a second caution expressed in Williams' review; that a person may remain vulnerable in the sense that they will tend to react to stress in a more catastrophic way. Such a tendency might be revealed by applying a stressor such as mood manipulation. Teasdale and Dent (1987) gave recovered depressed patients a mood-induction procedure, and found that, compared with some 'never-depressed' subjects who became equally disturbed by the MIP, these patients showed greater tendency to show negative self-reference biases.

It is noticeable that these investigations of vulnerability have all been concerned with depression. Although Martin (1985) has examined self-reference bias associated with the neuroticism trait, there have been to date few studies of recovered anxious patients comparable to those on depressives. This is perhaps because anxiety problems tend to be less episodic, but also because cognitive accounts of anxiety have not been elaborated to the same extent as those for depression. However, two types of evidence on the state–trait question for anxiety are available. First, partial correlations between cognitive measures and trait and state anxiety as assessed by questionnaire have been examined. Some tasks (e.g. homophone spelling) have not distinguished between state or trait, but the emotional Stroop task appeared to be associated more with the state than the trait level of anxiety (Mathews and MacLeod, 1985). The second type of evidence comes from research on college students who are about to take exams, and are tested at one month and at one day before the exams. High trait anxious subjects appear to react differently as the state anxiety increases, becoming more pessimistic about a wider range of possible negative outcomes (Butler and Mathews, 1983).

This notion that a high trait anxious person is particularly prone to develop pathological cognitive changes as state anxiety increases is similar to the findings of Teasdale and Dent (1987) that people who are vulnerable to depression react differently to a state mood manipulation from those who have never been clinically depressed.

In terms of the model, the high trait anxious or depression prone person may show little evidence of psychopathology when transient emotional disturbance is low. As state mood increases, however, the predisposition to allocate processing resources towards or away from negative stimuli at the preattentive or elaboration stages becomes more evident. In addition to increasing the likelihood that such people will exhibit greater psychopathology in response to smaller degrees of affective disturbance, the effect of such tendencies would be to prolong any episode of emotional disturbance. The recovery process is likely to be retarded if any small increase in affective disturbance produces a greater amount of biased processing. Such a prolongation of the emotional disturbance has been found for people currently depressed who have great cognitive disturbance, assessed by self-report measures (Lewinsohn et al., 1981) and for depressed patients who have remitted but who continue to have more dysfunctional attitudes (Rush et al. 1987).

10.4 OTHER IMPLICATIONS

10.4.1 Phenomenology of Anxiety and Depression

The model is based largely on studies with word stimuli. The question arises whether it is generalizable. Especially, can one talk about 'priming' and 'elaboration' outside the context of individual words? At the moment the answers to these questions remain speculative since the appropriate research has not been done. However, clinical observation would suggest that these notions are generalizable. The evidence reviewed in this book suggests that anxiety may arise from the interaction of stimuli and the pre-attentive mechanisms which operate upon them. Attention will be more likely to switch to a threatening location, threatening items become more activated and more likely to prime subsequently ambiguous stimuli. The result is that they too will be dissambiguated as negative. The significance of this becomes clear when it is realized how many stimuli in the environment are potentially mildly threatening. 'On the road, oncoming vehicles are potentially lethal, in dark streets passers by are potential assailants, and ... minor somatic sensations are potentially symptoms of some serious malady' (MacLeod et al., 1986, p. 18). The model emphasizes how, by the time a person becomes aware of the stimulus, it may already have been disambiguated as negative. For example, an anxious patient may not first feel a chest pain and subsequently interpret it as a heart attack. He or she may experience the pain as a heart attack.

If depression is less associated with biased pre-attentive priming, but rather more with bias in the active strategic aspect of encoding, it may explain why depressed patients attribute the source of their negative mood to themselves and attribute the causes of events that happen to them in a self schematic way. This contrasts with anxious and phobic patients who tend to attribute the source of their negative mood to specifiable bodily or external sources (e.g. chest pain or supermarkets).

This way of characterizing the nature of emotional disturbance may offer clinicians a framework which may help them notice aspects of their patients' problems they had not noticed before. The clinician may now not simply wish to take account of level of anxiety or depression or the situations in which these occur, but also how specific are the stimuli which the person notices, and whether it relates to external or bodily stimuli or to self-schemata. They might wish to assess to what extent the mood is being maintained by enhanced attention to negative items or to disambiguation (in a negative way) of neutral or ambiguous items. Alternatively, the mood may be being maintained by enhanced elaboration of negative items when encoded, or the biased selection of cues to recall events from the past at retrieval. The more exactly such assessments coincide with the processes which underlie dysfunction in emotional disturbance, the more helpful they are likely to be in generating specific remedial strategies.

10.4.2 Cognitive Impairments on Neutral Tasks

Deficits in performing neutral tasks can be understood in terms of the switching of resources (pre-attentive or elaborative) towards mood-congruent items and away from mood-neutral or incongruent material. In anxious patients reaction time to a neutral stimulus is impaired in both the dichotic listening paradigm (see section 4.2.1.) and the visual dot-probe task (section 4.4) when negative material is presented in another message or location. These deficiencies in performance in anxiety may arise from the pre-attentive switching of attention away from a task in hand to other mood-relevant current concerns. Such switching is likely to occur even when neutral or ambiguous stimuli occur in the environment of the individual if such material is easily disambiguated as negative. He or she need not be aware of their existence for them to disrupt performance.

In depressed patients, memory for neutral material is often impaired. Chapter 3 reviewed evidence suggesting that such memory impairment was not due to cautious response criteria (see section 3.2). Neither do depressive memory deficits occur because depressed patients do not bother to make the effort to recall material they have learnt. It appears that such patients are unable to structure material at encoding. This can be seen as representing a deficiency at the elaboration stage of encoding. The affective decision (how negative is this item?) which is made on the to-be-remembered material at the elaboration stage determines the extent to which material will be rehearsed, structured and elaborated. Neutral material will not receive priority in the allocation of resources.

10.4.3 Dissociation between Judgement and Memory

A further implication of the contention that emotional disorders may affect different aspects of processing is that it becomes easier to understand why some aspects of conscious experience do not correlate with some aspects of underlying cognitive biases. For example, the availability heuristic described by

Tversky and Kahneman (1982) has often been adduced as an explanation of how memory (the ease with which relevant instances come to mind) may affect judgements of frequency and probability. However, research (section 8.5.3) has suggested that judgements do not correlate with the speed of recollection of relevant instances from the past. These findings imply that modifying speed of recollection may have little effect on judgements of future probability. The model allows us to see, however, that a link between memory and judgements is not precluded by these results. Speed of recollection reflects the active, strategic aspect of memory (generating and refining the cues, searching for relevant episodes, checking their appropriateness, etc.). As such it may be relatively independent of the more automatic form of memory demonstrated in perceptual memory experiments discussed above. Judge-ments may be a function of the extent to which the memory system has been primed by differential exposure to salient instances. It is possible that such priming might be more readily assessed by word completion or tachistoscopic recognition tasks than by strategic recall tasks, and that these would be found to relate more closely to judgements of frequency or probability. As yet this possibility remains unexamined, however.

10.4.4 Implications for Processes Underlying Remediation

The relationship between judgements and memory discussed in the previous section represents only part of a much needed re-examination of the relation between underlying biases and conscious experience. Some of these issues have been discussed in the previous chapter (section 9.2.1) in relation to Nisbett and Wilson's contention that only the product but not the processes of cognitive bias can be introspectively accessed. It was suggested that even if nonconscious and conscious processes represent fundamentally different processes, the patient may, over time, acquire 'blueprints' for becoming more aware of the way perceptual hypotheses are contributing to current mental events (section 9.4).

But even if a person became more aware of his own errors and biases, the question still remains whether any such conscious knowledge could itself modify the biases themselves. There is very little evidence on whether cognitive and behavioural therapies do in fact modify underlying processing biases (though see Foa and McNally, 1986; Watts et al., 1986b; reviewed in Chapter 4). If they do so, it is because they provide opportunities for emotional processing to take place which may previously have been impeded.

First, treatments which involve confrontation with situations the patients previously found difficult may overcome the tendencies for patients cognitively to avoid stimuli they find threatening. This possibility arises from ˙he findings that the relationship between increased imageability of feared ˙uli and relaxation during the course of therapy is reciprocal. Watts (1974) found that increased detail in desensitization produced longer between-session reductions in anxiety, and more recent work has confirmed the extent to which phobic patients are impoverished in the amount of detail they encode about their feared stimuli (Watts et al., 1986d). It is an interesting outcome of this research that such impoverished detail of an image may also be associated in these patients with impoverished detail about what to do and how to cope with the feared subject (Watts et al., 1986c), reminiscent of the effect that imagining an outcome has on behavioural scripts (8.5.1). This implies that encouraging the patient to encode previously avoided stimuli in a detailed way will facilitate extinction and allow the development of adequate behavioural scripts for how to cope in previously feared situations.

Second, if the affective disturbances associated with exposure to a stimulus can be reduced, in terms of our model this will reduce the output of the affective decision mechanisms (see Figures 10.1a and 10.1b). At the pre-attentive stage this will reduce attentional deployment towards the source of threat for anxious patients. At the elaboration stage this will reduce the spread to associated negative concepts for depressed patients.

Third, the fact that most treatments involve explicit discussion of positive aspects of the patient's past and current life may alter the accessibility of these events in memory, providing a richer set of cues which the patients may use between sessions for recollecting aspects of their past. Information-processing tasks offer a potentially important tool in helping to determine whether these treatments perform all or any of these functions, and which techniques do so maximally for which patient.

Fourth, the information-processing paradigm has made available a framework to help understand which assessment techniques are best suited to assess which cognitive functions. For example, the model proposes that anxiety involves biased allocation of attention at the preattentive stage, and depression involves biased use of mnemonic cueing at the elaboration stage. This suggests that the use of attention biasing measures as measures of process or the outcome of therapy in depressed patients will be inappropriate. It will be similarly inappropriate to attempt to use incidental recall tasks to measure process or outcome of therapy with anxious patients.

Finally, an important role for such assessments may be to help to predict relapse in those patients who appear to have responded to treatment. For example, in the recent treatment outcome trial on depression by Murphy et al. (1984), it was found that cognitive behaviour therapy alone, drugs alone, and drugs in combination with CBT all resulted in very similar outcomes. Importantly, when they assessed the dysfunctional attitudes of their patients using the Dysfunctional Attitude Scale they found that all groups improved similarly on this questionnaire despite the fact that it purports to measure variables which were to be the specific target of the cognitive treatment. When these patients were followed up a year later (Simons et al., 1986) there were large differences in the relapse rate of patients who had apparently recovered in response to drugs (66 per cent relapse rate) or cognitive therapy (20 per cent relapse rate) or their combination (43 per cent relapse rate). This could have been either because different patients responded to the different treatments in the first place so that the proportion of relapse reflects individual differences in the initial response to treatment. Or it could have been because cognitive therapy taught the patients how to deal with the recurrence of symptoms so that when the symptoms tended to recur they did not return to the clinic to seek help whereas the drug patients would have done so. But there is a third possibility: that there *was* a change brought about in these patients who underwent the cognitive behaviour therapy but which was not assessed successfully by the self- and observer-rated questionnaires used in the trial. The advantage of these tasks is that they may assess vulnerability better than questionnaires on which an individual may be simply responding to the hedonic tone of the questions. It is possible that if some experimental cognitive tasks had been used to assess these patients it may have been possible to make more predictable which patients who *appeared* to be well nevertheless required more treatment.

10.5 CONCLUDING REMARKS

Part of the attraction of specifying a model which distinguishes between initial priming and subsequent elaboration is that it maps more readily onto the nature of anxiety and depression. Anxiety is a multi-component system which, in normal living, helps an individual to anticipate and avoid danger. It makes sense that it should include, as one of its components, a system which reacts rapidly to even a partial representation of a possibly threatening stimulus. The organism may need to take quick avoidant action, so there is little reason (at that time) to recruit a further system which elaborates the stimulus, which might only interfere with the necessary action.

However, there are likely to be differences between different types of anxious patient in the nature of the bias shown. For example, for some patients (especially those characterized by general worry) such elaboration of a threat stimulus may take place over a longer time-interval. It will be necessary to ensure that the entire time-course of possible elaboration bias in anxiety is assessed before one will be able to obtain a full picture of the nature of the cognitive psychopathology for these patients. Perhaps just as important is the distinction between those patients whose anxiety is an object or feeling which may occur at unpredictable times (for example, suddenly seeing a spider, or suddenly feeling a pain) and patients (such as agoraphobics) who know which situations are likely to cause anxiety and how to avoid them. In other words, there may be important differences in cognitive processing between those anxious patients who can provide themselves with adequate safety signals, and those who cannot.

Depression is also a multi-component system, part of the function of which in day-to-day living may be to help come to terms with loss. In its more severe form, depression loses its adaptive significance and becomes characterized by rumination over past failures and disappointments. In neither mild nor severe depression, however, does the problem which causes or exacerbates the depression require very quick avoidant or escape action. It is not surprising then to find that depressives do not in general show enhanced 'pick-up' of negative information. Of course, depressives may very quickly interpret an ambiguous situation as negative, but this may result from biased elaboration, rather than enhanced priming. The significance of this distinction is that the biased elaboration encodes the event in a form that can be strategically retrieved later; enhanced priming does not. If depression is, in some form, a response to an event which requires longer-term problem solving behaviour (rather than immediate avoidance or escape), then it can be seen why it is adaptive for it to involve a system that allows strategic access to previous problem-solving attempts.

Just as further research into anxiety will need to distinguish different types of anxiety so different subtypes of depression will need to be differentiated. For example, although the onset of many depressions is preceded by a stressful event, patients vary in how much they link their depression to the event in question (Matussek and Luks, 1981). Those patients who do not link their current feelings to the occurrence of the stress event tend to be the same patients whose mood is less reactive to changes in their moment-to-moment environment. There are likely to be important differences in the way their processing of mood-congruent material is biased compared with other depressed patients, which only further research will determine.

These differences that exist between different subtypes of anxiety and between different subtypes of depression remind us of the caution expressed at the outset about attributing dissociations between attention and memory bias simply to differences between anxiety and depression. There are too many differences between different studies — in paradigms, materials, task demands, diagnoses, severity of mood disturbance — to make sweeping conclusions. However, even on the basis of current evidence we can be fairly confident that not all emotional states will be found to affect cognitive processing in the same way. The usefulness of exploiting a simple distinction between anxiety and depression is to help make clear what dissociations may exist between different emotions and between different aspects of cognitive processing. Having derived a model which allows such distinctions to be made, we can now reassert that the picture is likely to be complex.

It is very unlikely that anxiety will never be found to affect memory and depression never found to affect pre-attentive processes. For one thing, anxiety and depression often co-occur. Although we should expect that anxious patients will be especially characterized by over-vigilance for threat cues on the basis of which immediate action might be necessary, some depressed patients might also show similar over-vigilance. In the same way, view the pick-up of negative material and its elaboration as distinct aspects of events. What the distinction between priming and elaboration offers is a framework within which such phenomena can be understood whether they occur in patients with a diagnosis of anxiety, depression or any other emotional disorder. It helps us to understand why a bias in one aspect of processing does not necessitate biases in other aspects. It suggests that we view the pick-up of negative material and its elaboration as distinct aspects of emotional disturbance needing distinct assessment and remediation. There is now sufficient evidence to suggest that the field needs to move away from general statements about the effects of mood on cognitive processing. There will be a need to specify which mood and what aspect of processing is affecting what bias.

When clinical psychologists assess patients' problems they do not simply make diagnoses, but also carry out a functional analysis. This includes description of those aspects of behaviour the patient wishes to decrease, and which aspects the patient wishes to increase. It includes a detailed analysis of the activities, places, people and times when the symptoms are most apparent and when they are least apparent. It includes a detailed analysis of the different components of the mood disturbance itself: behaviour (e.g. what objects or situations are avoided?); somatic symptoms (e.g. heart-rate increase, reduced weight); and experiential symptoms (e.g. thoughts and images). The work reviewed in this book has shown that progress can be made in understanding how perception, attention and memory contribute to these phenomena. It represents the first step along the road towards greater specification of remedial strategies based on this understanding.

References

Abelson, R.P. (1981) 'Psychological status of a script concept'. *Amer. Psychol.* **36**, 715–729.

Abramson, L.T., Seligman, M.E.P. and Teasdale, J.D. (1978) 'Learned helplessness in humans; critique and reformulation'. *J. Abnorm. Psychol.*, **87**, 49–74.

Adams, M.J. and Collins, A.A. (1979) 'A schematic-theoretic view of reading'. In R.O. Freedle (ed.), *New Directions in Discourse Processing*. Vol. II. Norwood, New Jersey: Ablex.

Adler, A. (1927) *Practise and Theory of Individual Psychology*. New York: Harcourt, Brace and World.

Adler, A. (1944) 'Disintegration and restoration of optic recognition in visual agnosia'. *Arch. Neurol. Psychiat.*, **51**, 243–259.

Alba, J.W. and Hasher, L. (1983) 'Is memory schematic?' *Psychol. Bull.*, **93**, 203–231.

Allison, J. (1963) 'Cognitive structure and receptivity to low intensity stimulation'. *J. Abnorm. Soc. Psychol.*, **67**, 132–138.

Alloy, L.B. and Abramson, L.Y. (1979) Judgement of contingency in depressed and non-depressed students: sadder but wiser? *J. Exp. Psychol.*, **108**, 441–485.

Alloy, L.B. and Abramson, L.Y. (1982) 'Learned helplessness, depression, and the illusion of control'. *J. Personal. Soc. Psychol.*, **42**, 1114–1126.

Allport, D.A. (1980) 'Attention and performances'. In G. Claxton (ed.), *Cognitive Psychology: New Directions*. London: Routledge and Kegan Paul.

Allport, T.A. (1977) On knowing the meaning of words we are unable to report: the effects of visual masking. In S. Dornic (ed.), *Attention and Performance*, Vol 6. New York and London: Academic Press.

Anderson, A., Garrod, S.C. and Sanford, A.J. (1983) 'The accessibility of pronominal antecedents as a function of episode shifts in narrative text'. *Quart. J. Exp. Psychol.*, **35a**, 427–440.

Anderson, C.A. (1983) 'Imagination and expectation: The effect of imagining behavioural scripts on personal intentions'. *J. Person. Soc. Psychol.*, **45** (2), 293–305.

Anderson, J. and Bower, G.H. (1973) *Human Associative Memory*. Washington, D.C.: Winston.

Anderson, M.P. (1981) 'Assessment of imaginal processes: Approaches and issues'. In T.V. Merluzzi, C.R. Glass and M. Genest (eds), *Cognitive Assessment*. New York: Guildford Press.

Anderson, R.C. and Pichert, J.W. (1978) 'Recall of previously unrecallable information following a shift in perspectives'. *J. Verb. Learn. & Verb. Behav.*, **17**, 1–12.

Anderson, R.C., Pichert, J.W., Goetz, E.T., Schallert, D.L., Stevens, K.V. and Trollip, S.R. (1976) 'Instantiation of general terms'. *J. Verb. Learn, & Verb. Behav.*, **15**, 667–679.

Andreasen, N.C. (1976) 'Do depressed patients show thought disorder?'. *J. Nerv. & Ment. Dis.*, **163**, 186–192.

Antell, M. (1969) 'The effect of subliminal activation of sexual and aggressive drives derivatives on literary creativity'. Doctoral dissertation, New York University.

Anthony, B.J. and Graham, F.K. (1983) 'Evidence for sensory-selective set in young infants'. *Science*, **220**, 742–744.

Arian, S. (1979) 'The effect of subliminal symbiotic stimuli in Hebrew on academic performance of Israeli high school students'. Unpublished PhD thesis, New York Universtiy.

Ausubel, D.P. (1968) *Educational Psychology: A Cognitive View.* New York: Holt, Rinehart and Winston.

Baddeley, A.D. (1966) 'The capacity for generating information by randomisation'. *Quart. J. Exp. Psychol.*, **18**, 119–129.

Baddeley, A.D. (1982) 'Domains of recollection'. *Psychol. Rev.*, **89**, 708–729.

Baddeley, A.D. (1986) *Working Memory.* Oxford: Clarendon Press.

Baddeley, A.D. and Hitch, G. (1974) 'Working memory'. In G.H. Bower (ed.), *The Psychology of Learning and Motivation*, Vol. 8. London: Academic Press.

Baddeley, A.D. and Liberman, K. (1980) 'Spatial working memory'. In R. Nickerson (ed.), *Attention and Performance VIII*. Hillsdale, N.J.: Lawrence Erlbaum.

Baker, L.E. (1937) 'The influence of subliminal stimuli upon verbal behaviour'. *J. Exp. Psychol.*, **20**, 84–100.

Baker, L.L. and Jessup, B.A. (1980) 'The psychophysiology of affective verbal and visual information processing in dysphoria'. *Cog. Ther. & Res.*, **4**, 135–148.

Balint, R. (1909) 'Seelenlanhnung des 'Schauens' optische ataxie raumliche storung der aufnerksankeit'. *Nonatsschrift für Psychiatrie und Neurologie*, **25**, 57–71.

Balota, D.A. (1983) 'Automatic semantic activation and episodic memory encoding'. *J. Verb. Learn. Verb. Behav.*, **22**, 88–104.

Bandura, A. (1977) 'Self-efficacy: towards a unifying theory of behavioural change'. *Psychol. Rev.*, **84**, 191–215.

Bara, B.G. (1983) 'Modification of knowledge by memory process. In M.A. Reda and M.J. Mahoney, (eds), *Cognitive Psychotherapies*. Cambridge, Mass.: Ballinger.

Bargh, J.A. (1982) 'Attention and automaticity in the processing of self-relevant information'. *J. Person. Soc. Psychol.*, **43** (3), 425–436.

Bargh, J.A. and Pietromonaco, P. (1982) 'Automatic information processing and social perception: the influence of trait information presented outside of conscious awareness on impression formation'. *J. Pers. Soc. Psychol.*, **43**, 437–449.

Baron, R. and Treiman, R. (1980) 'Some problems in the study of differences in cognitive processes'. *Mem. & Cog.*, **8**, 313–321.

Bartlett, F.C. (1932) *Remembering*. Cambridge: Cambridge University Press.

Bartlett, F.C. (1941) 'Fatigue following highly skilled work'. *Proc. Roy. Soc. London B*, **131**, 247–257.

Beck, A.T. (1976) *Cognitive Therapy and the Emotional Disorders*. New York: International Universities Press.

Beck, A.T., Rush, A.J., Shaw, B.F. and Emery G. (1979) *Cognitive Therapy of Depression*, New York: Guildford Press.

Beck. A.T., Emery, G. and Greenberg, R.C. (1986) *Anxiety disorders and phobias: A cognitive perspective*. New York: Basic Books.

Becker, C.A. and Killion, T.H. (1977) 'Interaction of visual and cognitive effects in word recognition'. *J. Exp. Psychol.: Human Perc. & Perf.*, **3**, 389–401.

Bellezza, F.S. and Bower, G.H. (1981) 'The representation and processing characteristics of scripts'. *Bull. Psychonom. Soc.*, **18**, 1, 4.

Berry, D.C. and Broadbent, D.E. (1984) 'On the relationship between task performance and verbal knowledge'. *Quart. J. Exp. Psychol.*, **36a**, 209–231.

Biederman, I. (1982) 'On the semantics of a glance at a scene'. In N. Kubovy and J.R. Pomerantz (eds), *Perceptual Organisation*. Hillsdale, N.J.: Lawrence Erlbaum.

Black, J. and Bower, G. (1979) 'Episodes as narrative chunks in memory'. *J. Verb. Learn. Verb. Behav.*, **18**, 309–310.

Blackburn, I.M. (1975) 'Mental and psychomotor speed in depression and mania'. *Br. J. Psychiat.*, **126**, 329–335.

Blaney, P.H. (1986) 'Affect and memory: a review'. *Psychol. Bull.*, **99**, 229–246.

Block, N. (1981) *Imagery*. Cambridge, Mass.: MIT Press.

Bolles, R.C. and Bailey, D.E. (1956) 'Importance of object recognition in size constancy'. *J. Exp. Psychol.*, **51**, 222–225.

Bootzin, R.R. and Natsoulas, T. (1965) 'Evidence for perceptual defence uncontaminated by response bias'. *J. Person. Soc. Psychol.*, **1**, 461–468.

Bootzin, R.R. and Stephens, M.W. (1967) 'Individual differences and perceptual defence in the absence of response bias'. *J. Person. Soc. Psychol.*, **6**, 408–412.

Borkovec, T.D. and Sides, J.K. (1979) 'The contribution of relaxation and expectancy to fear reduction via graded imaginal exposure to feared stimuli'. *Behav. Res. & Ther.*, **17**, 529–540.

Bower, G.H. (1981) 'Mood and memory'. *Amer. Psychol.*, **36**, 129–148.

Bower, G.H. (1983) 'Affect and cognition'. *Phil. Trans. Roy. Soc.*, London, **B302**, 387–402.

Bower, G.H. (1985) 'A review of research on mood and memory', Paper presented at Symposium on Affect and Cognition, Cognitive Psychology Section, British Psychological Society, Oxford, September 1985.

Bower, G.H. and Cohen, P.R. (1982) 'Emotional influences in memory and thinking: data and theory'. In S. Fiske and M. Clark (eds), *Affect and Cognition*. Hillsdale, N.J.: Lawrence Erlbaum.

Bower, G.H., Black, J.B. and Turner, T.J. (1979) 'Scripts in memory for text'. *Cog. Psychol.*, **11**, 177–220.

Bower, G.H., Gilligan, S.G. and Monteiro, K.P. (1981) 'Selectivity of learning caused by affective states'. *J. Exp. Psychol.: Gen.*, **110**, 451–473.

Bower, G.H. and Mayer, J.D. (1985) Failure to replicate mood-dependent retrieval'. *Bull. Psychonom. Soc.*, **23**, 39–42.

Bower, G.H., Monteiro, K.P. and Gilligan, S.G. (1978) 'Emotional mood as a context for learning and recall'. *J. Verb. Learn. Verb. Behav.*, **17**, 573–587,

Bradley, B. and Mathews, A. (1983) 'Negative self-schemata in clinical depression'. *Br. J. Clin. Psychol.*, **22**, 173–182.

Bradley, B. and Mathews, A. 'Memory bias in recovered clinical depressives'. (Submitted for Publication).

Braff, D.L. and Beck, A.T. (1974) 'Thinking disorder in depression'. *Arch. Gen. Psychiat.*, **31**, 456–460.

Bransford, J.D. (1979) *Human Cognition: Learning, Understanding and Remembering*. Belmont, California: Wadsworth.

Bransford, J.D. and Johnson, M.K. (1971) 'Semantic prerequisites for comprehending prose'. Paper presented at Eastern Verbal Investigators League Meetings, October 1971.

Bransford, J.D. and MacCarrell, N.S. (1975) 'A sketch of a cognitive approach to comprehension'. In E.B. Weimer and D.F. Palermo (eds), *Cognition and the Symbolic Processes*. Hillsdale, N.J.: Lawrence Erlbaum.

Breslow, R., Kocsis, J. and Belkin, B. (1981) 'Contribution of the depressive perspective to memory function in depression'. *Amer. J. Psychiat.*, **138**, 227–230.

Bressler, J. (1931) 'Illusion in the case of subliminal visual stimulation'. *J. Gen. Psychol.*, **5**, 244–251.

Brewer, W.F. and Treyens, J.C. (1981) 'Role of schemata in memory for places'. *Cog. Psychol.*, **13**, 207–230.

Briars, D.J. (1983) An information-processing analysis of mathematical ability. In R.F. Dillon and R.R. Schmeck, *Individual Differences in Cognition* Vol. I. New York: Academic Press.

Broadbent, D.E. (1958) *Perception and Communication*. New York: Pergamon Press.

Broadbent, D.E. (1971) *Decision and Stress*. London: Academic Press.

Broadbent D.E. (1977a) 'The hidden pre-attentive processes'. *Amer. Psychol.*, **32**, 109–118.

Broadbent, D.E. (1977b) 'Levels hierarchies, and locus of control'. *Quart. J. Exp. Psycho.*, **29**, 181–201.

Broadbent, D.E. (1982) 'Task combination and selective intake of information'. *Acta Psychologica*, **50**, 253–290.

Broadbent, D.E. (1984) 'The Maltese Cross; A new simplistic model for memory'. *Behav. Brain Sci.*, **7**, 55–94.

Broadbent, D.E. and Gregory, M. (1967) 'Perception of emotionally toned words'. *Nature*, **215**, 581–584.

Broadbent, D.E., Broadbent, M.H.P. and Jones, J.L. (1986) 'Performance correlates of self-reported cognitive failure and obsessionality', *Brit. J. Clin. Psychol.*, **25**, 285–299.

Broadbent, D.E., Fitzgerald, P. and Broadbent, M.H.T. (1986) 'Implicit and explicit knowledge in the control of complex systems'. *Brit. J. Psychol.*, **77**, 33–50.

Broadbent, D.E. and Gregory, N. (1967) 'Perception of emotionally toned words'. *Nature*, **215**, 581–584.

Brown, T. (1820) *Lectures on the philosophy of the human mind*. Edinburgh: Trait, Longman.

Brown, W.P. (1961) 'Conceptions of perceptual defence'. *Brit. J. Psychol. Monograph Supplements*, **35**.

Bruch, M.A., Juster, H.R. and Kaflowitz, N.G. (1983) 'Relationships of cognitive components of text anxiety to test performance: Implications for assessment and treatment'. *J. Couns. Psychol.*, **30**, 527–536.

Bruch, M.A., Kaflowitz, N.G. and Keuthe, M. (1986) 'Beliefs and the subjective meaning of thoughts: analysis of the role of self-statements in academic test performance'. *Cog. Ther. & Res.*, **10**, 51–69.

Bruner, J.S. and Postman, L. (1947a) 'Emotional selectivity in perception and reaction'. *J. Person.*, **16**, 69–77.

Bruner, J.S. and Postman, L. (1947b) 'Tension and tension-release as organising factors in perception'. *J. Person.*, **15**, 300–308.

Bruner, J.S., Postman, L. and Rodrigues, J. (1951) 'Expectation and the perception of color. *Amer. J. Psychol.*, **64**, 216–227.

Burgess, I.S., Jones, L.N., Robertson, S.A., Radcliffe, W.N., Emerson, E., Lawler, P. and Crow, T.J. (1981) 'The degree of control exerted by phobic and non-phobic verbal stimuli over the recognition behaviour of phobic and non-phobic subjects. *Behav. Res. Ther.* **19**, 223–234.

Buschke, H. and Schaier, A. (1979) 'Memory units, ideas, and propositions in semantic remembering'. *J. Verb. Learn. Verb. Behav.*, **18**, 549–563.

Butler, G. and Mathews, A. (1983) 'Cognitive processes in anxiety'. *Adv. Behav. Ther.*, **5**, 51–62.

Butler, G. and Mathews, A. (1987) 'Anticipatory anxiety and risk perception'. *Cog. Ther. & Res.*, **91**, 551–565.

Butterfield, E.C. and Belmont, J.M. (1971) 'Relations of storage and retrieval strategies as short-term memory processes'. *J. Exp. Psychol.*, **89**, 319–328.

Button, E.J. (1983a) 'Construing the anorexic'. In J.R. Adams-Webber and J.C. Mancuso (eds), *Applications of Personal Construct Theory*, London: Academic Press.

Button, E. (1983b) 'Personal construct theory and psychological well-being'. *Brit. J. Med. Psychol.*, **56**, 323–237.

Byrne, D. (1961) 'The repression-sensitisation skill: rationale, reliability, and validity'. *J. Personal.*, **29**, 334–349.

Byrne, D. (1964) 'Repression-sensitisation as a dimension of personality'. In B.A. Maher (ed.), *Progress in Experimental Personality Research*. New York: Academic Press.

Byrne, D.G. (1975a) 'A psychophysiological distinction between different types of depressive states'. *Aust. & N.Z. J. Psychiat.*, **8**, 261–267.

Byrne, D.G. (1975b) 'Note on decision time/movement, time relationships in normal and depressed subjects'. *Percept. Mot. Skills.*, **41**, 907–910.

Byrne, D.G. (1976a) 'Choice reaction times times in depressive states'. *Brit. J. Soc. & Clin. Psychol.*, **15**, 149–156.

Byrne, D.G. (1976b) 'Vigilance on arousal in depressive states'. *Brit. J. Clin. Psychol.*, **15**, 267–274.

Byrne, D.G. (1977). 'Affect and vigilance performace in depressive illness'. *J. Psychiat. Res.*, **13**, 185–191.

Calev, A. (1984) 'Recall and recognition in chronic nondemented schizophrenics: use of matched task'. *J. Abnorm. Psychol.*, **93**, 172–177.

Calev, A. and Erwin, P.G. (1985) 'Recall and recognition in depressives: use of matched task'. *Brit. J. Clin. Psychol.*, **24**, 127–128.

Campbell, D. (1957) 'A study of some sensory-motor functions in psychiatric patients'. Unpublished PhD thesis, University of London.

Cane, D.B. and Gotlib, I.H. (1985) 'Depression and the effects of positive and negative feedback on expectations, evaluations and performance'. *Cog. Ther. & Res.*, **9** (2) 145–160.

Cantela, J.R. and Baron, M.G. (1977) 'Covert conditioning: A theoretical analysis'. *Behav. Mod.*, **1**, 351–368.

Carr. T.H., McCauley, C., Sperber, R.D. and Parmelee, C.M. (1982) 'Words, pictures, and priming: on semantic activation, conscious identification, and automaticity of information processing'. *J. Exp. Psychol.: Hum. Perc. & Perf.*, **8**, 757–777.

Carroll, J.M., Thomas, J.C. and Malhotra, A. (1980) 'Presentation and representation in design problem solving'. *Br. J. Psychol.*, **71**, 143–153.

Carroll, J.S. (1978) 'The effect of imagining an event on expectations for the event: An interpretation in terms of the availability heuristic'. *J. Exp. Soc. Psychol.*, **14**, 88–96.

Casscells, W., Schoenberger, A. and Grayboys, T. (1978) 'Interpretations by physicians of clinical laboratory results'. *New Eng. J. Med.*, **299**, 999–1000.

Cermak, L.S. and Craig, F.I.M. (1979) *Levels of Processing in Human Memory*. Hillsdale, N.J.; Lawrence Erlbaum.

Chambers, D. and Reisberg, D. (1985) 'Can mental images be ambiguous?'. *J. Exp. Psychol: Hum. Perc. & Perf.*, **11**, 317–328.

Chapman, C.R. and Feather, B.W. (1972) 'Modification of perception by classical conditioning procedures'. *J. Exp. Psychol.*, **93**, 338–342.

Chapman, L.J. (1967) 'Illusory correlation in observation reports'. *J. Verb. Learn. Verb. Behav.*, **6**, 151–155.

Chapman, L.J. and Chapman, J.P. (1967) 'Genesis of popular but erroneous psychodiagnostic observations'. *J. Abnorm. Psychol.*, **72**, 193–204.

Chapman, L.J. and Chapman, J.P. (1969) 'Illusory correlation as an obstacle to the use of valid psychodiagnostic signs'. *J. Abnorm. Psychol.*, **74**, 271–280.

Chapman, L.J. and Chapman, J.P. (1973) *Disordered Thought in Schizophrenia*. New York: Appleton-Century-Crofts.

Charniak, E. (1972) 'Towards a model of children's story comprehension'. Technical Report 266, Artificial Intelligence Laboratory, Massachusetts Institute of Technology.

Cherry, E.C. (1953) 'Some experiments on the recognition of speech, with one and with two ears'. *J. Acoustic. Soc. Amer.*, **25**, 975–979.

Cherry, E. (1976) 'Subliminal fantasy activation and the avoidance of success'. Doctoral dissertation, Adelphi University.

Chi, M.T.H. (1978) 'Knowledge structures and memory development'. In R.S. Siegler (ed.), *Children's Thinking: What Develops?* Hillsdale, N.J.: Lawrence Erlbaum.

Christian, J., Bickley, W., Tarka, M. and Clayton, K.T. (1978) 'Measures of free recall of 900 English nouns: Correlations with imagery, concreteness, meaningfulness and frequency'. *Mem. & Cog.*, **6**, 379–390.

Cirilo, R.K. (1981) 'Referential coherence and text structure in story comprehension'. *J. Verb. Learn. Verb. Behav.* **2**, 358–367.

Clark, D.A. and de Silva, P. (1985) The nature of depressive and anxious intrusive thoughts: distinct or uniform phenomena. *Behav. Res. Ther.*, **23**, 383–393.

Clark, D.M. and Teasdale, J.D. (1982) 'Diurnal variations in clinical depression and accessibility of memories of positive and negative experiences'. *J. Abnorm. Psychol.*, **91**, 87–95.

Clark, D.M. and Teasdale, J.D. (1985) 'Constraints of the effects of mood on memory'. *J. Person. Soc. Psychol.*, **48**, 1598–1608.

Clark, H.H. and Chase, W.G. (1972) 'On the process of comparing sentences against pictures'. *Cog. Psychol*, **3**, 452–517.

Clark, H.H. and Marshall, C.R. (1981) 'Definite reference and mutual knowledge'. In A.K. Joshi, B.L. Webber and I.A. Sag (eds), *Elements of Discourse Understanding.* Cambridge: Cambridge University Press.

Cohen, R.M., Weingartner, H., Smallberg, S.A., Pickar, D. and Murphy, D.L. (1982) 'Effort and cognition in depression'. *Arch. Gen. Psychiat.*, **39**, 593–597.

Condon, T.J. and Allen, G.J. (1980) 'The role of psychoanalytic merging fantasies in systematic desensitisation: a rigorous methodological examination'. *J. Abnorm. Psychol.*, **89**, 437–443.

Cooper, A. and Marshall, P.H. (1985) Spatial location judgements as a function of intention to learn and mood state: an evaluation of an alleged automatic encoding operation. *Amer. J. Psychol.*, **98**, 261–269.

Coover, J.E. (1917) *Experiments in Psychical Research at Leland Stanford Junior University, California.* Stanford, California: Stanford University Press.

Cornell, D.G., Suarez, R. and Berent, S. (1984) 'Psychomotor retardation in melancholic and nonmelancholic depression: cognitive and motor components. *J. Abnorm. Psychol.*, **93**, 150–157.

Corteen, R.S. and Wood, B. (1972) 'Autonomic responses to shock associated words'. *J. Exp. Psychol.*, **9**, 308–313.

Corteen, R.S. and Dunn, D. (1974) 'Shock associated words in a non-attended message: a test for momentary awareness'. *J. Exp. Psychol.*, **102**, 1143–1144.

Covington, M.V., Omelich, C.L. and Schwarzer, R. (1986) 'Anxiety, aspirations and self-concept in the achievement process: a longitudinal model with latent variables'. *Motiv. & Emot.*, **10**, 71–88.

Cowley, J.J., Johnson, A.L. and Brooksbanck, B.W.L. (1977) 'The effect of two odorous compounds on performance in an assessment-of-people text'. *Psychoneuroendocrin.*, **2**, 159–172.

Coyne, J.C. and Gotlib, I. (1983) 'The role of cognition in depression: a critical appraisal'. *Psychol. Bull.*, **94**, 472–505.

Coyne, J.C. and Gotlib, I. (1986) 'Studying the role of cognition in depression: well-trodden paths and cul-de-sacs'. *Cog. Ther. & Res.*, **10**, 695–705.

Craig, M.J., Humphreys, M.S., Rocklin, T. and Revelle, W. (1979) 'Impulsivity, neuroticism and caffeine: Do they have additive effects on arousal'. *J. Res. Person.*, **13**, 404–419.

Craik, F.I.M. and Lockhart, R.S. (1972) 'Levels of processing: a framework for memory research'. *J. Verb. Learn. Verb. Behav.*, **11**, 671–684.

Craik, K.J.W. (1966) *The Nature of Psychology*. Cambridge: Cambridge University Press.

Cromwell, R.L. and Levenkron, J.C. (1984) 'Psychological care of acute coronary patients'. In A. Steptoe and A. Mathews (eds), *Health Care and Human Behaviour*. London: Academic Press.

Cronholm, B. and Ottosson, J.-O. (1961) 'The experience of memory function after electroconvulsive therapy'. *Brit. J. Psychiat.*, **109**, 251–258.

Crossman, E.R.S.W. (1953) 'Entropy and choice-time: The effect of frequency on balance on choice response'. *J. Exp. Psychol.*, **5**, 41–51.

Danaher, B. and Thoresen, C. (1972) 'Imagery assessment of self-report and behavior measures'. *Behav. Res. & Ther.*, **10**, 131–138.

Davis, H. (1979) Self-reference and the encoding of personal information in depression. *Cog. Res. & Ther.*, **4**, 97–110.

Dawes, R.M. 1964) Cognitive distortion. *Psychological Reports*, **14**, 443–459.

DeMonbreun, B.G. and Craighead, W.E. (1977) 'Selective recall of positive and neutral feedback'. *Cog. Ther. & Res.*, **1**, 311–329.

Den Uyl, M. and Van Oostendorp, H. (1980) 'The use of scripts in text comprehension'. *Poetics*, **9**, 275–294.

Derry. P.A. and Kuiper, N.A. (1981) 'Schematic processing and self-reference in clinical depression'. *J. Abnorm. Psychol.*, **90**, 286–297.

Deutsch, J.A., and Deutsch, D. (1963) 'Attention: some theoretical considerations'. *Psychol. Rev.*, **70**, 80–90.

DiCaprio, N.S. (1970) 'Essentials of verbal satiation therapy: A learning-theory-based behaviour therapy'. *J. Couns. Psychol.*, **17**, 419–424.

Dillon, R.F. (ed.) (1985) *Individual Differences in Cognition*, Vol. 2. Orlando, Fl, Academic Press.

Dillon, R.F. and Schmeck, R.R. (1982) *Individual Differences in Cognition*, Vol. 1. New York: Academic Press

Dixon, N.F. (1968) 'Perception without awareness. A reply to K.M. Banreti-Fuchs'. *Acta Psychologica*, **28**, 171–180.

Dixon, N.F. (1971) *Subliminal Perception: the Nature of a Controversy*. London: McGraw Hill.

Dixon, N.F. (1981) *Preconscious Processing*. London: John Wiley.

Dobson, K.S. and Shaw, B.F. (1987) 'Specificity and stability of self-referent encoding in clinical depression'. *J. Abnorm. Psychol.*, **96**, 34–40.

Doctor, R.M. and Altman, F. (1969) 'Worry and emotionality as components of test anxiety, with replication and further data'. Psychol. Rep., **24**, 563–568.

Donnelly, E.F., Waldman, I.N., Murphy, D.L., Wyatt, R.J. and Goodwin, F.K. (1980) 'Primary affective disorder; thought disorder in depression'. *J. Abnorm. Psychol.*, **89**, 315–319.

Dooling, D.J. and Lachman, R. (1971) 'Effects of comprehension on retention of prose'. *J. Exp. Psychol.*, **88**, 216–222.

Dooling, D.J. and Mullet, R. (1973) 'Locus of thematic effects in retention of prose'. *J. Exp. Psychol.*, **97**, 404–406.

Dorfman, D.D. (1967) 'Recognition of taboo words as a function of *a priori* probability'. *J. Person. Soc. Psychol.*, **7**, 1–10.

Dorfman, D.D., Grosberg, J.M. and Kroeker, L. (1965) 'Recognition of taboo stimuli as a function of exposure time'. *J. Person. Soc. Psychol.*, **2**, 552–562.

Dornic, S. (1977) Mental Load, effort and individual differences. *Reports of the Department of Psychology University of Stockholm*, No. 509.

Dreyfus, H.L. (1979) *What Computers Can't Do: A Critique of Artificial Reason*, 2nd edition. New York: Harper and Row.

Dulany, E. (1957) 'Avoidance learning of perceptual defence and vigilance'. *J. Abnorm. Soc. Psychol.*, **55**, 333–338.

Dunbar, D.C. and Lishman, W.A. (1984) 'Depression, recognition-memory, and hedonic tone: a signal detection analysis'. *Br. J. Psychiat.*, **144**, 376–382.

Duncan, J. (1980) 'The locus of interference in the perception of simultaneous stimuli'. *Psychol. Rev.*, **87**, 272–300.

Duncker, K. (1939) 'The influence of past experience upon perception of properties'. *Amer. J. Psychol.*, **52**, 255–265.

Dunlap, K. (1900) 'The effect of imperceptual shadows on judgement of distance'. *Psychol. Rev.*, **7**, 435–453.

Dutta, S. and Kanungo, R.N. (1975) *Affect and Memory: A Reformulation*. Oxford: Pergamon.

Dyckman, J. and Cowan, P. (1978) 'Imaging vividness and the outcome of in vivo and imagined scene desensitisation'. *J. Consult. & Clin. Psychol.*, **46**, 1155–1156.

Ebbinghaus, H. (1885) '*Über das Gedachtnis*'. Leipzig: Duncker and Humblot.

Edmundson, E.D. and Nelson, D.L. (1976) 'Anxiety, imagery and sensory interference'. *Bull. Psychonom, Soc.*, **8**, 319–322.

Ellis, H.C. and Ashbrook, P.W. (1987) 'Resource allocation model of the effects of depressed mood states on memory'. In K. Fiedler and J. Forgas (eds), *Affect, Cognition and Social Behaviour*. Toronto: Hogrefe.

Ellis, H., Thomas, R.L. and Rodrigez, I.A. (1984) 'Emotiorral mood states and memory: elaborative encoding, semantic processing and cognitive effort'. *J. Exp. Psychol.: Learn. Mem. & Cog.*, **69**, 237–243.

Ellis, H.C., Thomas, R.L., McFarland, A.D. and Lane, J.W. (1985) 'Emotional mood states and retrieval in episodic memory'. *J. Exp. Psychol.: Learn, Mem. & Cog.*, **11**, 363–370.

Erdelyi, M.H. (1974) 'A new look at the new look: perceptual defence and vigilance'. *Psychol. Rev.*, **81**, (1), 1–25.

Erdelyi, M. (1985) *Psychoanalysis: Freud's Cognitive Psychology*. New York: W.H. Freeman.

Erdelyi, M.H. and Goldberg, B. (1979) 'Let's not sweep repression under the rug: toward a cognitive psychology of repression'. In J.F. Kihlstrom and F.J. Evans (eds), *Functional Disorders of Memory*, Hillsdale, N.J.: Lawrence Erlbaum.

Ericsson, K.A. and Simon, H.A. (1984) *Protocol Analysis: Verbal Reports on Data*. Cambridge, Mass.: MIT Press.

Eriksen, C.W. (1963) 'Perception and personality'. In N.J. Wepman and R.W. Heine (eds), *Concepts of Personality*. Chicago: Aldine.

Eriksen, C.W. and Collins, J.F. (1964). 'Backward masking in vision'. *Psychom. Sci.*, **1**, 101–102.

Eriksen, C.W. and Collins, J.F. (1965) 'Reinterpretation of one form of backward and forward masking in visual perception'. *J. Exp. Psychol.*, **70**, 343–351.

Eysenck, M.W. (1979a) 'Anxiety, learning and memory: a reconceptualisation'. *J. Res. Personal.*, **13**, 363–385.

Eysenck, M.W. (1979b) 'Depth, elaboration, and distinctiveness'. In L.S. Cermak and F.I.M. Craik (eds), *Levels of Processing in Human Memory*, Hillsdale, N.J.: Lawrence Erlbaum.

Eysenck, M.W. (1982) *Attention and Arousal: Cognition and Performance*. Berlin: Springer-Verlag.

Eysenck, M.W., MacLeod, C. and Mathews, A. (1987) 'Cognitive functioning in anxiety'. *Psychol. Res.* **49**, 189–195.

Farné, M. (1963) 'Effects of so-called subliminal stimuli upon visual perception'. *Psychol. Res. Bull.* **3**, – .

Fehrer, E. and Smith, E. (1962) 'Effects of luminance ratio on masking'. *Perc. & Mot. Skills.*, **14**, 243–253.

Fennell, M.J.V., Teasdale, J.D., Jones, S. and Damle, A. (1987) 'Distraction in neurotic and endogenous depression: an investigation of negative thinking in major depressive disorders'. *Psychol. Med.*, **17**, 441–452.

Finger, R. and Galassi, J.P. (1977) 'Effects of modifying cognitive versus emotionality, responses in the treatment of text anxiety'. *J. Consult. & Clin. Psychol.*, **45**, 280–287.

Fischhoff, B. and Beyth, R. (1975) '"I knew it would happen" remembered probabilities of once-future things' *Organ. Behav. & Hum. Perf.*, **13**, 1–16.

Fischhoff, B., Slovic, P. and Lichtenstein, S. (1977) 'Knowing with certainty: The appropriateness of extreme confidence'. *J. Exp. Psychol.: Hum. Perc. & Perf.*, **3**, 552–564.

Fisher, C. (1960) 'Subliminal and supraliminal influences on dreams'. *Amer. J. Psychiat.*, **116**, 1009–1017.

Foa, E.G. and Kozak, M.J. (1986) 'Emotional processing and fear: exposure to corrective information'. *Psychol. Bull.*, **99**, 20–35.

Foa, E.B. and McNally, R.J. (1986) Sensitivity to feared stimuli in obsessive-compulsives: a dichotic listening analysis. *Cog. Ther. Res.*, **10**, 477–486.

Fodor, J.A. (1983) *The Modularity of Mind*. Cambridge, Mass.: MIT Press.

Fogarty, S.J. and Hemsley, D.R. (1983) 'Depression and the accessibility of memories: a longitudinal study'. *Br. J. Psychiat.*, **142**, 610–617.

Forster, P.M. and Govier, E. (1978) 'Discrimination without awareness'. *Quart. J. Exp. Psychol.*, **30**, 282–292.

Foulds, G.A. (1952) 'Temperamental differences in maze performance II: The effect of distraction and of electroconvulsive therapy on psychomotor retardation'. *Brit. J. Psychiat.*, **43**, 33–41.

Franks, J.J. (1974) 'Towards understanding understanding'. In W.B. Weimer and D.S. Palermo (eds), *Cognition and the Symbolic Processes*. Hillsdale, N.J.: Lawrence Erlbaum.

Fransson, A. (1977) 'On qualitative differences in learning IV: Effects of intrinsic motivation and extrinsic test anxiety on process and outcome'. *Brit. J. Educ. Psychol.*, **47**, 244–257.

Frederiksen, C.H. (1975) 'Acquisition of semantic information from discourse: Effects of repeated exposures'. *J. Verb. Learn. Verb. Behav.*, **14**, 158–169.

Freeman, J.T. (1954) 'Set or perceptual defence?'. *J. Exp. Psychol.*, **48**, 283–288.

Friedman, A. (1979) 'Framing pictures: The role of knowledge in automatised encoding and memory for gist'. *J. Exp. Psychol.: Gen.*, **108**, 316–355.

Friedman, A.B. and Polson, M.C. (1981) 'Hemispheres as independent resource systems: limited-capacity processing and cerebral specialisation'. *J. Exp. Psychol.: Human Perc. & Perf.*, **7**, 1031–1058.

Friedman, A.B., Polson, M.C., Defoe, C.G. and Gaskill, S.J. (1982) 'Dividing attention within and between hemispheres: testing a multiple resources approach to limited-capacity information processing'. *J. Exp. Psychol.: Hum. Perc. & Perf.*, **8**, 625–650.

Frisby, J.P. (1980) *Seeing, Illusion, Brain and Mind*. Oxford: Oxford University Press.

Frith, C.D., Stevens, N., Johnstone, E.C., Deakin, P.L., Lawler, P. and Crowe, T.J. (1983) 'Effects of ECT and depression on various aspects of memory'. *Br. J. Psychiat.*, **142**, 610–617.

Galambos, J.A. (1982) 'Normative studies of six characteristics of our knowledge of common activities'. *Cog. Sci. Tech. Rep.*, **14**, New Haven: Yale University.

Galambos, J.A. and Rips, L.J. (1982) 'Memory for routines'. *J. Verb. Learn. Verb. Behav.* **21**, 260–281.

Galassi, J.P., Frierson, H.T., Jr and Sharver, R. (1981a) 'The behavior of high, moderate, and low test anxious students during an actual test situation'. *J. Consult. & Clin. Psychol.*, **49**, 51–62.

Galassi, J.P., Frierson, H.T., Jr and Sharver, R. (1981b) 'Concurrent versus retrospective assessment in text anxiety research'. *J. Consult. & Clin. Psychol.*, **49**, 614–615.

Galassi, J.P., Frierson, H.T., Jr and Siegel, R.G. (1984) 'Cognitions, test anxiety, and test performance: A closer look'. *J. Consult. & Clin. Psychol.*, **51**, 292–293.

Ganzer, V.J. (1968) 'Effect of awareness presence and test anxiety on learning and, retention in a serial learning situation'. *J. Pers. Soc. Psychol.*, **8**, 194–199.

Garnham, A. (1982) 'On-line construction of representations of the content of texts'. Bloomington, Indiana: University Linguistics Club.

Garnham, A. (1983) 'What's wrong with story grammars'? . *Cognition*, **15**, 145–154.

Garnham, A., Oakhill, J.V. and Johnson-Laird, P.N. (1982) 'Referential continuity and the coherence of discourse. *Cognition*, **11**, 29–46.

Garrod, S.C. and Sanford, A.J. (1982) 'Bridging inferences and the extended domain of reference'. In J. Long and A. Baddeley (eds), *Attention and Performance IX*, Hillsdale, N.J.: Lawrence Erlbaum.

Garrod, S.C. and Sanford, A.J. (1983) 'Topic-dependent effects in language processing. In G.B. Flores D'Arcais and J. Jarvella (eds), *Processes of Language Understanding*. Chichester, John Wiley & Sons.

Gellatly, A.R.H. (1980) 'Perception of an illusory triangle with masked inducing figure'. *Perception*, **9**, 599–602.

Geller, V. and Shaver, P. (1976) 'Cognitive consequences of self-awareness'. *J. Exp. Soc. Psychol.*, **12**, 99–108.

Gentner, D.R. (1976) 'The structure and recall of narrative prose'. *J. Verb. Learn. Verb. Behav.*, **15**, 411–418.

Gerrig, R.J. and Bower, G.H. (1982) 'Emotional influences on word recognition'. *Bull. Psychonom. Soc.*, **19**, 197–200.

Gilligan, S.G. and Bower, G.H. (1984) 'Cognitive consequences of emotional arousal'. In C. Izard, J. Kagan and R. Zajonc (eds) *Emotions, Cognitions and Behaviour*, New York: Cambridge University Press.

Glaser, M.O. and Glaser, W.R. (1982) 'Time course analysis of the Stroop phenomenon'. *J. Exp. Psychol.: Hum. Perc. Perf.*, **8**, 875–894.

Glass, R.M., Uhlenhuth, E.H., Hastel, F.W., Matuzas, W. and Fischman, M.W. (1981) 'Cognitive dysfunction and imipramine in outpatient depressives'. *Arch. Gen. Psychiat.*, **38**, 1048–1051.

Glucksberg, S. and Cohen, N.J. (1970) 'Memory for non-attended auditory materal'. *Cog. Psychol.*, **1**, 149–156.

Godden, D.R. and Baddeley, A.D. (1975) 'When does context influence recognition memory?'. *Br. J. Psychol.*, **71**, 99–104.

Gogel, W.C. and Newton, R.E. (1969) 'Perception of off-sized objects'. *Perc. Psychophys.*, **5**, 7–9.

Going, M. and Read, J.D. (1974) 'Effects of uniqueness, sex of subject, and sex of photograph on facial recognition'. *Percept. & Mot. Skills.*, **39**, 109–110.

Goldiamond, I. (1958) 'Indicators of perception: I. Subliminal perception, subception, unconscious perception: an analysis in terms of psychophysical indicator methodology'. *Psychol. Bull.*, **55**, 373–411.

Goldiamond, I. (1962) 'Perception'. In A.J. Bachrach (ed.), *Experimental Foundations of Clinical Psychology*, New York: Basic Books.

Goldin, S.E. (1978) 'Memory for the ordinary: typicality effects in chess memory'. *J. Exp. Psychol.: Hum. Learn. & Mem.*, **4**, 605–616.

Goldstein, A.J. and Chance, J.E. (1985) 'Effects of training on Japanese face recognition: Reduction of the other-race effect'. *Bull. Psychonom. Soc.*, **23**, (3), 211–214.

Goldstein, M.J. and Barthol, R.P. (1960) 'Fantasy responses to subliminal stimuli'. *J. Abnorm. Soc. Psychol.*, **68**, 22–26.

Goodman, G.S. (1980) 'Picture memory: How the action schema affects retention'. *Cog. Psychol.*, **12**, 473–495.

Goodwin, A.M. and Williams, J.M.G. (1982) 'Mood induction research — its implications for clinical depression'. *Behav. Res. Ther.*, **20**, 373–382.

Gordon, G. (1967) *Semantic Determination by Subliminal Verbal Stimuli: A Quantitative Approach.* PhD Thesis, University of London.

Gordon, P.K. (1985) 'Allocation of attention in obsessional disorder'. *Br. J. Clin. Psychol.,* **24,** 101–107.

Gorham, D.R. (1956) 'A proverbs test for clinical and experimental user'. *Psychol. Rep.,* **2,** 1–12.

Gotlib, I.H. (1983) 'Perception and recall of interpersonal feedback: negative bias in depression'. *Cog. Ther. & Res.,* **7,** (5), 399–412.

Gotlib, I.H. and Asarnow, R.F. (1979) 'Interpersonal and impersonal problem-solving in mildly and clinically depressed university students'. *J. Consult. & Clin. Psychol.,* **47,** 85–95.

Gotlib, I.H. and McCann, C.D. (1984) 'Construct accessibility and depression: an examination of cognitive and affective factors'. *J. Person. Soc. Psychol.,* **47,** 427–439.

Govier, E. and Pitts, M. (1982) 'The contextual disambiguation of a polysemous word in an unattended message'. *Brit. J. Psychol.,* **73,** 537–545.

Graesser, A.C. (1981) *Prose Comprehension Beyond the Word.* New York: Springer-Verlag.

Graesser, A.C. and Nakamura, G.V. (1982) 'The impact of a schema on comprehension and memory'. *Psychol. of Learn. and Motiv.,* **16,** 59–109.

Graesser, A.C., Woll, S.B., Kowalski, D.J. and Smith, D.A. (1980) 'Memory for typical and atypical actions in scripted activities'. *J. Exp. Psychol.: Hum. Learn. & Mem.,* **6,** 503–513.

Graf, P. and Mandler, G. (1984) 'Activation makes words more accessible, but not necessarily more retrievable'. *J. Verb. Learn. Verb. Behav.,* **23,** 553–568.

Grayson, J.B., Foa, E.B. and Steketee, G. (1982) 'Habituation during exposure treatment: Distraction vs. attention focusing'. *Behav. Res. & Ther.,* **20,** 323–328.

Greenberg, L. and Safran, J.D. (1984a) 'Integrating affect and cognition: a perspective on the process of therapeutic change'. *Cog. Ther. & Res.,* **8,** 559–578.

Greenberg, L. and Safran, J.D. (1984b) 'Hot cognition — emotion coming in from the cold: a reply to Rachman'. *Cog. Ther. & Res.,* **8,** 591–598.

Gregory, W.L., Cialdini, R.B. and Carpenter, K.M. (1982) 'Self-relevant scenarios as mediators of likelihood estimates and compliance: Does imagining make it so?'*J. Person. Soc. Psychol.,* **43** (1), 89–99.

Griggs, S.S. and Green, D.W. (1983) 'How to make a good cup of tea: Exploring the scripts of thought-disordered and non-thought-disordered patients'. *Br. J. Med. Psychol.,* **56,** 125–133.

Grosz, B. (1977) 'The representation and use of focus in a system for understanding dialogues'. In *Proceedings of the 5th International Joint Conference on Artificial Intelligence.* Cambridge, Mass.: MIT.

Grosz, B. (1978) *Focusing in Dialogue. Tinlap-II. Theoretical Issues in Natural Language Processing, ACM and ACL.* New York: Academic Press.

Haber, R.N. and Hershenson, M. (1973) *The Psychology of Visual Perception.* London: Holt, Rinehart and Winston.

Hamilton, V. (1983) *The Cognitive Structures and Processes of Human Motivation and Personality.* Chichester: John Wiley.

Hammen, C., Marks, T., Mayol A. and de Mayo, R. (1985) 'Depressive self-schemas, life stress and vulnerability to depression'. *J. Abnorm, Psychol.,* **94,** 308–319.

Hammen, C., Dyck, D.G. and Miklowitz, D.J. (1986) 'Stability and severity parameters of depressive self-schema responding'. *J. Soc. Clin. Psychol.,* **4,** 23–45.

Hare, R.D. and Blevings, G. (1975) 'Defensive responses to phobic stimuli'. *Biol. Psychol.,* **3,** 1–13.

Harper, R.S. (1953) 'The perceptual modification of colored figures'. *Amer. J. Psychol.,* **66,** 86–89.

Hasher, L. and Zacks, R.T. (1979) 'Automatic and effortful processes in memory'. *J. Exp.*

Psychol.: Gen., **108**, 356–388.

Hasher, L., Rose, K.C., Zacks, R.T., Sanft, H. and Doren, B. (1985) Mood, recall and selectivity effects in normal college students'. *J. Exp. Psychol.: Gen.*, **114**, 104–118.

Haspel, K.C. and Harris, R.S. (1982) 'Effect of tachistoscopic stimulation to subconscious Oedipal wishes on competitive performance: a failure to replicate'. *J. Abnorm. Psychol.*, **91**, 437–444.

Healy, D. and Williams, J.M.G. 'Dysrhythmia, dysphoria, and depression: the interaction of learned helplessness and circadian dysrhythmia in the pathogenesis of depression'. *Psychol. Bull.* (in press).

Heilbrun, K. (1980) 'Silverman's subliminal psychodynamic activation: a failure to replicate'. *J. Abnorm. Psychol.*, **89**, 560–566.

Hemsley, D.R. and Zawada, S.L. (1976) 'Filtering' and the cognitive deficit in schizophrenia'. *Brit. J. Psychiat.*, **128**, 456–461.

Henderson, L. (1977) 'Word recognition'. In N.S. Sutherland (ed.), *Tutorial Essays in Experimental Psychology*, vol. 1. Hillsdale, N.J.: Lawrence Erlbaum.

Henley, S.H.A. (1975) 'Cross-modal effects of subliminal verbal stimuli'. *Scand. J. Psychol.*, **16**, 30–36.

Henley, S.H.A. and Dixon, N.F. (1974) 'Laterality differences in the effects of incidental stimuli upon evoked imagery'. *Brit. J. Psychol.*, **65**, (4), 529–536.

Henry, G.M., Weingartner, H. and Murphy, D.L. (1973) 'Influence of affective states and psychoactive drugs on verbal learning and memory'. *Amer. J. Psychiat.*, **130**, 966–971.

Hicks, W.E. (1952) 'On the rate of gain of information'. *Quart. J. Exp. Psychol.*, **4**, 11–26.

Hillyard, S.A. and Kutas, M. (1983) 'Electrophysiology of cognitive processing'. *Ann. Rev. Psychol.*, **34**, 33–61.

Hinton, G.E., McClelland, J.L. and Rumelhart, D.E. (1986) 'Distributed representations'. In J.L. McLelland and D.E. Rumelhart (eds), *Parallel Distributed Processing: Explorations in the Microstructure of Cognition.* Vol. 1: *Foundations.* Cambridge, Mass.: Bradford Books.

Hiscock, M. (1978) 'Imagery assessment through self-report: What do imagery questionnaires really measure?'. *J. Consult. Clin. Psychol.*, **46**, 223–231.

Hobbes, T. (1651) *Leviathan.* London: Andrew Crooke.

Hochberg, J.E. (1978) *Perception.* Engelwood Cliffs, N.J.: Prentice-Hall.

Hockey, G.R.J. (1986) 'A state control theory of adaptation to stress and individual differences in stress management'. In A.W.K. Gailland and M.G.H. Coles (eds), *Energetics and Human Information Processing.* Dordrecht: Nijhoff.

Holender, D. (1986) 'Semantic activation without conscious identification'. *Behav. Brain Sci.*, **9** (1), 1–66.

Homme, L.E. (1965) 'Control of coverants, the operants of the mind'. *Psychol. Rec.*, **15**, 501–511.

Horowitz, M.J. (1975) 'Intrusive and repetitive thoughts after experimental stress'. *Arch. Gen. Psychiat.* **32**, 1457–1463.

Horowitz, M.J. (1983) *Image Formation and Psychotherapy.* New York: Aronson.

Howes, D.H. (1954) 'A statistical theory of the phenomenon of subception'. *Psychol. Rev.*, **61**, 98–110.

Howie, D. (1952) 'Perceptual defence. *Psychol. Rev.*, **59**, 308–315.

Hume, D. (1739) *A Treatise of Human Nature*, Vols I and II. London: Noon.

Hirst, W. (1986) 'Aspects of divided and selective attention. In J. Le-Doux and W. Hurst (eds), *Mind and Brain.* New York: Cambridge University Press.

Hirst, W. and Kalmer, D. (1987) 'Characterising attentional resources'. *J. Exp. Psychol.: Gen.*, **116**, 68–81.

Hirst, W., Spelke, E., Reaves, C., Caharack, G. and Meisser, U. (1980) 'Dividing attention without alternation or automaticity'. *J. Exp. Psychol.: Gen.*, **109**, 98–117.

Hyman, R. (1953) 'Stimulus information as a determinant of reaction time'. *J. Exp. Psychol.*, **45**, 188–196.

Ingram, R. and Reed, M. (1986) Information encoding and retrieval processes in depression: findings, issues and future directions. In R. Ingram (Ed.) *Information Processing Approaches to Clinical Psychology*. Orlando, Florida: Academic Press.

Isen, A.M. (1984) 'Toward understanding the role of affect in cognition'. In R. Wyer and T. Srull (eds), *Handbook of Social Cognition* Hillsdale, N.J.: Lawrence Erlbaum.

Isen, A.M. (1985) 'The asymmetry of happiness and sadness in effects of memory in normal college students'. *J. Exp. Psychol.: Gen.*, **114**, 388–391.

Isen, A.M., Shalker, T.E., Clark, M. and Carp, L. (1978) 'Affect, accessibility of material in memory, and behavior: A cognitive loop'. *J. Person. Soc. Psychol.*, **36** (1), 1–12.

Isen, A.M., Johnson, M.M.S., Merts, E. and Robinson, G.S. (1985) 'The influence of positive affect on the unusualness of word associations'. *J. Person. Soc. Psychol.*, **48**, 1413–1426.

Jacoby, L.L. and Witherspoon, D. (1982) 'Remembering without awareness'. *Canad. J. Psychol.*, **36**, 300–324.

James, W. (1890/1950) *The Principles of Psychology*. New York: Dover.

Jensen, A.R. and Rohwer, W.D. (1966) 'The Stroop colour word test: A review'. *Acta. Psychol.*, **25**, 36–93.

Johnson, E.J. and Tversky, A. (1983) 'Affect, generalisation, and the perception of risk'. *J. Person. Soc. Psychol.*, **45**, (1), 20–31.

Johnson, M.H. and Magaro, P.A. (1987) 'Effects of mood and severity on memory processes in depression and mania'. *Psychol. Bull.*, **101**, 28–40.

Johnson, M.K. (1985) 'The origin of memories'. In *Advances in Cognitive-Behavioural Research and Therapy*, Vol. 4. New York: Academic Pres.

Johnson, R.E. and Scheidt, V.J. (1977) 'Organisational encoding in the serial learning of prose'. *J. Verb. Learn, Verb. Behav.*, **16**, 575–588.

Johnson-Laird, P.N. (1980) 'Mental models in cognitive science'. *Cog. Sci.*, **4**, 71–115.

Johnson-Laird, P.N. (1983a) *Mental Models: Towards a Cognitive Science of Language, Inference and Consciousness*. Cambridge: Cambridge University Press.

Johnson-Laird, P.N. (1983b) 'A computational analysis of consciousness'. *Cognition and Brain Theory*, **6**, 499–508.

Johsnon-Laird, P.N., Herrmann, D.J. and Chaffin, R. (1984) 'Only connections: a critique of semantic networks'. *Psychol. Bull.*, **96**, 292–315.

Johnston, W.A. and Dark, V.J. (1982) 'In defense of intra-perceptual theories of attention'. *J. Exp. Psychol.: Hum. Perc. Perf.*, **8**, 407–421.

Johnston, W.A. and Dark, V.J. (1985) 'Dissociable domains of selective processing'. In M.I. Posner and O.S.M. Marin, *Attention and Performance*, Vol. XI. Hillsdale, N.J.: Lawrence Erlbaum.

Johnston, W.A. and Dark, V.J. (1986) 'Selective attention'. *Ann. Rev. Psychol.*, **37**, 43–75.

Jonides, J. and Gleitman, H. (1972) 'A conceptual category effect in visual search: 'O' as letter or as digit'. *Percept. Psychophys.*, **12**, 457–560.

Kahneman, D. (1973) *Attention and Effort*. Englewood Cliffs, N.J.: Prentice-Hall.

Kahneman, D. and Treisman, A. (1984) 'Changing views of attention and automaticity'. In R. Parasuraman and D.R. Davies (eds), *Varieties of Attention*. Orlando, SL: Academic.

Kahneman, D., Treisman, A. and Burkell, J. (1983) 'The cost of visual filtering'. *J. Exp. Psychol.: Hum. Perc. Perf.*, **9**, 510–522.

Kahneman, D., Slovic, P. and Tversky, A. (eds) (1982) *Judgement under Uncertainty: Heuristics and Biases*. Cambridge: Cambridge University Press:

Kahneman, D. and Tversky, A. (1972) 'Subjective probability: A judgement of representativeness'. *Cog. Psychol.*, **3**, 430–454.

Kantowitz, B.H. and Knight, J. (1976) 'Test tapping and time-sharing II: use of auditory secondary task'. *Acta Psychol.*, **40**, 343–362.

Kavanagh, D.J. and Bower, G.H. (1985) 'Mood and self-efficacy: Impact of joy and sadness on perceived capabilities. *Cog. Ther. & Res.*, **9** (5), 507–525.

Kaye, N. (1975) 'The therapeutic value of three merging stimuli for male schizophrenics'. Unpublished doctoral thesis, Yeshiva University.

Keele, S.W. (1973) *Attention and Human Performance*. Pacific Pallisades, California: Good Year.

Kepecs, J.G. (1954) 'Observations on screens and barriers in the mind'. *Psychoanal. Quart.*, **23**, 62–77.

Kerr, B. (1973) Processing demands during mental operations'. *Mem. & Cog.*, **1**, 401–412.

Kieras, D. (1978) 'Beyond pictures and words: alternative information-processing models for imagery effects in verbal memory'. *Psychol. Bull.*, **85**, 532–554.

Kinsbourne, M. and Hicks, R. (1978) 'Functional cerebral space'. In J. Requin (ed.), *Attention and Performance VII*. Hillsdale, N.J.: Lawrence Erlbaum.

Kinsbourne, M. and Warrington, E.K. (1962) 'A disorder of simultaneous form perception'. *Brain*, **85**, 461–486.

Kinsbourne, M. and Warrington, E.K. (1963) 'The localising significance of limited simultaneous visual form perception'. *Brain*, **86**, 697–702.

Kirk-Smith, M., Booth, D.A., Carroll, D. and Davies, P. (1978) 'Human social attitudes affected by androstenol'. *Research on Community, Psychological and Psychiatric Behaviour*, **3**, 379–384.

Klapp, S.T. and Lee, P. (1974) 'Time of occurrence cues for 'unattended' auditory material'. *J. Exp. Psychol.*, **102**, 176–177.

Klein, F.B. and Kihlstrom, J.F. (1986) 'Elaboration organisation and the self-reference effect in memory'. *J. Exp. Psychol.: Gen.*, **115**, 26–38.

Klein, G.S. (1964) 'Semantic power measured through the interference of words with colour naming'. *Amer. J. Psychol.*, **77**, 576–588.

Kleinsmith, L.J. and Kaplan, S. (1963) Paired associate learning as a function of arousal and interpolated interval. *J. Exp. Psychol.*, **65**, 190–193.

Klinger, E. (1978) 'Dimensions of thought and imagery in normal waking states'. *J. Alt. States Consc.*, **4**, 97–113.

Klinger, E. (1980) 'Therapy and the flow of thought'. In J.E. Shorr, G.E. Sobel, P. Robin and J.A. Cornella (eds), *Imagery: Its many dimensions and applications*. New York: Plenum.

Klinger, E., Barter, S.G. and Maxeiner, M.E. (1981) 'Current concerns: assessing therapeutic relevant motivation'. In P.C. Kendall and S.D. Hollon (eds), *Assessment Strategies for Cognitive Behavioural Interventions*. New York: Academic Press.

Koh, S.D., Kayton, L. and Berry, R. (1973) 'Mnemonic organization in young non-psychotic schizophrenics'. *J. Abnorm. Psychol.*, **81**, 299–310.

Kolers, P.A. (1983) 'Perception and representation'. *Annual Rev. Psychol.*, **34**, 129–166.

Kolers, T.A. (1962) 'Intensity and contour effects in visual masking'. *Vis. Res.*, **2**, 277–294.

Kolodner, J. (1985) 'Memory for experience'. In G.H. Bower (ed.), *Psychology of Learning and Motivation*, Vol. 19. Hillsdale, N.J.: Lawrence Erlbaum.

Kosslyn, S.M. (1980) *Image and the Mind*. Cambridge, Mass.: Harvard University Press.

Kosslyn, S.M., Ball, T.M. and Reiser, B.J. (1978) 'Visual images preserve metric spatial information: evidence from studies of imagery scanning'. *J. Exp. Psychol.: Hum. Perc. & Perf.* **4**, 47–60.

Kovacs, M. and Beck, A.T. (1978) Maladaptive cognitive structures in depression. *Amer. J. Psychiatry.*, **135**, 525–533.

Kragh, U. and Smith, G.W. (1970) *Percept-Genesis Analysis*. Lund, Sweden: Gleerups.

Krames, L. and McDonald, M.R. (1985) 'Distraction and depressive cognition'. *Cog. Ther. & Res.*, **9**, 561–573.

Krueger, L.E. (1981) 'Is identity or regularity more salient than difference or irregularity?'. Paper presented at the meeting of the American Psychological

Association, Los Angeles, California.

Kuhn, T.S. (1962) *The Structure of Scientific Revolutions*. Chicago: Chicago University Press.

Kuiper, N. and MacDonald, M. (1982) Self and other perception in mild depressives. *Social Cognition*, **1**, 223–239.

Kukla, A. (1972) 'Foundations of an attributional theory of performance'. *Psychol. Rev.*, **79**, 454–470.

Kyllonen, P.C., Woltz, D.J. and Lohman, D.F. (1981) Models of strategy and strategy-shifting in spatial visual performance. Tech. Rep. No. 17. Stanford, Calif.: Aptitude Research Project, School of Education, Stanford University.

LaBerge, D. (1981) 'Automatic information processing: a review'. In J. Long and A.D. Baddeley (eds), *Attention and Performance*, **IX**. Hillsdale, N.J.: Lawrence Erlbaum.

LaBerge, D. and Samuels, S.J. (1974) 'Towards a theory of automatic information processing in reading'. *Cog. Psychol.*, **6**, 293–323.

Lacy, O.W., Lewinger, N. and Adamson, J.F. (1953) 'Foreknowledge as a factor affecting perceptual defence and alertness'. *J. Exp. Psychol.*, **45**, 169–174.

Landau, R.J. (1980) 'The role of semantic schemata in phobic word interpretation'. *Cog. Ther. & Res.*, **4**, 427–434.

Lang, P.J. (1977) 'Fear imagery: an information-processing analysis'. *Behav. Ther.*, **8**, 862–886.

Lang, P.J. (1979) 'A bio-informational theory of emotional imagery'. *Psychophysiol.*, **16**, 495–512.

Lang, P.J. (1984) 'Cognition in emotion: concept and action'. In C.E. Izard, R.R. Zajonc and J. Kagan (eds), *Emotions, Cognition and Behaviour*. Cambridge: Cambridge University Press.

Lang, P.J. (1985) The cognitive psychophysiology of emotion: fear and anxiety'. In A.H. Tuma and J. Maser (eds), *Anxiety and the Anxiety Disorders*. Hillsdale, N.J.: Lawrence Erlbaum.

Lang, P.J., Kozak, M.J., Miller, G.A., Levin, D.N. and MacLean, A. (1980) 'Emotional imagery: conceptual structure and pattern of somato-visceral response'. *Psychophysiol.*, **17**, 179–192.

Lang, P.J., Levin, D.N., Miller, G.A. and Kozak, M.J. (1983) 'Fear behaviour, fear imagery and the psychophysiology of emotion: the problem of affective response integration'. *J. Abnorm. Psychol.*, **92**, 276–306.

Lang, P.J., Melamed, B.G. and Hart, J. (1970) A psychophysiological analysis of fear modification using an automated desensitisation procedure'. *J. Abnorm. Psychol.*, **76**, 229–234.

Lazarus, R.S. (1966) *Psychological Stress and the Coping Process*. New York: McGraw Hill.

Lazarus, R.S. (1982) 'Thoughts on the relations between emotion and cognition'. *Amer. Psychol.*, **37**, 1019–1010.

Lazarus, R.G. (1984) 'On the primacy of cognition'. *Amer. Psychol.*, **39**, 124–129.

Lee, I. and Tyrer, P. (1980) 'Responses of chronic agoraphobics to subliminal and supraliminal phobic motion pictures'. *J. Nerv. Ment. Dis.*, **168** (1), 34–40.

Lee, I., Tyrer, P. and Horn, S. (1983) 'A comparison of subliminal, supraliminal and faded phobic cine-films in the treatment of agoraphobia'. *Brit. J. Psychiat.*, **143**, 356–361.

Leeper, R.W. (1935) 'A study of a neglected portion of the field of learning — the development of sensory organisation'. *J. Genetic Psychol.*, **46**, 41–75.

Leight, K.A. and Ellis, H.D. (1981) 'Emotional mood states, strategies and state-dependency in memory'. *J. Verb. Learn. Verb. Behav.*, **20**, 251–266.

Levene, M. (1966) 'Hypothesis behaviour by humans during discrimination learning'. *J. Exp. Psychol.*, **71**, 331–338.

Leventhal, H. (1984) A perceptual-motor theory of emotion. In L. Berkowitz (ed.), *Advances in Experimental Social Psychology.*, Vol. 17. New York: Academic Press.

Leventhal, H. and Cupchik, G. (1976) 'A process model of human judgement'. *J. Commun.*, **26**, 190–204.

Leventhal, H. and Scherer, K. (1987) 'The relationship of emotion to cognition: a functional approach to a semantic controversy', *Cog. & Emot.*, **1**, 3–28.

Levy, L.H. (1958) 'Perceptual defence in tactual perception'. *J. Personal.*, **26**, 467–478.

Levy, R. and Maxwell, A.E. (1968) 'The effect of verbal context on the recall of schizophrenics and other psychiatric patients'. *Brit. J. Psychiat.*, **114**, 311–316.

Lewinsohn, P.M., Steinmetz, J.L., Larson, D.W. and Franklin, J. (1981) 'Depression-related cognitions: antecedents or consequences?' *J. Abnorm. Psychol.*, **90**, 213–219.

Lewis, J.L. (1970) 'Semantic processing of unattended messages during dichotic listening'. *J. Exp. Psychol.*, **85**, 225–228.

Leyens, J., Cisneros, T. and Hossay, J. (1976) 'Decentration as a means for reducing aggression after exposure to violent stimuli'. *Europ. J. Soc. Psychol.*, **6**, 459–473.

Lichtenstein, E.H. and Brewer, W.F. (1980) 'Memory for goal-directed events'. *Cog. Psychol.*, **12**, 412–445.

Lichtenstein, S., Slovic, P., Fischhoff, B., Layman, M. and Combs, B. (1978) 'Judged frequency of lethal events'. *J. Exp. Psychol.: Hum. Learn. & Mem.*, **4** (6), 551–578.

Liepmann, H. (1908) 'Über die agnostischen Storungen'. *Neurologisches, Zenpralblatt.*, **27**, 609–617.

Light, L.L., Kayra-Stuart, F. and Hollander, S. (1979) 'Recognition memory for typical and unusual faces'. *J. Exp. Psychol.: Hum. Learn. & Mem.*, **5**, 212–218.

Linville, P.W. (1982) Affective consequences of complexity regarding the self and others. In M. Clark and S. Fiske (eds.) *Affect and Cognition*. New Jersey: Lawrence Erlbaum.

Lloyd, G.G. and Lishman, W.A. (1975) 'Effect of depression on the speed of recall of pleasant and unpleasant experiences'. *Psychol. Med.*, **5**, 173–180.

Locke, J. (1960) *An Essay Concerning Human Understanding*. London: T. Basset.

Loewenstein D.A. and Hokanson, J.E. (1986) 'The processing of social information by mildly and moderately dysphoric students'. *Cog. Ther. & Res.*, **10**, 447–460.

Loftus, E.F. (1979) *Eyewitness Testimony*. Cambridge, Mass.: Harvard University Press.

Long, J. (1976) 'Effect of task difficulty on the division of attention between non-verbal signals: independence or interaction'. *Quart. J. Exp. Psychol.*, **28**, 179–192.

Lonski, M. and Palumbo, P. (1978) 'The effects of subliminal stimulation on competitive dart-throwing performance'. Unpublished, Hofstra University.

Lord, C.G. (1980) Schemas and images as memory aides: two modes of processing social information. *J. Personality Soc. Psychol.*, **38**, 257–269.

Lundh, L.G. (1979) 'Introspection, consciousness, and human information processing'. *Scand. J. Psychol.*, **20**, 223–238.

McAllister, T.W. (1981) 'Cognitive functioning in the affective disorders'. *Comp. Psychiat.*, **22**, 572–586.

McClelland, J.L. (1979) 'On the time relations of mental processes: an examination of systems of processes in cascade'. *Psychol. Rev.*, **86**, 287–330.

McClelland, J.L. and Rumelhart, D.E. (1981) 'An interactive model of the effect of context in perception, Part I.'. *Psychol. Rev.*, **88**, 375–407.

McClelland, J.L. and Rumelhart, D.E. (1985) 'Distributed memory and the representation of general and specific information'. *J. Exp. Psychol.: General*, **114**, 159–188.

McDowell, J. (1984) 'Recall of pleasant and unpleasant words in depressed subjects'. *J, Abnorm. Psychol.*, **93**, 401–407.

MacKay, D.G. (1973) 'Aspects of a theory of comprehension, memory and attention'. *Quart. J. Exp. Psychol.*, **25**, 22–40.

McLemore, C.W. (1972) 'Imagery in desensitisation'. *Behav. Res. & Ther.*, **10**, 51–57.

McLemore, C.W. (1976) 'Factorial validity of imagery measures'. *Behav. Res. & Ther.*, **14**, 399–408.

MacLeod, C., Mathews, A. and Tata, P. (1986) 'Attentional bias in emotional disorders'. *J. Abnorm. Psychol.*, **95**, 15–20.

McLeod, P. (1977) 'A dual task response modality effect: support for multi-processor models of attention'. *Quart. J. Exp. Psychol.*, **29**, 651–667.

McLeod, P. (1978) 'Does probe RT measure central processing demand'?. *Quart. J. Exp. Psychol.*, **30**, 83–89.

McNair, D.M., Lorr, M. and Droppleman, L.F. (1981) *Manual for the profile of mood states*, 2nd edition. San Diego, Edits.

Mahoney, M.J. (1984) 'Integrating cognition, affect and action: a comment'. *Cog. Ther. & Res.*, **8**, 585–589.

Makhlouf-Norris, F., Jones, H.G. and Norris, H. (1970) 'Articulation of the conceptual structure in obsessional neurosis'. *Brit. J. Soc. & Clin. Psychol.*, **9**, 264–274.

Mandel, R.G. and Johnson, N.S. (1984) 'A developmental analysis of story recall and comprehension in adulthood'. *J. Verb. Learn. Verb. Behav.*, **23**, 643–659.

Mandler, G. (1975) 'Consciousness: respectable, useful and probably necessary'. In R. Solsol (ed.), *Information Processing and Cognition: the Loyola Symposium*, Hillsdale, N.J.: Lawrence Erlbaum.

Mandler, G. (1982) The structure of value: accounting for taste. In M.S. Clark and S.T. Fiske (eds), *Affect and Cognition*. Hillsdale, N.J.: Lawrence Erlbaum.

Mandler, G. (1984) *Mind & Body: Psychology of Emotion and Stress*. New York: Norton.

Mandler, J. (1975) *Mind and Emotion*. New York: John Wiley.

Mandler, J. (1978) 'A code in the node: the use of a story schema in retrieval'. *Discourse Processes*, **1**, 14–35.

Mandler, J.M. and De Forest, M. (1979) 'Is there more than one way to recall a story?' *Child Development*, **50**, 86–89.

Mandler, J.M. and Goodman, M.S. (1982) 'On the psychological validity of story structure'. *J. Verb. Learn. Verb. Behav.*, **21**, 507–523.

Marcel, A.J. (1978) 'Unconscious reading: experiments on people who do not know that they are reading'. *Visible Language*, **12** (4), 391–404.

Marcel, A.J. (1980) 'Conscious and preconscious recognition of polysemous words: locating the selective effects of prior verbal context'. In R.S. Nickerson (ed.), *Attention and Performance*, XII. Hillsdale, N.J.: Lawrence Erlbaum.

Marcel, A.J. (1983a) 'Conscious and unconscious perception: experiments on visual masking and word recognition'. *Cog. Psychol.*, **15**, 197–237.

Marcel, A.J. (1983b) 'Conscious and unconscious perception: an approach to the relations between phenomenal experience and perceptual processes'. *Cog. Psychol.*, **15**, 238–300.

Marcel, A.J., Katz L. and Smith, M. (1974) 'Laterality and reading proficiency'. *Neuropsychologia*, **12**, 131–139.

Marcel, A.J. and Patterson, K.E. (1978) 'Word recognition and production: reciprocity in clinical and normal studies'. In J. Requin (ed.), *Attention and Performance*, VII, Hillsdale, N.J.: Lawrence Erlbaum.

Marcus, H. (1977) Self-schemata and processing information about the self. *J. Personality Soc. Psychol.*, **35**, 63–78.

Marks, D. (1972) 'Individual differences in the vividness of visual imagery and their effect on function'. In P. Sheehan (ed.), *The Nature and Function of Imagery*. New York: Academic Press.

Marr, D. (1980) 'Visual information processing: the structure and creation of visual representations'. *Phil. Trans. Roy. Soc. Lond., Series B*, **290**, 199–218.

Martin, D.G., Hawryluk, G.A. and Guse, L.L. (1974) 'Experimental study of unconscious influences: ultrasound as a stimulus'. *J. Abnorm. Psychol.*, **83**, 589–608.

Martin, D.J., Abramson, L.Y. and Alloy, L.B. (1984) 'Illusion of control for self and others in depressed and nondepressed college students'. *J. Person. Soc. Psychol.*, **46**, 125–136.

Martin, M. (1985) 'Neuroticism as predisposition towards depression: a cognitive mechanism'. *Person. Individ. Diff.*, **6**, 353–365.

Martin, M. and Clark, D.M. (1985) 'Constraints on the effects of mood on accessibility'. Paper given at the Symposium on Affect and Cognition, Cognitive Psychology Section, British Psychology Society, Oxford, September 1985.

Martin, M. and Clark, D.M. (1986a) 'On the response bias explanation of selective memory effects in depression'. *Cog. Ther. & Res.*, **10**, 267–270.

Martin, M. and Clark, D.M. (1986b) 'Selective memory, depression and response bias: an unbiased response'. *Cog. Ther. & Res.*, **10**, 275–278.

Marton, F., Hounsell, D. and Entwistle, N. (1984) *The Experience of Learning*. Edinburgh: Scottish Academic Press.

Marzillier, J.S., Carroll, D. and Newland, J.R. (1979) 'Self-report and physiological changes accompanying repeated imagining of a phobic scene'. *Behave. Res. & Ther.*, **17**, 71–77.

Mathews, A.M. (1971) 'Psychophysiological approaches to the investigation of desensitization and related procedures'. *Psychol. Bull.*, **76**, 73–91.

Mathews, A. and Bradley, B. (1983) 'Mood and the self-reference bias in recall'. *Behav. Res. & Ther.*, **21**, 233–239.

Mathews, A.M. and MacLeod, C. (1985) 'Selective processing of threat cues in anxiety states'. *Behav. Res. & Ther.*, **23**, 563–569.

Mathews, A.M. and MacLeod, C. (1986) 'Discrimination of threat cues without awareness in anxiety states'. *J. Abnorm. Psychol.*, **95**, 131–138.

Matussek, P. and Luks, P. (1981) 'Themes of endogenous and nonendogenous depressions'. *Psychiat. Res.*, **5**, 235–242.

Meichenbaum, D. (1977) *Cognitive Behaviour Modification*. New York: Plenum.

Mendelsohn, E. and Silverman, L.H. (1982) 'Effects of stimulating psychodynamically relevant unconscious fantasies on schizophrenic psychopathology'. *Schizophrenia Bull.*, **8**, 532–547.

Merrill, J. *Analysis of the Phenomena of the Human Mind*. London: Baldwin.

Meyer, B., Haring, M., Brandt, D. and Walker, C. (1980) 'Comprehension of stories and expository text'. *Poetics*, **9**, 203–210.

Meyer, D.E., Schvaneveldt, R.W. and Ruddy, N.G. (1972) *Activation of Lexical Memory*. Paper presented at the meeting of the Psychonomic Society, St. Louis, Missouri, November 1972.

Millar, D.G. (1980) 'A repertory grid study of obsessionality distinctive cognitive structure or distinctive content'. *Brit. J. Med. Psychol.*, **53**, 59–66.

Miller, E. and Lewis, P. (1977) 'Recognition memory in elderly patients with depression and dementia'. *J. Abnorm. Psychol.*, **86**, 84–86.

Miller, G.A. (1962) *Psychology: The Science of Mental Life*. New York: Harper and Row.

Miller, J.G. (1939) 'Discrimination without awareness'. *Amer. J. Psychol.*, **52**, 562–578.

Miller, J.G. (1940) 'The role of motivation in learning without awareness'. *Amer. J. Psychol.*, **53**, 229–239.

Miller, J. (1973) 'The effects of aggressive stimulation upon adults who have experienced the death of a parent during childhood and adolescence'. Unpublished Doctoral Dissertation, New York Univertiy.

Miller, S.M. and Mangan, C.E. (1983) 'Interacting effects of information and coping style in adapting to gynaecological stress: should the doctor tell all?'. *J. Person. Soc. Psychol.*, **45**, 223–236.

Miller, S.M. (1987a) 'Monitoring and blunting: validation of a questionnaire to assess styles of information seeking under threat'. *J. Person. Soc. Psychol.*, **52** (2), 345–353.

Miller, S.M. (1987b) 'To see or not to see: cognitive informational styles in the coping process'. In M. Rosenbaum (ed.), *Learned Resourcefulness: on coping skills, self-regulation and adaptive behaviour*. New York: Springer Press.

Miller, W.R. (1975) 'Psychological deficit in depression'. *Psychol. Bull.*, **82**, 238–260.

Minard, J.G. (1965) 'Response-bias interpretation of perceptual defense'. *Psychol. Rev.*, **72**, 74–88.

Mineo, A. and Kahneman, D. (1974) 'Reaction time in focussed and in divided attention'. *J. Exp. Psychol.*, **103**, 394–399.

Minsky, M. (1975) 'A framework for representing knowledge'. In P.H. Winston (ed.), *The Psychology of Computer Vision*. New York: McGraw Hill.

Mogg, K., Mathews, A. and Weinman, J. (1987) 'Memory bias in clinical anxiety'. *J. Abnorm. Psychol.*, **96**, 94–98.

Moore, R.G., Watts, F.N. and Williams, J.M.G. The specificity of personal memories in depression. *Brit. J. Clin. Psychol.* (in press).

Moray, N. (1959) 'Attention and dichotic listening: effect of cues and the influence of instructions'. *Quart. J. Exp. Psychol.*, **11**, 56–60.

Morris, L.W., Brown, N.R. and Halbert, B.L. (1977) 'Effects of symbolic modelling on the arousal of cognitive and affective components of anxiety in pre-school children'. In C.D. Spielberger and I.G. Sarason (eds), *Stress and Anxiety*, Vol. 4. London: Halsted.

Morris, P., Gruneberg, M.M., Sykes, R.N. and Merrick, A. (1981) 'Football knowledge and the acquisition of new results'. *Br. J. Psychol.*, **72**, 479–483.

Mueller, J.H. (1976) 'Anxiety and cue utilization in human learning and memory'. In M. Zuckerman and C.D. Spielberger (eds), *Emotions and Anxiety: New Concepts, Methods and Applications*. Hillsdale, N.J.: Lawrence Erlbaum.

Mueller, J.H. (1977) 'Test anxiety, input modality, and levels of organization in free recall'. *Bull. Psychonom. Soc.*, **9**, 67–69.

Mueller, J.H. (1978) 'The effects of individual differences in test anxiety and type of orienting task on levels of organization in free recall'. *J. Res. Pers.*, **12**, 100–116.

Mueller, J.H. (1980) Test anxiety and the encoding and retrieval of information. In I. Sarason (ed.) *Test Anxiety: Theory, Research and Applications*. New Jersey: Lawrence Erlbaum.

Murphy, G.E., Simons, K.D., Wetzel, R.D. and Lustman, P.J. (1984) 'Cognitive therapy and pharmacotherapy; singly and together in the treatment of depression'. *Arch. Gen. Psychiat.*, **41**, 33–41.

Mykel, N. and Daves, W.F. (1979) 'Emergence of unreported stimuli into imagery as a function of laterality of presentation: a replication and extension of research by Henley and Dixon'. *Brit. J. Psychol.*, **70**, 253–258.

Naish, P.L.M. (1985) 'The locus of the stroop effect: one site masquerading as two?'. *Br. J. Psychol.*, **76**, 303–310.

Nakamura, G.V. and Graesser, A.C. (1985) 'Memory for script-typical and script-atypical actions: A reaction time study'. *Bull. Psychonom. Soc.*, **23**, (4), 384–386.

Navon, D. (1977) 'Forest before trees: the presence of global features in perception'. *Cog. Psychol.*, **9**, 353–383.

Navon, D. (1984) 'Resources — a theoretical soup stone?'. *Psychol. Rev.*, **91**, 216–234.

Navon, D. and Gopher, D., (1979a) 'Interpretation of task difficulty in terms of resources: efficiency, load, demand and cost-composition'. In R. Nickerson (ed.), *Attention and Performance*, VIII. Hillsdale, N.J.: Lawrence Erlbaum.

Navon, D. and Gopher, D. (1979b) 'On the economy of the human-processing system'. *Psychol. Rev.*, **86** (3), 214–255.

Navon, D. and Margalit, B. (1983) 'Allocation of attention according to informativeness in visual recognition'. *Quart. J. Exp. Psychol.*, **35(a)**, 497–512.

Neisser, U. (1963) 'The multiplicity of thought'. *Brit. J. Psychol.*, **54**, 1–14.

Neisser, U. (1967) *Cognitive Psychology*. New York: Appleton-Century-Crofts.

Neisser, U. (1976) *Cognition and Reality: Principles and Implications of Cognitive Psychology*. San Francisco: W.H. Freeman.

Neisser, U. and Becklen, R. (1975) 'Selective looking: Attending to visually specific events'. *Cog. Psychol.*, **7**, 480–494.

Nelson, J.G. and Mazure, C. (1985) 'Ruminative thinking: a distinctive sign of melancholia'. *J. Affect. Dis.*, **9**, 41–46.

Nelson, K. (1977) 'Cognitive development and the acquisition of concepts. In R.C. Anderson, R.J. Spiro, and W.D. Montague (eds), *Schooling and the Acquisition of Knowledge.* Hillsdale, N.J.: Lawrence Erlbaum.

Nelson, R.E. and Craighead, W.E. (1977) 'Selective recall of positive and negative feedback, self-control behaviors, and depression'. *J. Abnorm. Psychol.*, **86**, 379–388.

Newstead, S.E. and Dennis, I. (1979) Lexical and grammatical processing of unshadowed messages: a re-examination of the Mackay effect. *J. Exp. Psychol.*, **31**, 477–88.

Nicholson, W.M. (1958) 'The influence of anxiety upon learning: interference or drive increment'. *J. Person.*, **26**, 303–319.

Nisbett, R.E. and Wilson, T.D. (1977) 'Telling more than we can know: verbal reports on mental processes'. *Psychol. Rev.*, **84**, 231–259.

Norman, D.A. and Bobrow, D.G. (1975) 'On data-limited and resource-limited processes. *Cog. Psychol.*, **7**, 44–64.

Norman, D.A. and Bobrow, D.G. (1976) 'On the role of active memory processes in perception and cognition'. In C.N. Cofer (ed.), *The Structure of Human Memory.* San Francisco: Freeman.

Norman, D.A. and Bobrow, D.G. (1979) 'Descriptions: an intermediate stage in memory retrieval'. *Cog. Psychol.*, **11**, 107–123.

Norman, D.A. and Shallice, T. (1986) 'Attention to action: willed and automatic control of behaviour'. In R.J. Davidson (eds), *Consciousness and Self-Regulation*, Vol. IV. New York: Plenum.

Nunn, J.D., Stevenson, R. and Whalan, G. (1984) Selective memory effects in agaraphobic patients. *Br. J. Clin. Psychol.*, **23**, 195–201.

Oatley, K. and Johnson-Laird, P. (1987) 'Towards a cognitive theory of emotions'. *Cog. & Emot.*, **1**, 29–50.

Oatman, L.C. (1984) 'Auditory evoked-potential amplitude during simultaneous visual stimulation'. Presented at the Annual Meeting of the Psychonomic Society, San Antonio.

Oliver, J.M. and Burkham, R. (1982) 'Subliminal psychodynamic activation in depression: a failure to replicate'. *J. Abnorm. Psychol.*, **92**, 337–342.

O'Sullivan, J.T. and Pressley, M. (1984) Completeness of instruction and strategy transfer. *J. Exp. Child Psychol.*, **38**, 275–288.

Pachella, R.G. (1974) 'The interpretation of reaction time in information processing research'. In B. Kantowitz, (ed.), *Human Information Processing: tutorials in performance and cognition*, Hillsdale, N.J.: Lawrence Erlbaum.

Paivio, A. (1986) *Mental Representations: A Dual Coding Approach.* Oxford: Clarendon Press.

Palmer, S.E. (1975) 'The effects of contextual scenes on the identification of objects'. *Mem. & Cog.*, **3**, 519–526.

Paris, S.G., Lindauer, B.K. and Cox, G.L. (1977) 'The development of inferential comprehension'. *Child Devt*, **48**, 1728–1733.

Parker, K. (1977) 'The effects of subliminal merger stimuli on the academic performance and psychological adjustment of college students'. Doctoral dissertation, New York University.

Parkes, C.M. (1972) *Bereavement: Studies of Grief in Adult Life.* London: Tavistock.

Parkinson, L. and Rachman, S. (1981) 'Intrusive thoughts: the effects of an uncontrived stress'. *Adv. Behav. Res. Ther.*, **3**, 111–118.

Paul, I.H. (1959) 'Studies in remembering: the reproduction of connected and extended verbal material'. *Psychol. Issues*, **1**, (2), WHO, No. 2.

Payne, R.W. and Hewlett, J.H.G. (1960) 'Thought disorders in psychotic patients'. In H.J. Eysenck (ed.), *Experiments in Personality*, Vol. 2. London: Routledge and Kegan Paul.

Persons, J.B. and Foa, E.B. (1984) 'Processing of fearful and neutral information by obsessive-compulsives'. *Behav. Res. & Ther.*, **22**, 26–265.

Peterson, C. and Seligman, M.E.P. (1984) 'Causal explanations as a risk factor for depression: theory and evidence'. *Psychol. Rev.*, **91**, 347–374.

Philpott, A. and Wilding, J. (1979) 'Semantic interference from subliminal stimuli in a dichoptic viewing situation'. *Brit. J. Psychol.*, **70**, 559–563.

Pieters, J.P.M. (1983) 'Sternberg's additive factor method and underlying psychological processes: some theoretical considerations'. *Psychol. Bull.*, **93**, 411–426.

Poppel, E., Held, R. and Frost, D. (1973) 'Residual function of brain wounds involving the central visual pathways in man'. *Nature*, **243**, 295–296.

Porterfield, A.L. and Golding, S.L. (1985) 'A failure to find an effect of subliminal psychodynamic activation upon cognitive measures of pathology in schizophrenia'. *J. Abnorm. Psychol.*, **94**, 630–639.

Posner, M.I. and Boies, S.W. (1971) 'Components of attention'. *Psychol. Rev.*, **78**, 391–408.

Posner, M., Klein, R., Summers, J. and Buggie, S. (1973) 'On the selection of signals'. *Mem. & Cog.*, **1**, 2–12.

Posner, M.I. and McLeod, P. (1982) 'Information processing models — in search of elementary operations'. *Annual Rev. Psychol.*, **33**, 477–514.

Postman, L. (1953) 'On the problem of perceptual defence'. *Psychol. Rev.*, **60**, 298–306.

Postman, L. (1954) 'Learned principles of organisation in memory'. *Psychol. Mono.*, **68**, 374.

Postman, L., Bronson, W.C. and Gropper, G.L. (1953) 'Is there a mechanism of perceptual defence?'. *J. Abnorm. Soc. Psychol.*, **48**, 215–224.

Poulton, E.C. (1956) 'Listening to overlapping calls'. *J. Exp. Psychol.*, **52**, 334–339.

Poulton, E.C. (1957) 'On prediction in skilled movements'. *Psychol. Bull.*, **54**, 467–478.

Powell, G.E. and Watts, F.N. (1973) Determinants of expectation in imaginal desensitisation'. *Percept. & Mot. Skills.*, **37**, 246.

Powell, M. and Hemsley, D.R. (1984) 'Depression: a breakdown of perceptual defence?'. *Brit. J. Psychiat.*, **145**, 358–362.

Power, M.J. and Champion, L.A. (1986) 'Cognitive approaches to depression: a theoretical critique'. *Brit. J. clin. Psychol.*, **25**, 201–212.

Pylyshyn, Z. (1983) 'What the mind's eye tells the brain: a critique of mental imagery'. *Psychol. Bull.*, **80**, 1–22.

Pylyshyn, Z. (1984) *Computation and Cognition: Towards a Foundation in Cognitive Science.* Cambridge, Mass.: The MIT Press.

Quillan, M.R. (1968) 'Semantic memory'. In M.L. Minsky (ed.), *Semantic Information Processing.* Cambridge, Mass.: MIT Press.

Rachman, S. (1980) 'Emotional processing'. *Behav. Res. & Ther.*, **18**, 51–60.

Rachman, S. (1981) 'The primacy of affect: some theoretical implications'. *Behav. Res. & Ther.*, **19**, 279–290.

Rachman, S. (1984) 'A reassessment of the 'primacy of affect'. *Cog. Ther. & Res.*, **8**, 579–584.

Ranney, M. (1987) 'The role of structural context in perception: syntax in the recognition of algebraic expressions'. *Mem. & Cog.*, **15**, 29–41.

Ray, C. (1979) 'Examination stress and performance on a colour word interference test'. *Perc. Mot. Skills*, **49**, 400–402.

Reed, G.F. (1969a) 'Under-inclusion' — a characteristic of obsessional personality: I'. *Brit. J. Psychiat.*, **115**, 781–785.

Reed, G.F. (1969b) 'Under-inclusion' — a characteristic of obsessional personality: II'. *Brit. J. Psychiat.*, **115**, 787–790.

Reed, G.F. (1977) 'Obsessional cognition: performance on two numerical tasks'. *Brit. J. Psychiat.*, **130**, 184–185.

Reed, G.F. (1985) *Obsessional Experience and Compulsive Behaviour: A Cognitive-Structural Approach.* New York: Academic Press.

Rehm, L. (1973) 'Relationships among measures of visual imagery. *Behav., Res. & Ther.,* **11**, 265–270.

Reiser, B.J. Black, J.B. and Abelson, R.P. (1985) 'Knowledge structures in the organisation and retrieval of autobiographical memories'. *Cog. Psychol.,* **17**, 89–137.

Reyher, J. and Smeltzer, W. (1968) 'Uncovering properties of visual imagery and verbal association: a comparative study'. *J. Abnorm. Psychol.,* **73**, 218–222.

Riggs, L.A. and Whittle, P. (1967) 'Human occipital and retinal potentials evoked by subjectively faded visual stimuli'. *Vis. Res.,* **7**, 441–451.

Rimm, D. and Bottrell, J. (1969) 'Four measures of visual imagination'. *Behav. Res. & Ther.,* **7**, 63–69.

Roberts, R.B. and Goldstein, I.T. (1977) 'The FRL Manual'. Memo 409, Artificial Intelligence Laboratory, MIT.

Robinson, A. and Reading, C. (1985) 'Imagery in phobic subjects: a psychophysiological study. *Behav. Res. & Ther.,* **23**, 247–253.

Roediger, H.L. Knight, J.L. and Kantowitz, D.H. (1977) 'Inferring decay in short-term memory: the issue of capacity'. *Memory and Cognition,* **5**, 167–176.

Rogers, T.B., Kuiper, N.A. and Kirker, W.S. (1977) Self-reference and the encoding of personal information. *J. Personality Soc. Psychol.,* **35**, 677–688.

Rollins, H.A. and Hendricks, R. (1980) 'Processing of words presented simultaneously to eye and ear'. *J. Exp. Psychol.: Hum. Perc. & Perf.,* **6**, 99–109.

Rosenberg, S.T. (1977) 'Frame-based test processing'. Memo 431, Artificial Intelligence Laboratory, MIT.

Ross, L. (1977) 'The intuitive psychologist and his shortcomings: distortion in the attributional process'. In L. Berkowitz (ed.), *Adv. in Exper. Soc. Psychol.,* Vol. 10. New York: Academic Press.

Ross, L., Lepper, M.R. and Hubbard, M. (1975) 'Perseverance in self-perception and social perception: Biased attributional processes in the debriefing paradigm'. *J. Person. Soc. Psychol.,* **32**, 880–892.

Ross, L., Lepper, M.R., Strack, F. and Steinmetz, J. (1977) 'Social explanation and social expectation: Effects of real and hypothetical explanations on subjective likelihood'. *J. Person. Soc. Psychol.,* **35** (11), 817–829.

Rothbart, M. (1981) 'Memory processes and social beliefs'. In D.L. Hamilton (ed.), *Cognitive Processes in Stereotyping and Intergroup Behavior.* Hillsdale, N.J.: Lawrence Erlbaum.

Roy-Byrne, P.J., Weingartner, H., Bierer, L.M., Thompson, K. and Post, R.M. (1986) 'Effortful and automatic cognitive processes in depression'. *Arch. Gen. Psychiat.,* **43**, 265–267.

Rozeboom, W.M. (1972) 'Problems in the psychophilosophy of knowledge'. In J.R. Royce and W.M. Rozeboom (eds), *The Psychology of Knowing.* New York: London and Breech.

Rubin, D.C. and Friendly, M. (1986) 'Predicting which words get recalled: measures of free recall, availability, goodness, emotionality and pronunciability for 925 nouns'. *Mem. & Cog.,* **14**, 79–94.

Ruddock, K.H. and Waterfield, V.A. (1978) 'Selective loss of function associated with a central visual field defect'. *Neuroscience Letters,* **8**, 93–98.

Rumelhart, D.E. (1975) 'Notes on a schema for stories'. In D.G. Bobrow and A. Collins (eds), *Representing and Understanding: Studies in Cognitive Science.* New York: Academic Press.

Rumelhart, D.E. (1978) 'Schemata: the building blocks of cognition'. In R. Spiro, B. Bruce and W. Brewer (eds), *Theoretical Issues in Reading Comprehension.* Hillside, N.J.: Lawrence Erlbaum.

Rumelhart, D.E. and McClelland, J.L. (1986) 'On learning the past tenses of English verbs'. In J.L. McClelland D.E. Rumelhart (eds), *Parallel distributed Processing: Explorations in the Microstructure of Cognition*, Vol. II: *Applications*. Cambridge, Mass.: Bradford Books.

Rush, A.J., Weissenburger, J. and Eaves, G. (1987) 'Do thinking patterns predict depressive symptoms?'. *Cog. Ther. Res.*, **10**, 225–236.

Russell, J. (1987) 'Comments on articles by Frijda and by Conway and Bekerian'. *Cog. & Emot.*, **1**, 193–197.

Russell, J.A. and Woudzia, L. (1986) 'Affective judgments, common sense and Zajonc's thesis of independence'. *Motiv. & Emot.*, **10**, 169–183.

Russell, P.W. and Beekhuis, M.E. (1976) 'Organization in memory'. *J. Abnorm. Psychol.*, **85**, 527–534.

Ryle, A. and Breen, D. (1972) 'Some differences in the personal constructs of neurotic and normal subjects'. *Brit. J. Psychiat.*, **120**, 483–489.

Sackeim, H.A., Packer, I.K. and Gur, R.C. (1977) 'Hemisphericity, cognitive set and susceptibility to subliminal perception'. *J. Abnorm. Psychol.* **86**, 624–630.

Sadeim, H. (1977) 'Self-deception: motivational determinants of the non-awareness of cognition'. Doctoral Dissertation, University of Pennsylvania.

Salavoy, P. and Singer, J.A. (1985) 'Mood and recall of autobiographical memories'. Paper given at APA, Los Angeles, August 1985.

Sales, B.D. and Haber, R.N. (1968) 'A different look at perceptual defence for taboo words'. *Percept. & Psychophys.*, **3**, 156–160.

Sanders, A. (1979) *Mental Work-load: Its Theory and Measurement*. New York: Plenum Press.

Sanford, A.J. (1983) *Models, Mind and Man*. Press Gang: Glasgow University.

Sanford, A.J. (1985) *Cognition and Cognitive Psychology*. London: Weidenfeld and Nicolson.

Sanford, A.J. and Garrod, S.C. (1980) 'A demonstration of the situational bases of text comprehension through implicit assignments of roles to entities'. Unpublished manuscript, Department of Psychology, University of Glasgow.

Sanford, A.J. and Garrod, S.C. (1981) *Understanding Written Language: Explorations of Comprehension beyond the Sentence*. New York: John Wiley.

Sanford, A.J. and Garrod, S.C. (1982) 'Towards a psychological model of written discourse comprehension'. In J.F. Le Ny and W. Kintsch (eds), *Language and Comprehension: Advances in Psychology*, 9. Amsterdam: North-Holland.

Sartory, G., Rachman, S. and Grey, S.J. (1982) 'Return of fear: the role of rehearsal'. *Behav. Res. & Ther.*, 123–133.

Schank, R. and Abelson, R.P. (1975) *Scripts, Plans, and Knowledge*. Advance Papers of the 4th International Joint Conference on Artificial Intelligence. Tblisi, USSR.

Shank, R. and Abelson, R. (1977) *Scripts, Plans, Goals and Understanding: An Enquiry into Human Knowledge Structures*, Hillsdale, N.J.: Lawrence Erlbaum.

Schare, M.L., Lisman, S.A. and Spear, N.E. (1984) 'The effects of mood variation on state dependent retention. *Cog. Ther. & Res.*, **8**, 387–408.

Scheibe, K.E., Shaver, P.R. and Carrier, S.C. (1967) 'Colour association values and response interference on variants of the Stroop test'. *Acta. Psychol.*, **26**, 286–295.

Scherer, K.R. (1984) 'On the nature and function of emotion: a component process approach'. In K.R. Scherer and P. Ekman (eds), *Approaches to Emotion*. Hillsdale, N.J.: Lawrence Erlbaum.

Schneider, W., Dumais, S.T. and Shiffrin, R.M. (1984) 'Automatic and control processing in attention'. In R. Parasuraman and D.R. Davies (eds), *Varieties of Attention*. Orlando, SL.: Academic.

Schneider, W. and Fisk, D. (1984) 'Automatic category search and its transfer'. *J. Exp. Psychol.: Learn. Mem. & Cog.*, **10**, 1–15.

Schneider, W. and Shiffrin, R.M. (1977) 'Controlled and automatic human information processing: (1) Detection, search and attention'. *Psychol. Rev.*, **84**, 1–66.

Schvaneveldt, R.W. and Meyer, D.E. (1973) 'Retrieval and comparison processes in semantic memory'. In S. Kornblum (ed.), *Attention and Performance*, IV. New York: Academic Press.

Schwartz, S. (1975) 'Individual differences in cognition: some relationships between personality and memory'. *J. Res. Person.*, **9**, 217–225.

Schwarz, N. and Clore, G.L. (1983) 'Mood, misattribution, and judgments of well-being: Informative and directive functions of affective states'. *J. Person, Soc. Psychol.*, **45**, (3), 513–523.

Schweller, K.G., Brewer, W.F. and Dahl, D.A. (1976) 'Memory for illocutionary forces and perlocutionary effects of utterances'. *J. Verb. Learn. Verb. Behav.*, **15**, 325–337.

Scott, J.D. and Nelson, D.L. (1979) 'Anxiety and encoding strategy'. *Bull. Psychonom. Soc.*, **13**, 297–299.

Searle, J. (1980) 'Minds, brains and programs'. *Behav. & Brain Sci.*, **3**, 417–457.

Selfridge, O.G. (1959) 'Pandemonium: a paradigm for learning'. In *The Mechanisation of the Thought Process*. London: HMSO.

Seligman, M.E.P., Abramson, L., Semmel, A. and von Baeyer, C. (1979) 'Depressive attributional style'. *J. Abnorm. Psychol.*, **88**, 242–248.

Sergeant, H. (1965) 'Systematic desensitisation'. Unpublished DPM thesis, University of London.

Severance, L.J. and Dyer, F.N. (1973) 'Failure of subliminal word presentations to generate interference to colour-naming'. *J. Exp. Psychol.*, **101**, 186–189.

Shadbolt, N. (1983) 'Processing reference'. *J. of Semantics*, **2**, 63–98.

Shallice, T. (1972) 'Dual functions of consciousness'. *Psychol. Rev.*, **79**, 383–393.

Shallice, T. (1978) 'The dominant action system: an information-processing approach to consciousness'. In K.S. Hope and J.L. Singer (eds), *The Stream of Consciousness: scientific investigations into the flow of human experience*. New York: Plenum.

Shallice, T. (1982) Specific impairments of planning. *Phil. Trans. Roy. Soc. Lond. B.*, **298**, 199–209.

Sheehan, M.J. (1981) 'Constructs and "conflict" in depression'. *Brit. J. Psychol.*, **72**, 197–209.

Sheikh, A.A. and Jordan, C.S. (1983) 'Clinical uses of mental imagery'. In A.A. Sheikh (ed.), *Imagery: Current Theory, Research and Application*. New York: John Wiley.

Sheikh, A.A. and Panagiotou, N.C. (1975) 'Use of mental imagery in psychotherapy: A critical review'. *Percept. & Mot. Skills*, **41**, 555–585.

Shepard, R.N. and Cooper, L.A. (1982) *Mental Images and Their Transformations*. Cambridge, Mass.: MIT Press.

Sher, K.J., Frost, R. and Otto, R. (1983) 'Cognitive deficits in compulsive checkers: An exploratory study'. *Behav. Res. & Ther.*, **21**, 357–363.

Sher, K.J., Mann, B. and Frost, R.O. (1984) 'Cognitive dysfunction in compulsive checkers: further explorations'. *Behav. Res. & Ther.*, **22**, 493–502.

Sherman, S.J., Zehner, K.S., Johnson, J. and Hirt, E.R. (1983) 'Social explanation: The role of timing, set, and recall on subjective likelihood estimates'. *J. Person. Soc. Psychol.* **44**, (6), 1127–1143.

Shevrin, H. and Dickman, S. (1980) 'The psychological unconscious: A necessary assumption for all psychological theory?'. *Amer. Psychol.*, **35**, (5), 421–434.

Shiffrin, R.M. (1976) 'Capacity limitations in information processing, attention and memory'. In W.K. Estes (ed.), *Handbook of Learning and Cognitive Processes*, Vol. 4. Hillsdale, N.J.: Lawrence Erlbaum.

Shiffrin, R.M. (1985) 'Attention'. In R.C. Atkinson, R.J. Herrnstein, G. Lindsey and R.D. Luce (eds), *Stevens' Handbook of Experimental Psychology*. New York: John Wiley.

Shiffrin, R.M. and Schneider, W. (1977) 'Controlled and automatic human processing: (2) Perceptual learning, automatic attending, and a general theory'. *Psychol. Rev.*, **84**, 127–190.

Sidis, B. (1898) *The Psychology of Suggestion*. New York: Appleton.

Silberman, E.K., Weingartner, H., Laraia, M., Byrnes, S. and Post, R.M. (1983a) 'Processing of emotional properties of stimuli by depressed and normal subjects'. *J.*

Nerv. & Ment. Dis., **171**, 10–14.

Silberman, E.K., Weingartner, H. and Post, R.M. (1983b) 'Thinking disorder in depression'. *Arch. Gen. Psychiat.*, **40**, 775–780.

Silver, E.A. (1981) 'Recall of mathematical problem information: solving related problems' *J. for Res. in Maths Educ.*, **12**, 54–64.

Silverman, L.H. (1980) 'A comprehensive report of studies using the subliminal psychodynamic activation method'. *Psychol. Res. Bull.*, **20**, (3), 1–22.

Silverman, L.H. (1983) 'The subliminal psychodynamic activation method: overview and comprehensive listing of studies'. In J. Masling (ed.), *Empirical Studies of Psychoanalytic Theories*, Vol. 1. Hillsdale, N.J.: Lawrence Erlbaum.

Silverman, L.H. (1984) 'Further comments on subliminal psychodynamic activations studies (revised)'. Unpublished manuscript. (Available from Department of Psychology, New York University, 6 Washington Place, New York, 1003.)

Silverman, L.H. (1985) 'Comments on three recent subliminal psychodynamic activation investigations'. *J. Abnorm. Psychol.*, **94**, (4), 640–643.

Silverman, L.H., Bronstein, A. and Mendelsohn, E. (1976) 'The further use of the subliminal psychodynamic activation method for the experimental study of the clinical theory of psychoanalysis: on the specificity of relationships between manifest psychopathology and unconscious conflict'. *Psychother.: Theory, Res. & Pract.*, **13**, (1), 22–16.

Silverman, L.H. and Candell, P. (1970) 'On the relationship between aggressive activation, symbiotic merging, intactness of body boundaries and manifest pathology in schizophrenics'. *J. Nerv. Ment. Dis.*, **150**, 387–399.

Silverman, L.H., Clinger, H., Lustbader, L., Farrel, J. and Martin, A.D. (1972) 'The effects of subliminal driver stimulation on the speech of stutters'. *J. Nerv. Ment. Dis.*, **155**, 14–21.

Silverman, L.H. Kwawer, J.S., Wolitzky, C., and Coron, M. (1973) 'An experimental study of aspects of the psychoanalytic theory of male homosexuality'. *J. Abnorm. Psychol.* **82**, 178–188.

Silverman, L.H., Frank, S. and Dachinger, P. (1974) 'A psychoanalytic interpretation of the effectiveness of systematic desensitisation: experimental data bearing on the role of merging fantasies'. *J. Abnorm. Psychol.*, **83**, 313–318.

Silverman, L.H., Martin, A., Ungaro, R. and Mendelsohn, E. (1978) 'Effect on subliminal stimulation of symbiotic fantasies on behaviour modification treatment of obesity'. *J. Consult. Clin. Psychol.*, **46** (3), 432–441.

Silverman, L.H., Ross, D.L., Adler, J.N. and Lustig, D.A. (1978) 'Simple research paradigm for demonstrating subliminal dynamic activation: effects of Oedipal stimuli on dart-throwing accuracy in college males'. *J. Abnorm. Psychol.*, **87**, 341–357.

Silverman, L.H. and Silverman, D.K. (1964) 'A clinical-experimental approach to the study of subliminal stimulation'. *J. Abnorm. Soc. Psychol.*, **69** (2), 158–172.

Silverman, L.H. and Spiro, R.H. (1968) 'The effects of subliminal, supraliminal and vocalised aggression on the ego functioning of schizophrenics'. *J. Nerv. Ment. Dis.*, **1456**, 50–61.

Simon, H.A. (1982) 'Comments'. In S. Fiske and M. Clark (eds), *Affect and Cognition*. Hillsdale, N.J.: Lawrence Erlbaum.

Simons, A.D., Murphy, G.E., Levine, J.L. and Wetzel, R.D. (1986) 'Cognitive therapy and pharmacotherapy for depression'. *Arch. Gen. Psychiat.*, **43**, 43–50.

Simpson, P.J. (1972) 'High-speed scanning: stability and generality'. *J. Exp. Psychol.*, **96**, 239–246.

Singer, J.L. (1974) *Imagery and Daydream Methods in Psychotherapy and Behaviour Modification*. New York: Academic Press.

Smith, D.A. and Graesser, A.C. (1981) 'Memory for actions in scripted activities as a function of typicality, retention interval, and retrieval task'. *Mem. & Cog.*, **9**, 550–559.

Smith, E.R. and Miller, F.D. (1978) 'Limits on perception of cognitive processes: A reply to Nisbett and Wilson'. *Psychol. Rev.*, **85** (4), 355–362.

Smith, G.J.W. and Danielson, A. (1979) 'On how to compensate for inadequate ego defences: an experimental description'. *Psychol. Res. Bull.*, **XIX**, 1–2. University of Lund, Sweden.

Smith, G.J.W. and Henriksson, M. (1955) 'The effect on an established percept of a perceptual process beyond awareness'. *Acta Psychol.*, **2**, 346–355.

Smith, G.J.W., Spence, D.P. and Klein, G.S. (1959) 'Subliminal effects of verbal stimuli'. *J. Abnorm. Soc. Psychol.* **59**, 167–176.

Smith, G.J.W. and Westerlundh, B. (1980) 'Perceptgenesis: A proces perspective on perception-personality'. In L. Wheeler (ed.), *Review of Personality and Social Psychology*, Vol. 1. London: Sage Publications.

Snyder, M. and Swann, W.B. Jr (1978) 'Hypothesis-testing processes in social interaction'. *J. Person. Soc. Psychol.*, **36** (11), 1202–1212.

Snyder, M. and Uranowitz, S.W. (1978) 'Reconstructing the past: some cognitive consequences of person perception'. *J. Person. Soc. Psychol.*, **36**, 941–950.

Solomon, R.L. and Postman, L. (1952) 'Frequency of usage as a determinant of recognition thresholds for words'. *J. Exp. Psychol.*, **43**, 195–201.

Somekh, D.E. and Wilding, J.M. (1973) 'Perception with awareness in a dichoptic viewing situation'. *Brit. J. Psychol.*, **64**, 339–349.

Spelke, E., Hirst, W. and Meisser, U. (1976) 'Skills of divided attention'. *Cognition*, **4**, 215–230.

Spence, D.P. and Holland, B. (1962) 'The restricting effects of awareness: a paradox and an explanation'. *J. Abnorm Soc. Psychol.*, **64**, 163–174.

Sperling, G. (1967) 'Successive approximations to a model for short-term memory'. *Acta Psychol.*, **27**, 285–292.

Spiro, R.J. (1980) 'Accommodative reconstruction in prose recall'. *J. Verb. Learn. Verb. Behav.*, **19**, 84–95.

Sprock, J., Braff, D.L., Saccuzzo, D.P. and Alkinson, J.H. (1983) 'The relationship of depression and thought disorder in pain patients'. *Brit. J. Med. Psychol.*, **56**, 351–360.

Srull, T.K. (1981) 'Person memory: some tests of associative storage and retrieval models'. *J. Exper. Psychol.: Hum. Learn. & Mem.*, **47**, 440–463.

Stein, N.L. and Glenn, C.G. (1979) 'An analysis of story comprehension in elementary school children'. In R. Freedle (ed.), *New Directions in Discourse Processing*. Norwood, N.J.: Ablex.

Stent, G.S. (1981) 'Cerebral hermeneutics'. *J. Soc. and Biol. Structures*, **4**, 107–124.

Sternberg, D.E. and Jarvik, M.E. (1976) 'Memory functions in depression'. *Arch. Gen. Psychiat.*, **33**, 219–224.

Sternberg, R.J. (1977) *Intelligence, Information Processing, and Analogical Reasoning*. Hillsdale, N.J.: Lawrence Erlbaum.

Sternberg, S. (1969) 'The discovery of processing stages: extensions of Donder's method'. *Acta Psychol.*, **30**, 276–315.

Storms, M.D. and Nisbett, R.E. (1970) 'Insomnia and the attribution process'. *J. Person. Soc. Psychol.*, **2**, 319–328.

Strosahl, K.D. and Ascough, J.C. (1981) 'Clinical uses of mental imagery: experimental foundations, theoretical misconceptions and research issues'. *Psychol. Bull.*, **89**, 422–438.

Strack, F., Schwarz, N. and Gschneidinger, E. (1985) 'Happiness and reminiscing: the role of time perspective, affect, and mode of thinking'. *J. Person. Soc. Psychol.*, **49**, 1460–1469.

Stroh, N., Shaw, A.M. and Washbourn, M.F. (1908) 'A study in guessing'. *Amer. J. Psychol.*, **1908**, 243–245.

Stroop, J.R. (1935) 'Studies of interference in serial verbal reactions'. *J. Exp. Psychol.*, **18**, 643–662.

Suinn, R.M. (1983) 'Imagery and sports'. In A.A. Sheikh (ed.), *Imagery: Current Theory, Research and Application*. New York: John Wiley.

Sutherland, G., Newman, B. and Rachman, S. (1982) 'Experimental investigations of the relations between mood and intrusive unwanted cognitions'. *Brit. J. Med. Psychol.*, **55**, 127–138.

Taylor, S.E. and Crocker, J. (1981) 'Schematic bases of social information processing'. In E.T. Higgins, C.P. Herman and M.P. Zanna (eds), *Social Cognition: The Ontario Symposium*, Vol. I. Hillsdale, N.J.: Lawrence Erlbaum.

Teasdale, J.D. (1983) 'Affect and accessibility'. In D.E. Broadbent (ed.), *Functional Aspects of Memory*. The Royal Society, London.

Teasdale, J.D. (1983a) 'Negative thinking in depression: cause, effect or reciprocal relationship?'. *Adv. Behav. Res. & Ther.*, **5**, 3–25.

Teasdale, J.D. and Dent, J. (1987) 'Cognitive vulnerability to depression: an investigation of two hypotheses'. *Br. J. Clin. Psychol.*, **26**, 113–126.

Teasdale, J.D. and Fogarty, S.J. (1979) 'Differential effects of induced mood on retrieval of pleasant and unpleasant events from episodic memory'. *J. Abnorm. Psychol.*, **88**, 248–257.

Teasdale, J.D. and Russell, M.L. (1983) 'Differential effects of induced mood on the recall of positive, negative and neutral words'. *Br. J. Clin. Psychol.*, **22**, 163–172.

Teasdale, J.D. and Spencer, P. (1984) 'Induced mood and estimates of past success'. *Br. J. Clin. Psychol.*, **23**, 149–150.

Teasdale, J.D. and Taylor, R. (1981) 'Induced mood and accessibility of memories: an effect of mood states or of induction procedure?'. *Brit. J. Clin. Psychol.*, **20**, 39–48.

Teasdale, J.D., Taylor, R. and Fogarty, S.J. (1980) 'Effects of induced elation–depression on the accessibility of memories of happy and unhappy experiences'. *Behav. Res. Ther.*, **18**, 339–346.

Thorndike, E.L. (1931) *Human Learning*. New York: Appleton-Century Crofts.

Thorndike, E.L. and Lorge, I. (1944) *The Teacher's Word-Book of Thirty Thousand Words*. New York: Columbia University, Teacher's College, Bureau of Publications.

Thorndyke, P.W. (1975) 'Cognitive structures in human story comprehension and memory'. *Technical Report P-5513*. Santa Monica: The Rand Corporation.

Thorndyke, P.W. (1976) 'The role of interferences in discourse comprehension'. *J. Verb. Learn. Verb. Behav.*, **15**, 437–446.

Thorndyke, P.W. (1977) 'Cognitive structures in comprehension and memory of narrative discourse'. *Cog. Psychol.*, **9**, 77–110.

Titchener, A.B. and Pyle, W.H. (1907) 'The effect of imperceptual shadows on the judgement of distance'. *Practical . Amer. Philosoph. Soc.*, **46**, 94–109.

Treisman, A.M. (1960) 'Contextual cues in selective listening'. *Quart. J. Exp. Psychol.*, **12**, 242–248.

Treisman, A.M., Squire, R. and Green, G. (1974) 'Semantic processing in dichotic listening? A replication'. *Mem. & Cog.*, **2**, 641–646.

Trimble, R. and Eriksen, C.W. (1966) 'Subliminal cues in the Muller-type illusion'. *Percept. & Psychophys.*, **1**, 401–404.

Tulving, E. (1983) *Elements of Episodic Memory*. Oxford: Oxford University Press.

Tulving, E. and Thomson, D.N. (1973) 'Encoding specificity and retrieval processes in episodic memory'. *Psychol. Rev.*, **80**, 352–373.

Turk, D.C. and Salovey, P. (1986) 'Clinical information processing: bias inoculation'. In R. Ingram (ed.), *Information Processing Approaches to Clinical Psychology*, Orlando: Academic Press.

Turvey, M. (1973) 'On peripheral and central processes in vision: inferences from an information-processing analysis of masking with patterned stimuli'. *Psychol. Rev.*, **80**, 1–52.

Tversky, A. and Kahneman, D. (1973) 'Availability: A heuristic for judging frequency and probability'. *Cog. Psychol.*, **5**, 207–232.

Tversky, A. and Kahneman, D. (1974) 'Judgement under uncertainty: heuristics and biases'. *Science*, **185**, 1124–1131.

Tversky, A. and Kahneman, D. (1982) 'Judgement under uncertainty: heuristics and biases'. In D. Kahneman, P. Slovic and A. Tversky (eds), *Judgement under Uncertainty: Heuristics and Biases*. Cambridge: Cambridge University Press.

Tyler, H.R. (1968) 'Abnormalities of perception with defective eye movements (Balint's Syndrome)'. *Cortex*, **4**, 154–171.

Tyrer, P., Horn, S. and Lee, I. (1978) 'Treatment of agoraphobia by subliminal and supraliminal exposure to phobic cine-film'. *Lancet*, **1**, 358–360.

Underwood, G. (1976) 'Semantic interference from unattended printed words'. *Brit. J. Psychol.*, **67**, 327–338.

Underwood, G.L. (1977) 'Facilitation from attended and unattended messages'. *J. Verb. Learn. Verb. Behav.*, **16**, 99–106.

Upper, D. and Cantela, J.R. (1979) *Covert Conditioning*. New York: Pergamon Press.

Velten, E. (1968) 'A laboratory task for induction of mood states'. *Behav. Res. & Ther.*, **6**, 473–482.

Vestre, N.D. and Caulfield, B.P. (1986) 'Perception of neutral personality descriptions by depressed and nondepressed subjects'. *Cog. Ther. & Res.*, **10** (1), 31–36.

Volans, P.J. (1976) 'Styles of decision-making and probability appraisal in selected obsessional and phobic patients'. *Brit. J. Soc. & Clin. Psychol.*, **15**, 305–317.

Von Wright, J.N., Anderson, K. and Stenman, U. (1975) 'Generalisation of conditioned GSRs in dichotic listening'. In P.M.A. Rabbitt and S. Dorric (eds), *Attention and Performance*. New York: Academic Press.

Walker, C.H. and Meyer, B.J.F. (1980) 'Integrating different types of information in text'. *J. Verb. Learn. Verb. Behav.*, **19**, 263–275.

Walker, C.H. and Yekovich, F.R. (1984) 'Script-based inferences: Effects of text and knowledge variables on recognition memory'. *J. Verb. Learn. Verb. Behav.* **23**, 357–370.

Walker, P. and Myer, R.R. (1978) 'The subliminal perception of movement and the course of autokinesis'. *Brit. J. Psychol.*, **69**, 225–231.

Warren, R.E. (1972) 'Stimulus encoding and memory'. *J. Exp. Psychol.*, **94**, 90–100.

Warren, R.E. (1974) 'Association, directionality and stimulus encoding'. *J. Exp. Psychol.*, **102**, 151–158.

Wason, P.C. (1971) 'Problem-solving and reasoning'. *Brit. Med. Bull.*, **27**, 206–210.

Wason, P.C. and Shapiro, D. (1971) *Quart. J. Exp. Psychol.*, **23**, 63.

Watson, D. and Clark, L.A. (1984) 'Negative affectivity: the disposition to experience aversive emotional states'. *Psychol. Bull.*, **96** (3), 465–490.

Watson, J.B. (1925) *Behaviourism*. New York: W.W. Norton.

Warrington, E.K. and Weiskrantz, L. (1974) The effect of prior learning on subsequent retention in amnesic patients. *Neuropsychologia*, **12**, 419–428.

Watts, F.N. (1974) 'The control of spontaneous recovery of anxiety in imaginal desensitisation'. *Behav. Res. & Ther.*, **12**, 57–59.

Watts, F.N. (1979) 'Habituation model of systematic desensitisation'. *Psychol. Bull.*, **86**, 627–637.

Watts, F.N. (1983) Affective cognitive: sequel to Zajonc and Rachman. *Behav. Res. & Ther.*, **21**, 89–90.

Watts, F.N. (1984) 'Cognitive paradigms for the study of depression'. Paper presented at British Psychological Society Conference, Warwick, April 1984.

Watts, F.N. (1985) 'Individual-centred cognitive counselling for study problems'. *Brit. J. Couns. & Guid.*, **13**, 238–247.

Watts, F.N. (1986) 'Cognitive processing in phobias'. *Behav. Psychother.*, **14**, 295–301.

Watts, F.N. 'Experimental abnormal psychology'. In G. Parry and F.N. Watts (eds), *Skills and Methods in Mental Health Research*, in press. Brighton: Lawrence Erlbaum.

Watts, F.N. and Blackstock, A. (1987) 'Lang's theory and emotional imagery'. *Cog. & Emot.*, **1**, in press.

Watts, F.N., Herbert, J., Moore, G.F. and Levey, A. (1986a) 'Approaches to studying, personality and examination'. *Person. Indiv. Diff.*, **7**, 243–245.

Watts. F.N., McKenna, F.P., Sharrock, R. and Trezise, L. (1986b) 'Colour naming of phobia related words'. *Br. J. Psychol.*, **77**, 97–108.

Watts, F.N., MacLeod, A.K. and Morris, L. 'Associations between phenomenal and objective aspects of concentration problems in depressed patients'. *Brit. J. Psychol.* (in press a).

Watts, F.N., MacLeod, A.K. and Morris, L. 'A remedial strategy for memory and concentration problems in depressed patients'. *Cog. Ther. & Res.* (in press b).

Watts, F.N., Morris, L. and MacLeod, A.K. 'Recognition memory in depression'. *J. Abnorm. Psychol.* (in press c).

Watts, F.N. and Sharrock, R. (1985a) 'Description and measurement of concentration problems in depressed patients'. *Psychol. Med.*, **15**, 317–326.

Watts, F.N. and Sharrock, R. (1985b) 'Relationships between spider constructs in phobics'. *Brit. J. Med. Psychol.*, **58**, 149–153.

Watts, F.N. and Sharrock, R. (1987) 'Cued recall in depression'. *Brit. J. Clin. Psychol.*, **26**, 149–150.

Watts, F.N., Sharrock, R. and Trezise, L. (1986c) 'Detail and elaboration in phobic imagery'. *Behav. Psychother.*, **14**, 115–123.

Watts, F.N., Trezise, L. and Sharrock, R. (1986d) 'Processing of phobic stimuli'. *Brit. J. Clin. Psychol.*, **25**, 253–261.

Wegman, C. (1985) *Psychoanalysis and Cognitive Psychology.* New York: Academic Press.

Weingartner, H., Cohen, R.M., Murphy, D.L., Martello, J. and Gerdt, C. (1981) 'Cognitive processes in depression'. *Arch. Gen. Psychiat.*, **38**, 42–47.

Weingartner, H. and Silberman, E. (1982) 'Models of cognitive impairment: cognitive changes in depression'. *Psychopharm. Bull.*, **18**, 27–42.

Weiskrantz, L. (1977) Trying to bridge some neurological gaps between monkey and man. *Brit. J. Psychol.*, **68**, 431–45.

Weiskrantz, L., Warrington, K., Sanders, M.D. and Marshall, J. (1974) 'Visual capacity of the hemianopic field following a restricted occipital ablation'. *Psychonom. Sci.*, **2**, 75–76.

Welford, A.T. (1967) 'Single channel operations in the brain'. *Acta Psychol.*, **27**, 15–24.

White, J.D. and Carlston, D.E. (1983) 'Consequences of schemata for attention, impressions, and recall in complex social interactions'. *J. Person. Soc. Psychol.*, **45**, (3), 538–549.

White, P. (1980) 'Limitations on verbal reports of internal events: a refutation of Nisbett and Wilson and of PEM'. *Psychol. Rev.*, **87** (1), 105–112.

Whitehead, A. (1973) 'Verbal learning and memory in elderly depressives'. *Brit. J. Psychiat.*, **123**, 203–208.

Whitehead, A. (1974) 'Factors in the learning deficit of elderly depressives'. *Brit. J. Soc. Clin..Psychol.*, **13**, 201–208.

Whyte, L.L. (1978) *The Unconscious Before Freud.* London, Longwood.

Wickelgren, W. (1976) Network strength theory of storage and retrieval dynamics. *Psychol. Rev.*, **83**, 466–478.

Wickens, C.D. (1979) 'The structure of attentional resources'. In R. Nickerson (ed.), *Attention and Performance*, VIII. Hillsdale, N.J.: Lawrence Erlbaum.

Wickens, C.D. (1984) 'Processing resources in attention'. In R. Parasuraman and D.R. Davies (eds), *Varieties of Attention.* Orlando, SL.: Academic.

Williams, A. (1938) 'Perception of subliminal visual stimuli'. *J. Psychol.*, **6**, 187–199.

Williams, J.M.G. (1984) *The Psychological Treatment of Depression: A guide to the theory and practice of cognitive behaviour therapy.* London: Croom Helm/New York: Free Press.

Williams, J.M.G. and Broadbent, K. (1986) 'Autobiographical memory in attempted suicide patients'. *J. Abnorm. Psychol.*, **95**, 144–149.

Williams, J.M.G. and Broadbent, K. (1986) 'Distraction by emotional stimuli: Use of a Stroop task with suicide attempters'. *Br. J. Clin. Psychol.*, **25**, 101–110.

Williams, J.M.G. and Nulty, D.D. (1986) 'Construct accessibility, depression and the emotional Stroop task: Transient mood or stable structure?. *Person. Individ. Diff.*, **7**, 485–491.

Williams, J.M.G. and Teasdale, J.D. (1982) 'Facilitation and helplessness: the interaction of perceived difficulty and importance of a task'. *Behav. Res. & Ther.*, **20**, 161–171.

Williams, K.W. and Durso, F.T. (1986) 'Judging category frequency: automaticity or availability?'. *J. Exper. Psychol.: Learn. Mem. & Cog.*, **12**, 387–396.

Williams, M.D. and Hollan, J.D. (1981) 'Process of retrieval from very long-term memory'. *Cog. Sci.*, **5**, 87–119.

Wine, J. (1971) 'Test anxiety and direction of attention'. *Psychol. Bull.*, **76**, 92–104.

Wine, J.D. (1980) 'Cognitive-attentional theory of test anxiety'. In I.G. Sarason (ed.), *Test Anxiety: Theory, Research, and Application*. Hillsdale, N.J.: Lawrence Erlbaum.

Winter, D.A. (1983) 'Logical inconsistency in construction relationships: Conflict or complexity?'. *Brit. J. Med. Psychol.*, **56**, 79–87.

Wolpe, J. (1958) *Psychotherapy by Reciprocal Inhibition*. Stanford: Stanford University Press.

Worthington, A.G. (1964) 'Effect of Worthingsubliminal structural cues on reproductions of a simple line drawing'. *Percept. & Mot. Skills*, **19**, 823–882.

Wright, J. and Mischel, W. (1982) 'Influence of affect on cognitive special learning person variables'. *J. Person. Soc. Psychol.*, **43**, (5), 901–914.

Yates, J. (1985) 'The content of awareness is a model of the world'. *Psychol. Rev.*, **92** (2), 249–284.

Yekovich, F.R. and Thorndyke, T.W. (1981) 'An evaluation of alternative functional models of narrative schemata'. *J. Verb. Learn. Verb. Behav.*, **20**, 454–469.

Zajonc, R.B. (1980) 'Feeling and thinking: preferences need no inferences'. *Amer. Psychol.*, **35**, 151–175.

Zajonc, R.B. (1984) 'On the primacy of affect'. *Amer. Psychol.*, **39**, 117–123.

Zajonc, R.B., Pietromonaco, P. and Bargh, J. (1982) 'Independence and interaction of affect and cognition'. In M.S. Clark and S.T. Fiske, (eds), *Affect and Cognition*. Hillsdale, N.J.: Lawrence Erlbaum.

Zarantonello, M., Slaymaker, F., Johnson, J. and Petzel, T. (1984) 'Effects of anxiety and depression on anagram performance, ratings of cognitive interference, and the negative subjective evaluation of performance'. *J. Clin. Psychol.*, **40**, (1), 20–25.

Zimbardo, P.G., Cohen, A., Weisenberg, M., Dworkin, L. and Firestone, I. (1969) 'The control of experimental pain'. In P.G. Zimbardo (ed.), *The Cognitive Control of Motivation*. Glenview, Illinois: Scott Foreman.

Zuroff, D.C., Colussy, S.A. and Wielgus, M.S. (1983) 'Selective memory and depression: a cautionary note concerning response bias'. *Cog. Ther. & Res.*, **7**, 223–232.

Author Index

Subject Index

Debiasing, 142–144
Defence, 18, 60–61, 69
Depression (*see also* Mood)
    integrated model of, 168–184
    learned helplessness, theory of, 7,
        48, 176
    memory bias in, 8, 20, 73–90
    neutral materials and, 32–52
    phenomenology of, 178–179
    processing resources and, 47–48
    treatment (*see also* Treatments),
        50–52
    types of, 35, 37
Desensitization, 63, 114, 122–124
Diary studies, 78
Dichotic listening tasks, 57–58, 64, 72,
        150–151, 166, 171, 179
Double dissociation
    of memory and judgement,
        179–180
    of priming and elaboration,
        166–184
Dual task performance, 36–37, 46–48, 50

Effort
    cognitive, 43–46
Elaboration, 27, 68–69, 71, 73, 166–184
Emotions
    basic, 4, 5
    complex, 4, 5
    computational model of, 22
    theories of, 9–11

Frames (*see also* Schema), 97–100, 160

Habituation, 114
Happiness
    negative, 86–87
Hemispheres, 16
Heuristics (*see also* Judgement), 127–130
    anchoring, 129–130
    availability, 127–128, 132, 138–140
    representativeness, 128–129
Hierarchies, 26, 31
Hindsight, 131

Imagery, 51, 52, 78, 110–125, 180
    effect on judgement, 134–136
    Lang's theory of, 4, 111, 113–114
    pictorialist–descriptionalist debate,
        111–113, 114, 116

properties of, 115–120
Information processing paradigm, 1, 5, 6,
        13–31, 181
Insomnia, 147–148
Integration (*see also* Priming), 68–69,
        166–184
Integrative model, 166–184

Judgement, 8, 85–86, 126–144, 147
    heuristics of, 127–130
    of ambiguity, 13, 140–142
    of contingency, 134
    of difficulty, 48
    of probability, 13, 131, 166, 174,
        180

Learned helplessness, 7, 48, 178
Learning (*see* Memory)
Levels
    Leventhal's theory at, 9–11
    of cognitive system, 2, 9–11,
        26–28
    of processing, 42–43, 68, 71, 172
Lexical decision, 84–85, 167

Masking, 37, 153–157
Memory, 73–90
    autobiographical, 76–79, 174
    for neutral materials, 40–46
    for prose (*see* Prose)
    for word lists, 79–81
    mood and, 73–90
    specificity of, 88–90
Mental models, 25, 110, 113, 124–125
Mind wandering, 48–50
Mood (*see also* Memory *and* Depression)
    congruency, 74–75, 82, 90
    memory asymmetry, 87–88
    memory bias, 73–90
    state dependency, 75, 83
Motor performance, 32, 35–36

Negative happiness, 86–87
Network models
    associative, 8, 75–76, 90, 116, 132,
        136, 166, 167
    problems with, 82–90
Neuroticism, 177
Neutral stimuli, 2, 32–52, 179
Nonconscious processing, 3, 8, 11, 29,
        145–165